Published by Lilyflower Publishing, Inc.
351 N. Congress Ave #139
Boynton Beach, FL 33426

ISBN 0-9819775-1-0

Written by:

Janice Hoetker Doherty

Cover Art and Book Layout by:

Jim Jung

Lilyflower
PUBLISHING

Lilyflower Publishing, Inc. is trademarked.

www.lilyflowerpublishing.com

Legal Disclaimer

Although all horticultural therapy references and benefits are acknowledged by the American Horticultural Therapy Association, this book is for entertainment purposes only and should not be considered medical advice. All subject matter and information provided and brought forth, is of a general nature and is not intended to address the circumstances of any particular medical or physical condition.

The projects, experiences and participants' responses are from the author's own personal creations and interactions and are not endorsed by any entity, nor should any of the above be considered psychiatric or medical evaluations or advice.

Please seek medical advice from a professional for specific queries.

Special Introduction By Jane Garee, Founder of *Lilyflower Publishing, Inc.*

A Calendar Year of Horticultural Therapy was definitely a long time in the making. It is my pleasure to inform you that the book you are holding is a limited edition.

We specifically timed the debut of this book, Jan's first, to coincide with the twentieth anniversary of the Cincinnati Flower Show. Jan is an award winning horticulturalist and also one of the speakers at the Cincinnati Flower Show for 2009.

Since we wanted to provide "that little something extra" in honor of this occasion, you will find that there are over fifteen special projects at the end of this book. The publication of these projects in a single volume is our gift to you, as we celebrate the twentieth anniversary milestone. Future editions of this book will not include the extra projects, so please enjoy this special first printing!

A Note From The Publisher

There truly is something about nature that soothes the soul. Each season brings its own glory and a feast for the eyes. We experience the splendor of newly fallen snow, the aching siren's song of autumn and the pure, fresh hope of spring. Add to that the sultriness of long summer days, and your spirit can't help but wonder at the gifts of nature.

This book is for anyone who appreciates the beauty in our world and knows that we are the richer for it.

A Note From The Author

Many years ago, I realized that my garden was a calming place where I could work out the stress of the day. I soon realized that many people used their gardening for therapy without realizing that horticultural therapy was a practice. But, what do you do if you can no longer actively garden? After seeing first hand the benefits of horticultural therapy in nursing homes and retirement communities, it became my passion to give all caregivers and shut-in gardening enthusiasts the tools and information that would encourage the practice of horticultural therapy, even if it's in a limited way. I hope that reading this book will cause you to find the same passion, excitement and love for nature that I have always experienced!

A Calendar Year of

Horticultural Therapy

How Tending to Your Garden Can Tend to Your Soul

Contents

Prologue

Connectedness, living in the moment, finding ourselves — these seem to be the new buzz words and phrases, the goals of everyone. There are classes offered to help us achieve these lofty ideals. There are weekend seminars to show us how to find that elusive peace within ourselves, and how-to manuals written on "awareness" and the "clearing of our minds" and the way to free our lives of stress.

Gardeners have a head start in those types of seminars. Give us a trowel, a spade and a pruning shears and within an hour, or less, we will be "living in the moment" and feeling a "connectedness" to the soil and to our souls. We find ourselves grounded, literally and figuratively. Somehow that elusive peacefulness isn't so elusive in the garden!

I wonder if the world leaders should be given a trowel, a spade and a pruning shears!

Important things in life are learned at our parents' knees. My love of gardening had its beginning there, literally. I was three-and-a-half years old when I was taught the difference between a weed and a seedling, with my mother kneeling at the edge of her flower garden. I wasn't too much older than that when I was taught how to plant a straight row of corn and beans, as my father knelt in the freshly tilled garden soil. Little did I know just how important these things would become in my life. Because there weren't many children in our neighborhood, I spent a lot of time with my parents in the garden. I graduated from pulling weeds to planting flower seeds, and finally I was old enough to help dad pick the corn for dinner. The seeds of gardening had taken root before I was five years old!

Twenty-one years passed and I found myself the young mother of three toddlers and their father was an Army captain in Vietnam. Because he was in the artillery, our stress level was off the charts. I took to gardening once again, this time in my own yard. Weeding was calming and almost hypnotizing and the fears of being an Army widow were lost in the good earth. Digging a garden in solid clay soil, with just a spade to cut through the gummy, yellow dirt, was the perfect way to release the tensions of a day. Who could tell if those were tears or beads of sweat rolling down my cheeks? I dug and beat the clay to death feeling my tensions become one with the clay, until darkness forced me inside for the day. Ralph Waldo Emerson knew the mind of a gardener when he wrote, "All my hurts my garden spade can heal."

That was "Connectedness 101" and this was a 52-week course.

It was during that horrible year of worry that dad would come to help me dig a new garden or lay rock edging, and preach to me the importance of digging a new garden "a spade's depth deep" into the clay before adding compost or peat. Mom babysat the children so that I could find my sanity in the garden. She could always judge the stress level of the week by how many new garden areas had been dug. At one point she commented, "I sure hope he comes home soon because there won't be any lawn left in this yard!" He did come home safely and the gardens bloomed beautifully for him the following summer. I had graduated with honors, from "Connectedness 101."

Twenty-five more years slipped by and I never lost my love of gardening. I continued to find immediate relaxation and stress release in weeding and digging; at "a spade's depth," of course!

My own daughters grew to maturity, married and have their own yards and gardens now. I hear myself instructing them to "be sure you dig that garden a spade's depth."

I have taught my three granddaughters, before they reached four years of age, the joy of planting seeds in a pot while kneeling next to me. I have seen their anticipation while they watch and wait for the first break in the soil and the first sign of a sprouting seedling. Their joy is real when the bloom finally appears. Little did my parents know they began a four-generation gardener legacy.

Dad died suddenly at the age of 96. Even though he suffered from macular degeneration, he had been gardening that afternoon, and was dead that same evening from a ruptured aneurysm. I hope that I am that fortunate.

In the week that followed the funeral, I once again found myself digging at a frantic pace. The feel of the dirt was soothing and it swallowed up those "beads of sweat" running down my cheeks. The smell of the soil was comforting. This time I planted a memorial garden in my yard and I could hear his voice saying, "It has to be dug a spade's depth." The gardening circle had been completed.

For more than two decades I worked as a microbiologist in a clinical lab. I had been trained to grow and harvest microorganisms for identification. It was an interesting, but stressful profession and after twenty five years, my soul cried out for the peace I had always found in the garden. It was time for a career change and the opportunity came quite unexpectedly while I was volunteering at The Cincinnati Flower Show. It was here that I learned that landscapers were designing "enabling gardens" and that what I had experienced for myself in my own gardening history, was actually a therapeutic profession! My interest and knowledge about horticultural therapy had begun!

The birth of my company, Growing Healthy Inc. occurred in 1995. For nine years I provided horticultural therapy to nursing home residents, senior centers, health care facilities and Alzheimer units throughout the area. Since I personally knew the therapeutic value of gardening, smelling flowers and playing in the dirt, I wanted to share that therapy with others who no longer had the opportunity to dig in their own garden. The powerful therapeutic tools of fragrance, color and texture are appreciated with these activities. They are the cause for remembrance, reflections on past gardens and smiles that come from playing in the potting soil; for feeling the softness of lambs ears or smelling lavender and other herbs. I took the joys of gardening to those who once loved the earth, but were now unable, through no choice of their own, to enjoy that pastime. We worked with dried and fresh flowers and herbs. The participants reminisced about the beautiful zinnias and roses that once gave them gardening pleasure, while smelling and touching the ones that I brought to them from my garden.

Sometimes we planted pansies or aloe or grass and I could always tell the real gardeners. They were the ones who let the dirt sift through their stiff fingers, the ones who refused the offer of gloves. They liked the feel and the smell, and they remembered.

Their gardens, but more often, their mothers' gardens were once again thought of, and talked about, and loved. For that hour, at least, they were connected and enjoying the moment! I saw agitated people come to my table and an hour later, leave the table laughing. That was horticultural therapy at work.

Horticultural therapy has different goals for different populations. It may be a garden club activity once a month for some groups, and that is okay. The nursing staffs often told me that the attitudes of the people changed the day before they learned I was on their schedules. They wondered what we'd be doing and they talked about what we had done the last time. That high-spirited conversation lingered throughout the next few days. I think their world, or at least their attitudes, became happier because of our gardening activity. It was an activity that they looked forward to with eagerness. That was also horticultural therapy at work.

I have found success with Growing Healthy Inc. in many ways. The business aspect of the company is good but the real success stories center around the changed attitudes, smiles, or thank you's that I've received from the people I have worked with that day. It is so rewarding for me to witness their feelings of accomplishment at the completion of an activity that they thought they could not do. At the end of my day, I'm not always sure who has benefited the most from the horticultural therapy that has been provided; the residents or me!

With this book, I hope to provide inspiration as well as guidelines, for others to be able to provide horticultural therapy to those who are in need of "finding themselves" or to realize the sense of contentment, connectedness and peacefulness that is associated with Mother Nature and her gifts to us. By reading the modules for each project, you will see how most of the sessions can be revised to accommodate the functioning level of the participants.

Come with me through the year of horticultural therapy projects, and experience for yourself the "mindfulness" and the therapy of gardening.

* *

A garden is a love story… a duet between a human being and Mother Nature.

- Jeff Cox

ACKNOWLEDGEMENTS

For my initial interest in gardening, I owe my parents, Helen and Bernard Hoetker, everything.

For the form-filling, boring business details of legally incorporating a company, I will be forever indebted to my business manager and husband, J. Dennis Doherty. He has been my support system, my critic and my sounding board! Thank you a hundred times over.

To Bill Donabedian who patiently worked with me in establishing a company identity and logo, I am most appreciative.

I am grateful for having had the opportunity to work with Pamscapes, a landscape designer, at The Cincinnati Flower Show. She showed me that Horticultural Therapy was indeed what I had experienced with my own gardening activities over the years.

I am grateful to Melanie Trelaine who informed me that horticultural therapy is a profession and felt that I could do it, and gave me the information I needed to set forth on my own.

Without the flowers, given to me by "Dan the Flower Man" (Vine Street Flowers) and the Florist Shop at the Eastgate Kroger store, I would have had a hard time realizing my dream of providing patients with fresh flowers and having enough material for drying purposes. I am most appreciative.

I owe many thanks to the Activity Directors for giving me a chance to prove how horticultural therapy can benefit and enrich the lives of their residents.

I acknowledge the patron saint of all gardeners, St. Fiacre. His blessings are welcomed by those who love springtime and planting, summertime and weeding, the fruits of the harvest, the smell of turned earth and the joy of a flowering land.

And last, but certainly not least, I am grateful to each and every resident who sat at my tables and taught me. You showed me the connectedness between people of all generations, and shared the benefits of your therapy with me. You have made my day!!!

PART 1

The Who, What, Where, and Why of Horticultural Therapy

When I told my family and friends that I was setting out on a new career, one of horticultural therapy, I received a lot of comments like, "oh that's nice," and "how interesting that must be," or, "how appropriate it is that you should take that path." When I told them that I was seeing patients at retirement homes and health care facilities, I could see the confusion on their faces. Later they told me that they thought my "new career" was one of tending to the plants in patients' rooms or in the facilities' lobbies! No wonder they had looked at me in a somewhat blank manner when I told them snippets of my rewarding experiences! They had put me into the position of a "horticulturist", whereas my new passion was that of a "horticultural therapist."

The function of the former is to tend to the plants' needs and has as its main focus, the health of that plant. Feeding, watering, insect removal, re-potting, or simply a change of lighting conditions are all needed for the plant's well being.

The focus of the horticultural therapist is on the well-being of the **participant** performing those acts of watering, feeding or re-potting.

Horticultural therapy is, **by definition**, "a supervised activity that uses plants, and plant material, along with horticultural procedures, to improve the social, physical and psychological well-being of people." That does sound like a rather grandiose, perhaps abstract theory, to think that a trowel or "spoon-shovel" could affect the social, and physical, much less the psychological conditions of people. But it does, as you will see as you get further into this book. My family and friends now make the distinction between the two professions and now when I tell them snippets of my days' activities, they understand why the rewards are great and why my days are fulfilled.

In hundreds of hospitals throughout the country, working with plants is a powerful form of therapy for patients of all ages, especially those with emotional and physical disabilities. For patients with physical disabilities, horticultural therapy can be designed to treat specific problems. The simple act of misting a plant with an atomizer or spooning dirt into a flowerpot or weeding a garden helps to strengthen muscle tone of stroke victims and patients with spinal cord or head injuries. The need to follow directions also aids in the cognitive development of the patient.

Therapists also use plants and flowers to help patients regain their sense of color, texture and smell.

The urge to put horticultural therapy in competition with the other professional therapies, such as occupational or physical therapy, should be immediately dismissed! The optimum condition is to have the therapists from those three distinct therapies work together at improving the condition of the patient. Many times the patient is intimidated by the use of the word "therapy" or by the sterile appearance of the treatment room. A greenhouse, or an activity room, or in some cases, their own room, seems to be a far less imposing atmosphere to work in, and the beneficial activity can be transferred from the threatening, clinical areas of a hospital or health care facility to a more pleasant, comfortable area.

Some patients lack enthusiasm for the standard physical therapy exercises and see no point in doing them at all. However, with the recommendations of their therapist, alternate activities centered on gardening, or other activities utilizing plant material, can achieve the same motor skill or muscle rehabilitation. The patient doesn't even realize that he is performing a therapy while he is busy at work doing something he is interested in doing. For an activity to be enticing, it should be fun or purposeful.

Squeezing a glue bottle or picking up a dried flower can be important in the physical improvement of the patient. Colors, textures and fragrances are used as stimulants in other therapies. Herbs and flowers provide all three of these elements.

Smell is directly related to memory, and specific smells immediately take patients back to their gardens or their mothers' gardens or even to their wedding days. Herbal smells that are culinary in nature immediately conjure up memories and stories of favorite foods or holiday fun. It's the sharing of these stories and the laughter that often follows that aid in the social development impact of this therapy.

Well-planned horticultural activities can play a major role in improving coordination, mobility, endurance and conditioning. The effects of weakened muscles, restricted range of motion, and joint stiffness can be greatly diminished through such activities.

It is here that I would like to point out the social development that comes from cooperation between patients. I have seen one patient help another accomplish a certain task when stiff fingers or poor eyesight hampers the other from completing the project. There is never a feeling of competition between the participants, but rather one of helpfulness. I think this is an important trait to be developed among people living in a confined situation. Horticultural therapy seems to bring out the best in people with its social interaction.

It has been noticed that working with plants or being around plants, or having a garden to view from the room, adds to the general positive, relaxed attitude of a patient. Blood pressure values and heart rates decrease, and oxygen consumption reduces when there is a green space to view instead of a street scene, or the patient has the opportunity to work with plant material. There is increased alpha brain wave activity and a feeling of calm and well-being ensues. This positive attitude, developed through horticultural therapy, helps the patient adjust to a confined living situation, become more relaxed and thereby be more receptive to other forms of medical treatment that may be necessary for recovery.

Plants and people go together like peanut butter and jelly, like ham and eggs. The plants are dependent on the person for their very survival. They rely on the person for their nutrients and care. The person benefits from taking care of the plant, by being needed, and by developing a sense of responsibility for the livelihood of that plant. That is something that the patients can control, when much of the rest of their lives is controlled by others.

The healing benefits of working with plants are deceptively simple but powerful. Experts agree that working with a plant, or in a garden, can relieve stress, heal physical or emotional wounds, rehabilitate injured muscles, improve motor skills and increase coordination. That's a big order to be filled by horticulture, but it does work!

Researchers are beginning to realize the potential of gardening as an activity that could be prescribed to improve mental wellness, as well as physical wellness. Dr. Mihaly Csikszentmhalyi has written a book entitled, "Flow: the Psychology of Optimal Experience," wherein he suggests that, "gardening is an activity, which when done correctly and skillfully, with the main focus on the activity and without concern about the outcome, can lead to the optimal experience", as far as physical well being is concerned. I like to think of horticultural therapy as medicine that needs no prescription, and has no limit on dosage amounts or administered frequency.

The modern history of horticultural therapy goes back as early as 1812, when Dr. Benjamin Rush, a Philadelphia physician and signer of the Declaration of Independence, noted the benefits of laboring in the garden for patients with mental disabilities in his "Medical Inquiries and Observations Upon Diseases of the Mind." Five years later, the Friends Asylum for the Insane was opened in Philadelphia and patients were involved in planting fruit trees and vegetables. A number of therapeutic gardening programs were created over the next century but the major impetus for horticultural therapy's development did not occur until the 1940's when the federal government established a number of new veterans' hospitals to care for wounded servicemen. Horticulture was viewed as a form of occupational therapy and volunteers from garden clubs brought the benefits of their love of gardening to thousands of patients. In reality, horticultural therapy is one of the world's oldest therapeutic activities. It's just that until recently, it has not been thought of as being a distinct discipline for therapeutic benefits. Thanks to The American Horticultural Therapy Association, which was founded in 1973, HT has gained acceptance as a unique and dynamic human service program.

Since the beginning of recorded history, gardens and landscapes have been places for spiritual, emotional and physical restoration. Ancient Chinese planted groves of sacred trees for spiritual enrichment. Ancient Romans enjoyed roof top gardens filled with flowers and vegetables and herbs. The early cultures of the Middle East placed high value on gardens, associating them with well-being and everlasting beauty. The paradise garden evolved and was considered a human built oasis. It was characterized by an enclosing wall that gave peace, security and a feeling of serenity to all within. These kinds of gardens have been used in present time, as the prototype for successful Alzheimer gardens. The cloistered gardens that surround the great cathedrals of the world have used this paradise garden design, as well, to provide a spiritual, contemplative atmosphere for the monks that is healing and restorative to both mind and body. It is their paradise, their Garden of Eden, here on earth. At some time in our week, we all need to find that special place where we can unwind or feel peace and serenity. For me and many others, that place is in a garden because we are so connected to the earth and can pull revitalizing energy from that place into ourselves.

<u>Everyone can be helped</u>, to some degree, by being involved with plants and horticultural procedures! There is no age or gender or educational limitations for those who can benefit from horticultural therapy. I have had college professors, as well as

grade school dropouts, sit at my table and we all learned from both of them! Many elementary schools have seen these benefits in action and now incorporate some kind of gardening into their activities or class schedules. Facilities with troubled children and young adults have noticed the changes in attitudes and personality traits. Prison systems are finding that greenhouse activities not only are therapeutic but also raise the self-esteem of the inmates and give them a potential job skill when they are released into the working world. It comes down to the simple fact that everyone can benefit from working with and enjoying horticulture, whether it's in the activity itself or just the enjoyment of the completed, peaceful area. Big corporations have noticed a change in their employees' productivity if they have a green space to go to on their breaks.

I have provided hands-on-sessions of horticultural therapy for many groups of Alzheimer patients, at varying stages of their disease, and I have seen their responses to various activities related to plants and plant material. I have seen the looks of achievement and the smiles on their faces that tell me that they are pleased and proud of what they have accomplished in that hour with me. I have heard the stories about their mothers' gardens. I have seen quiet, inactive people flourish when the materials necessary to arrange a vase of flowers have been placed in front of them. I have witnessed the transformation of individuals from irritated and angry, to calm and content. I have seen them smell the potting soil and enjoy the feel of it in their bare hands. These people were gardeners and thought that those days were a thing of the past. They were delightfully surprised to be playing in the dirt once again.

I have witnessed the light in their eyes as they smell a familiar fragrance, whether it be that of pine or cedar, lavender or roses. I have seen and heard the laughter, and sometimes the songs, that accompany some of the activities. I have been told by activity directors that they are impressed that their patients can be a captive audience for more than just a few minutes for my activity! Some residents, who won't participate in any other type of offered activity, will sit at my table for an hour. Their agitation seems to disappear with the flowers. Who could be grumpy with a beautiful flower to look at or to smell!

Some of the residents simply like the familiar motion of cleaning up after our project is completed. That is a good thing as well. They may not remember who I am from one week to the next, or even remember by the next day what we did together, but they do respond for that one hour that we are together. That one hour was a good one for them. They were happy and there were reminiscences.

Some Alzheimer units have a garden area where they can work, or wander throughout or sit in and visit with family members. The benefits to this type of situation are many. Although the Alzheimer patient may have difficulty expressing their thoughts in the spoken word, they can communicate in many other ways through their love of gardening. A garden is an opportunity for the patient, as well as the family members to share in the beauty and fragrance of flowers, and to enjoy the activities that a visit to a garden can bring. Listening to birds, watching the butterflies at work or hearing the wind chimes that hang from a limb bring enjoyment. A garden is a place where spoken language doesn't have to dominate the visit. Here there is tranquility and serenity where nothing is expected of the patient. After all, it is best to remain quiet so as not to disturb the birds and butterflies! The visit is certainly less stressful for both the patient and the visitor.

A garden viewed from the window of any confined patient is a source of enjoyment as well as a reference line for the time of day or the changing of the seasons.

They can look forward to the flower bud opening with the warmth of the sun or watch and identify the birds feast at the garden's feeder. The weather changes are observed and often times can be the start of a conversation when all other topics have been covered! There is a feeling of contentment within their souls when they feel warm and cozy as they see the snow flying, or the rain cascading down their window panes. "I'm sure glad I'm in here and don't have to go out in this" is a comment I hear quite often.

They feel the lilt and optimism of spring as they observe the first greening on the tree branches or see the cheerful yellow forsythia in bloom. They can spend many hours of their confinement watching the changes occur in the garden outside their window. This is also a form of horticulture therapy.

Let me summarize how horticultural therapy is used by the medical profession as a therapeutic tool for their patients:

a) ***Social development*** - promotes a sense of responsibility for living things, encourages interaction in a non-threatening environment and develops pride in accomplishments;
b) ***Psychological development*** - improves self-esteem, improves mental awareness and stimulation of the senses and achieves a sense of productivity by completing projects;

c) *Physical improvements* - helps maintain and develop musculoskeletal coordination, increases performance of cardiovascular system;

d) *Cognitive development* - is aided by following simple directions for project completion;

e) *Visual stimulation* - working with bright flowers or viewing photos;

f) *As a tension and stress reliever* - as demonstrated by lowering blood pressure and heart rates;

g) *Restores joy* - to daily life by enjoying floral and herbal fragrances, by experiencing different textures of plant material and by reminiscing about pleasant and/or humorous things that those fragrances bring to mind.

There are three distinctly different types of programs that I have found successful over the past years:

1) **The hands-on sessions** start with a discussion and exchange of information about a variety of horticultural subjects ranging from herbs to wildflowers and everything in between. This discussion is integrated with a hands-on related activity that is tailored to the abilities of the participants. A complete listing of all the tried and true sessions \will follow.

2) **The Garden on the Move program** puts the horticulture on a rolling cart that is taken to the rooms of the residents. I always include a "show and tell" bouquet of what's blooming in my own yard for them to see and smell, and conversation usually follows as they recognize the flowers from their own or, yes, from their mothers' gardens! If the blooming season is over, then other treasures from Mother Nature

are displayed, such as pine cones or wild-flowers or pumpkins or interesting winter seed pods. It brings the outside environment in to them. This program offers intense sensory therapy and often-times develops into a lengthy conversation and visit as they tell me their problems, share their fears and concerns with me, tell stories, or show me their newest great-grandchild's photo. "Just because you've taken the time to stand there and listen to me makes me feel better," was a powerful, poignant comment that was told to me by a forlorn lady. I try to remember that statement as I start my rounds with the garden cart each week.

I keep a list of all the patients visited so that it can be entered into their charts as a one on one visit. Before I leave, they have the opportunity to choose a fresh flower in a water pick that is self-standing, from a large selection on the cart. Such a decision! "Which color or variety should I pick this time?" "Which will stay fresh the longest?" "Which kind did I take the last time?" "Where shall I put it?" A cute Irish woman wanted me to place her flower somewhere in her room "so that everyone who passes by can see it and the old lady enjoying her flower."

Many times they'll ask how much it costs, and when I tell them the cost is just a smile, they immediately light up with a spontaneous one! One lady told me after she had paid for her flower with a beautiful smile that it was the first time she had reason to smile in a few days! I'm thankful she was on my list of visits that day! Most people think the trade of a smile for a flower is a good deal since they have no money available to them. Many of the patients also make it a point to save the water picks for me and it makes them feel good to be able to give me something in return for a fresh flower the next time I stop by. One resident thought she should keep her flower tubes in her medicine chest because, "Flowers are the best medicine you know, dear." That should have been my line!

I had a pleasant surprise on one of my return visits to a woman, when she handed me the following note to be read later: "Dear Flower Angel, God bless you for making those little flower arrangements. Thanks for distributing them in our room when we are not home. I can't tell you how happy it makes me. The one arrangement this week is especially pretty. It lifts the spirits of everyone who visits me. Thank you is all I can say, but I want you to know you are in my prayers." Clint Eastwood couldn't have said it better. "Go on. Make my day!"

You may think that those few garden cart minutes spent with each patient are just a few minutes out of their very long days. Those few minutes, however, can be magically transformed into horticultural therapy that is ongoing for weeks, or in a few cases, months and years. Let me explain. They have been told that if they keep fresh water in the tubes, the flower will remain fresh longer. This translates into something that they have to care for, as well as enjoy, for its beauty or fragrance.

They want to remember to save the tube for "the flower lady", as I am referred to, so that in itself is a memory stimulator. They check to see if their roommate received a flower and if she/he is not awake they will pick one out for them. That is interaction and social stimulation. "Flowers make the home, now this is my home," is a prevailing thought, and many memories are packed into that comment.

One woman took a flower that had a bud with it and wondered if it would open for her. It did within a week and she was pleased to report that fact back to me on my next visit to her room. She could hardly wait for me to come back! It takes some co-ordination to refill those little tubes with water, and since they want to keep the flower fresh as long as possible, they manage to do it.

One resident chose a brightly colored sultana stem. The next time I saw her was a month later and she was excitedly waiting for me at her doorway. "Do you think those are roots on that stem?", she asked. They were, and she had her son bring a little four inch pot of dirt on his next visit. She transplanted her cutting. By my next visit, her little rooting had taken hold in its pot of dirt and had another stem with a bud on it. She was so tickled with it! As the months went on she kept transplanting that little water-pick cutting to larger pots and enthusiastically beckoned me to her room for inspection. One year later, she had a big fourteen-inch pot just dripping with bright flowers from her rooted sultana! That was one whole year of therapy from one garden cart visit! The other residents all knew about Ruth's potted plant and they all kept up with the latest growth report given at meal times. She earned the reputation of having a green thumb and felt proud and accomplished and very pleased with herself.

Sometimes the residents don't want to return the empty water picks to me because they are using them for (gasp) artificial flowers! I've also seen them use the foam base of the pick as a pin cushion! Even that pleases me because it shows a mind at work.

There have been many appreciative comments over the months by the residents concerning the garden on the move visits. "These little flower tubes may be a small thing to you but they are a big thing for us." "I just needed something to cheer me up today!" "My day has taken a turn for the better because of your smile and this bright flower." "It's such a bleak day outside, this will brighten things up around here." Or, "Where have you been? I've missed you!" (It's nice being missed!) "You bring joy to our day." "I know that God is smiling on you because of the smiles that you give us with your flowers." "I've felt so lonely and scared and depressed today. Thank you for taking the time to talk to me today." "I like all kinds of flowers, house plants too, but I sure do like the garden flowers the best." "Your visit has made me feel warm all over." "This is something cheerful after a bad week." "I certainly need something to pick me up today." One man was teary as he identified all of the flower types in my vase. His wife had grown them all and he knew each by name. The lady slippers were her favorite. Hearing these comments makes my day worthwhile and causes my heart to sing as I know that I've made a difference in their lives.

As if the verbal comments are not enough, I've even been handed notes by a few of the residents. I look at these often when I need a pick-me-up:

"Thanks To the Flower Lady: Your lovely flower made me smile as I opened my eyes this morning. I thank you and praise God for your thoughtfulness and your creativity. Thank you for sharing!"

Below is a poem entitled "Lady of the Flowers" written by a 95-year-old resident:

My Lady of the flowers,
That's what I call her.
About once a month, she knocks on my door.
This special lady has a wonderful way of arranging a single carnation, or a small arrangement or a tiny bud and little spray of some cute color spray.

Because of these comments and notes, I know, without a doubt, how important horticultural therapy is, especially in the nursing home environment.

This is the last of my session types:

3) The slide show. This type of program is very strong visual therapy and is uplifting, educational and promotes conversation and material for reminiscing.

Since I love flowers, gardens, traveling and photography, this type of session fills the bill for my own personal therapy. I have created one-hour slide presentations on a big screen, ranging from visits to the Krohn Conservatory in Cincinnati to the deserts of the southwest. From my personal travels I have compiled presentations on everything from wildflowers to tropical flowers. Viewers can stroll through beautiful formal gardens of this country, Canada and Europe without ever leaving their wheelchairs! Cincinnati has a first class Flower Show each spring and many of the residents used to be able to attend this fabulous display. Now that they can no longer attend, I bring the show to them, through the hundreds of slides that I've taken of this world class event. They tell me that even when they were able to attend the show in person, they didn't see as much or learn as much as they do from these programs.

A woman named Margo told me she used to go to the flower shows on a regular basis. I invited her to the slide presentation on the flower show, which would follow my garden cart visit. She gave me a dozen reasons why she would not be able to come, all of which I negated. While she was fretting over not being able to come, I asked her aide to have her ready for the following hour's presentation. Was I ever surprised when I looked up from the slide projector and saw her dressed in a beautiful suit! It was the first time I had seen her in anything other than hospital gowns. She laughed and enjoyed herself and from that point on she attended other sessions and even went on the group outings. The activity director said, "She hasn't been out of her room in one-and-a-half years and you've initiated the change in her!" I put the credit where it belongs…to horticultural therapy!

Since many of the residents have expressed a desire to see my own gardens, I have put together a visit to my yard via the big screen. They will recognize most of the flowers from their own gardens or yes, their mothers' gardens! I encourage questions and comments throughout the show, so the stimulation is not only visual; there is also a lot of social interaction going on at the same time. This is therapeutic and they are not even aware of the therapy taking place. Even though I've referred to the slide shows as visual stimulation, residents who are visually impaired can also enjoy the flowers through an in-depth description of the flower and background setting. I have had both deaf and blind participants enjoy these presentations.

During one show on wildflowers, I had the therapeutic effects of these programs pointed out to me quite clearly. A gentleman who was watching the wildflowers intently on the screen, but not saying much, asked me to back up a few slides. I did and he studied the picture and its scenery a while longer before he asked, "Was that picture taken in Montana?" After I answered affirmatively he asked if it was in Glacier National Park. It was, and I was amazed at his recall. He studied it a few seconds longer and asked, "Was that on the trail going to Hidden Lake?" I said yes and obviously he knew the park very well. He then asked me how I had gotten to that trail. I was slightly perplexed as I told him we had driven to the park and hiked to the trailhead. I then asked him how he had gotten to that point. "Well", he said, "there weren't any roads going into the park when I was there. I took a train into the nearest town and picked up my mule and pack and camping gear", he replied. I was impressed. After the show was over and he came up to me to talk. I was not only impressed with his memory but I was ecstatic with his following comment. "I just wanted to thank you for taking me back there and making me feel young again! I haven't thought about that trip in over 60 years and now I'll be thinking about it for the rest of the night! Thank you for making me feel young again!" THAT is horticultural therapy!

During another slide presentation, a resident canary began singing along with my narration. Our feathery friend seemed to set the mood for a photographic stroll through my flower gardens. At the program's conclusion the comment was , "Thank you for a wonderful program. It was like a meditation!" I thought the slides were good, but I do believe the canary's song lifted that presentation to a higher level!

As you have now learned from reading, there are three very distinct types of horticultural therapy that I have provided to my clients over the years and each is extremely successful in its own way. None of these programs requires a greenhouse and all can be done in an activity room. There are a few books written on horticultural therapy utilizing a greenhouse but not all facilities have that luxury.

Following is a list of the programs that I have created for the calendar year, and these have been successful with the geriatric population. That is not to infer that these same sessions could not be successfully used in programs for other age groups and for different therapeutic reasons. I have just found my niche with the Alzheimer and health care population. Each one of these projects is complete in itself, providing gratification within the hour. I have also included the month of the year when I have used the programs to their best advantage in southwestern Ohio. For example, it would be difficult and really not appropriate, to have a session in the dead of winter that is geared towards wildflowers when the natural material would not be available. Your local growing conditions may vary from mine, and will therefore change this monthly guideline. Be creative! Plan ahead by drying or pressing plants that can be used at a later date.

Hands-on Programs that I have developed and the chapter where they are included in this book:

- Bulbs for All Seasons ~ January
- Lavender Bath Powder and Lavender Sachets ~ January
- Hearts and Flowers ~ February
- Mardi Gras Masks ~ February
- Red Clover ~ March
- Seed Art ~ March
- Everybody is Irish ~ March
- Pansies Mean Contentment ~ March
- Easter Grass ~ April
- Put on Your Easter Bonnet ~ April
- Spring Housecleaning with Mother Nature ~ April
- Heirloom Gardens ~ May
- Fairy Gardens ~ May
- Seeds of Sunshine ~ May
- Lilacs, the Mother of Memory ~ May
- Butterfly Gardening ~ June
- Water Gardens ~ June
- Bug Repellant Plants ~ July
- Colorful Coleus ~July

- Patriotic Petals ~ July
- Wild and Crazy Wildflowers ~ July
- Petal Painting ~ July
- The Grass Is Not Always Greener ~ July
- "Scent-sational" Geraniums ~ August
- Ferns and Frames ~ August
- Mint Madness ~ August
- The Language of Flowers ~ August
- A Taste of Lemon without the Pucker ~ August
- Forever and Ever Are Everlastings ~ September
- Remarkable Rosemary ~ September
- The Nose Knows ~ September
- Door Greeters ~ October
- Autumn Splendor ~ October
- The Wonderful World of Weeds and Seeds ~ October
- The Nose Knows ~ October
- Leaf Mosaic ~ October
- Turkey Thyme ~ November
- Pilgrim Herbs ~ November
- Pressed Flowers ~ November
- The Fragrance of Conifers ~ December
- Celebrating the Winter Solstice ~ December

- Happy Holidays, Naturally ~ December
- Osage Orange Ornaments, Flowers and Wreaths ~ December

The following are program ideas found in the **ADDITIONAL PROJECTS** section of this book. They are suitable for any month where you have the product available as fresh or dried plant material.

- Sweet Dreams (Sleep pillows/Sachets)
- Bath Thyme
- Terrific Topiaries
- Herbal Salt
- The Antiquity of Carnations
- Lavender Eye Pillows
- Cactus and Succulents
- The Enjoyment of Potpourri
- A Rose Is A Rose Is A Rose
- Sycamore Bark Painting
- Ivy League and Otherwise
- Fresh Flower Arranging
- Delightful Dish Gardens

PART 2

Twelve Months of Projects to Chase Away the Blues

Now that you have the background information, it is time for the actual therapeutic tools (trowels) to be put into action. I think you will find these program modules easy reading and thorough. They are complete, down to the scissors you must not forget to have with you! I have included photographs of the actual completed project so that you have a guideline to follow. I am sure you will develop your own varieties on the theme, but these will get you started on the fulfilling path of horticultural therapy.

~~ JANUARY ~~

* *

If Janiver's calends be summerly gay

Twill be wintry weather to the calends of May.

- Olde English words of wisdom

* *

To many people living in the Ohio Valley, January is a bleak, grey, cold, long month, with nothing to look forward to except more of the same in February! Some say the best thing about February is that it is a shorter month. The holidays are past and it is an anticlimactic time. Twilight seems to come at mid-day, the germs seem to proliferate like weeds in a flower garden and generally, people are in a slump unless you are a gardener! I personally like January! It is a new beginning to a year of garden ideas and plans. The house looks fresh and clean and uncluttered after the holiday decorations are packed and stored for another year. My calendar is new and empty and waiting in anticipation for an entry. My New Year's resolutions are still intact and I feel cozy inside the house with a gardening catalogue in my lap as I look out at the cold starkness of winter. I find beauty in the snow that glistens on the seedpods and grasses that I have intentionally left standing in my garden. The moonlight is brighter and casts long evening shadows across the blanket of snow under the spruces. My perennials are tucked in for the winter and that snow cover is an insulator. They are happy and so am I. The birds and squirrels are entertaining at the deck feeders and all is right with my world. I like the quiet, dormant beauty of winter and the anticipation of what the New Year will bring, in both my life and in my gardens.

However, I do not live in the confinement of a nursing home or health care facility and so it is easy for me to have those positive feelings about the long month after the holidays! This is the time when horticultural therapy plays a very important role in the mental attitude of the residents of nursing homes.

This is a great time for presenting a slide show on brightly colored tropical flowers from warm climates with blue skies and sunshine! Beautiful flowers do seem to chase away the post-holiday blues. I love sharing my tropical photos with the residents on one of those bleak days, and this always seem to spawn conversation about their travels or just the weather in general.

Another great January program is that of force-blooming spring bulbs. I like to use paper white narcissus because of the fun and ease of doing it in a container of gravel. Theoretically, it should be done earlier than January, but if you can keep the bulbs refrigerated, it is worth it.

The fragrance of my show and tell sample fills our work area and everyone can think, and smell spring as we talk about spring bulbs of other varieties.

Another favorite project in January is one that has the residents working with the delightful fragrance of lavender, whether it's put into a sachet or made into a bath powder.

If you read further, the complete modules for these projects follow:

SESSION TITLE: Bulbs for All Seasons

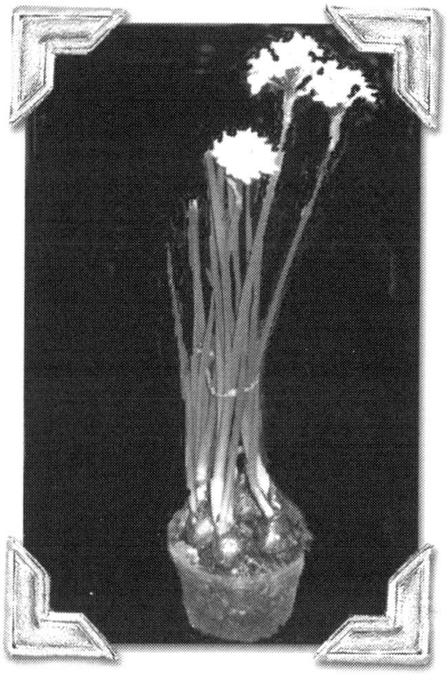

PROGRAM DESCRIPTION: This is a winter session where force-blooming Paperwhite Narcissus is the hands-on activity.

BACKGROUND INFORMATION: Bulbs are little food and energy warehouses. Food is taken in through the leaves, goes to the bulb and is stored there. That is why you never cut the leaves off bulbs until they have turned brown and wilted. The stored food and energy sustains the plant while it is resting up for the next growing season.

There are three kinds of bulbs:

1. *Hardy bulbs* - these can remain in the ground all year without worry of a freeze. Example: daffodils, crocus, tulips and hyacinths

2. *Half-hardy bulbs* - those that can remain in the ground in mild climates. Example: Grecian windflowers, oxalis

3. *Tender bulbs* - those that cannot be left in the ground over the winter unless you live in the tropics. Example: Canna bulbs and Dahlias.

All bulbs need a rest period and some need cold temperatures to bring them out of dormancy.

Bulbs blooming outside signal the end of winter. The sweet fragrances are good for the spirit! Bulbs and flowering branches forced indoors are even more appreciated on a cold, bleak winter day. Did you know that squirrels think that tulips are a gourmet lunch but they will leave daffodils alone? Spring bulbs are great to plant in areas that receive no sun during the summer months because of tree foliage. They bloom before the trees are in full leaf.

Most everyone thinks of bulbs as being only spring flowering bulbs. There are beautiful summer blooming bulbs as well, for example, Lilies, Caladium and the stately Gladiolas

MATERIALS REQUIRED:

- A four-inch–deep, clear saucer
- Medium-sized gravel
- Two Paperwhite Narcissus bulbs per participant
- A scoop for the gravel
- One plastic bag per person to work on
- A small watering can
- Black waterproof marker
- A sample of one you have pre-forced to show the results and to appreciate the heavy perfume

HANDS-ON INSTRUCTIONS:

1. Pass out the plastic bags to work on and the saucers to plant in.
2. Have each person scoop out enough gravel to fill the container about half way.
3. Distribute two bulbs to each participant and show them how to set the bulbs on top

of the gravel.

4. Give them more gravel to bury the bulb.
5. They can then add water up to the bottom of the bulb. Do not cover the bulb with water!
6. With the black marker, draw a line indicating the water line.

When they return to their rooms, they have to place the bulb container in a cool, dark place for about one week in order for a strong root system to develop. When the green sprouts have reached about 2” tall, they can bring the pot out of the dark and place it in a sunny windowsill. They will be able to see the roots developing and must keep the water level at the marker line to prevent the roots from drying out. Every day the container should be turned one-half turn so that the sunlight hits all sides. The foliage will lean towards the light. By rotating the pot, the foliage will grow straight. In approximately three-to-four weeks, they should be enjoying the sweetness of the flowers and thinking of spring!

SPECIAL NOTES: This is not a good session for those patients who tend to put everything in their mouths.

Include pictures of bulbs and/or flower catalogues for discussion purposes. Take any flowering branches that you have forced or potted, blooming bulbs, or even a bouquet of spring flowers for show and tell. It’s nice to fool Mother Nature!

RESPONSES TO THIS SESSION:

The month following this session brings a show and tell reaction from the participants. It turns into a competition that is ongoing for weeks. “How many flowers do you have?” “When did yours produce the first flower?” “How long did it last?” “I have one more bud, do you?” “It does help to think spring.”

SESSION TITLE: Lavender Bath Powder or Lavender Sachets

PROGRAM DESCRIPTION: This hands-on session begins with a discussion of the herb lavender and the reasoning behind the usage of bath powder throughout history. This is a good sensory stimulating session, utilizing the senses of smell, touch and sight. By the end of this session, each participant will have a small shaker top container of lavender scented bath powder to take with them.

BACKGROUND INFORMATION: In the 16th century, it was not customary to bathe daily. Both the men and women wore perfume and powders. Strewing herbs in their homes and fragrant water splashes on their bodies were used freely. These things were necessary since the fancy, puffed out clothing was rarely ever cleaned.

Powders of flour, cornstarch and a fragrance, became very popular during the 19th century in Queen Victoria's time and both men and women used them. The wigs were powdered as well as the body.

Lavender (Lavandula) is part of the mint family, which is evidenced by its square stem. There are twenty-eight different varieties of this "Herb of the Year 1999." In the language of flowers it means devotion and/or purity.

Lavender owes its name to the Latin word, "lavare," which means to wash. This is a reference to its use in scenting the water of the public baths in ancient Rome. It was known even then that the fragrance of lavender had a soothing and calming effect.

Lavender was cultivated for its fragrance, and English lavender is most desired for the perfumery business. The English have been in love with the genus forever. The "true" or English lavender came with the colonists to America and is a good drought-tolerant plant. It prefers to grow in slightly alkaline, well drained, not too rich soil and wants to be protected from high winds. The best color and scent is produced when it's planted in the full sun. The flowers range from a pale pink to burgundy to purple to a blue color and are used in many recipes where a subtle sweetness is desired. Lavender tea, cakes, jellies, sugars and ice cream are just a few of the lavender treats enjoyed by many gourmet cooks.

This herb gained a reputation as the herb of war as far back as the ancient Roman times. Because of its antiseptic qualities, the Roman soldiers always carried its essential oil in their first aid kits. The English battlefield nurses during WWI also made use of lavender's antiseptic quality when their supply of military antiseptics ran low. Sphagnum moss sprinkled with the oil of lavender made very effective bandages. Quite a few soldiers owed their arms and legs to this herb's antiseptic quality.

There are other medicinal uses for lavender. The oil of lavender is used to treat insect bites and to promote rapid healing of burns, as well as wounds and acne. It is used as a calming agent and therefore, migraines, insomnia and stress are relieved by its use. This beautiful herb also repels some insects, and sachets filled with lavender flowers will keep cupboards free of moths. Cotton balls soaked with the oil of lavender and tied in a muslin bag will keep a room free of flies.

In Elizabethan times, lavender was mixed with charcoal and used as a tooth cleaner. Because of so many varied uses for a single herb, it was recommended as the herb of choice if you only had space for one herb in your medicine chest.

Lavender was also considered a sacred herb in many of the ancient rituals honoring the gods. It was thought to help the person rise above difficulties and see things more clearly.

It is said that the oil of lavender is a soothing rub for arthritic joints. It is amazing to me that this delicate, beautiful flower has so many varied uses. It must have been a medicine man's dream come true!

It takes twelve pounds of lavender flowers to produce one ounce of the essential oil. The essential oil is the lifeblood of a plant. It is the essence of the plant. It is what makes lavender, lavender and a rose, a rose. These essential oils are produced by extracting the highly concentrated essences from flowers, leaves, stems, fruits, berries, resin or roots of plants.

MATERIALS REQUIRED:

- Mortar and pestle for grinding the lavender blossoms (optional)
- Stems of dried lavender flowers
- A tablespoon measure

- Wax paper to be used for mixing
- Teaspoons for mixing
- Containers and lids
- Lavender oil
- Corn starch (corn flour)
- White clay (Kaolin)
- Labels and a purple pen for labeling
- Narrow purple ribbon and scissors (optional)
- Various lavender scented items such as room sprays, shampoo, candles, and lotions
- Pictures of lavender fields or varieties of lavender from plant catalogues

White clay (kaolin), also called china clay or porcelain clay, is the purest form of clay. It consists mostly of the mineral kaolinite, which is formed by the decomposition of rocks containing feldspar. Eighty percent of USA kaolin is produced in Georgia for the production of dusting powders. Its fluffy nature wicks moisture away from the body.

Cornstarch stabilizes the mixture and retains the added scent of the lavender oil and flowers, which absorbs body odors, and leaves your skin feeling silky smooth.

HANDS-ON INSTRUCTIONS:

1. Show the different lavender scented items to everyone and let their noses enjoy the scents!
2. Distribute pieces of wax paper and teaspoons to everyone.
3. Measure out two tablespoons of both the clay and the cornstarch and place in separate piles on their wax paper pieces.

4. Give instructions on thoroughly blending the two mounds, using their teaspoon, and noticing the differences in the white and beige colors being mixed.
5. Add two drops of the essential oil to the mixture of clay and cornstarch and have them totally mix that into the powder.
6. Give all participants stems of dried lavender and show how to strip and crush the flowers off the stem to get the maximum fragrance released. You can have them grind the flowers using the mortar and pestle at this point, or have them just crush the flowers between their fingers if the mortar and pestle aren't available.
7. Blend these crushed flowers into the powder mix with the teaspoon provided. At this point, distribute the containers, minus the lids.
8. Using the purple pen, identify the contents, or the participant's initials, on the label and affix to the front of the container.
9. Show how to fill the containers using the teaspoons. All of the mixing and spooning into the containers help with small motor skills and eye-hand development. If any of the powder spills on their hands, just rub it in and have them enjoy the fragrance.
10. The snap on shaker caps are the last item given to them because once these caps are snapped into place, they cannot be removed!
11. Now it's time to cut a piece of purple ribbon and tie it in a bow around the neck of the container. The clean up for this project is also pleasant because I tell them that even the garbage cans will smell great.

SPECIAL INSTRUCTIONS: Keep the container closed for about a week before using it so that the fragrance permeates the powder sufficiently. Then enjoy after a bath or shower and feel the elegance of lavender!

A RESPONSE TO THIS SESSION:

After completing and enjoying the aroma of this lavender session, a woman commented to the others, "I've waited seventy years to smell this pretty." She told us that she had wanted to be like her school friends and wear fragrances. That was her Christmas gift request as a young girl. Her mother told her that was, "not a practical gift." She received shoes instead.

SESSION TITLE: Lavendar Sachets

These sachets can be used to scent dresser drawers or closets or to just enjoy the fragrance on top of the nightstand.

* * * * * * * * * * * * * * * * * * * *

Not all lavender varieties are purple

* * * * * * * * * * * * * * * * * * * *

MATERIALS REQUIRED:

- Dried lavender flowers
- Fine lavender colored netting precut to a 13" x 13" size/ participant
- A twelve inch piece of narrow purple ribbon per participant
- Wax paper to work on

HANDS-ON INSTRUCTIONS:

The above background information can be used for this project as well.

1. Distribute the wax paper and about a dozen stems of dried lavender per participant.
2. Show them how to remove the lavender from the stems by pressing it with their fingers (as in the project above).
3. Distribute the net squares and have them fill the center of the square with the lavender flowers.
4. Bundle up the netting and tie with the lavender ribbon forming a bow. The more often they touch the finished product, the more fragrance will surround them! Enjoy!

~~ FEBRUARY ~~

* *

Much February snow

A fine summer doth show.

- Olde English words of wisdom

* *

The groundhog provides a lot of joking and laughter this month. "Will he see his shadow? Will he be able to dig out of his burrow in the snow? Oh no, six more weeks of winter; or does that mean that spring will be just around the corner? Do you believe that groundhog gibberish anyway?" I personally feel that he should be part of pet therapy! He is joked about, criticized, and talked about, for days before and after his entrance into the cold morning.

Fortunately, Valentine's Day takes over where the groundhog lets off!

Hearts, roses, fragrances and flowers help bring smiles to the resident's faces this month.

Since I always give my groups a "garden report" of the happenings in my yard, I can happily report that the Lenten Rose (Helleborus) is in frosty bloom now and that the delicate, white snowdrops and bright yellow, shiny petals of the winter aconite have brightened the floor of the woods in my back yard. Everyone is anticipating the first crocus to poke through the frozen earth, and Mother Nature has brought optimism and the hope of springtime to the room.

I also have a slide show entitled, "The Beauty in All Seasons," and showing this provides a feeling of optimism and light heartedness. It seems to be uplifting to see the beauty of a snowy-capped thistle, the red berries on an icy crabapple branch, the yellow forsythia in bloom, or the persevering pansy wearing a cap of fluffy white snow.

This is also the month when those beautiful, enticing seed packets appear in the stores. I can never pass up that display. This is truly a case of my eyes being bigger than my garden space! How could I possibly think I would have space for all these varieties that I've purchased? Perhaps the best part of February is the garden that blooms in our mind's eye. There is always enough space, the flowers always grow to perfection and there are never bugs that demolish the fruits of our labor, nor bindweed choking the life out of their stems. They always look just like the picture on that seed packet!

Read on to see how you can use your extra seed packets or enjoy the hearts and flowers that this month signifies.

SESSION TITLE: Hearts and Flowers

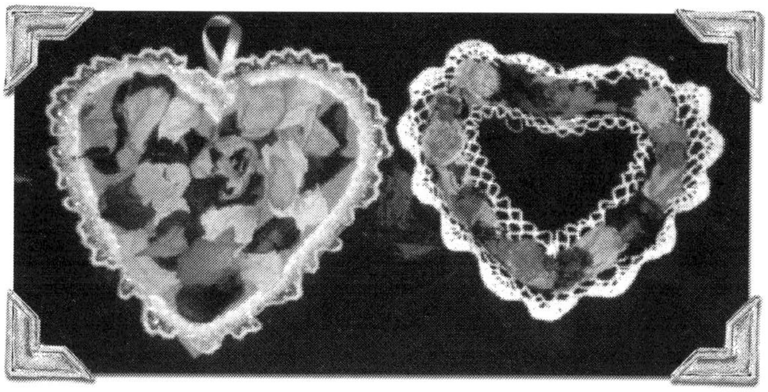

PROGRAM DESCRIPTION: Participants of any functioning level will enjoy this very simple hands-on session, depending on the materials used. I have used just dried rose petals for low functioning groups, and a combination of dried roses, carnations or other small dried flowers for more capable levels of residents.

Because of the familiarity of crocheted items in the older population, this activity stimulates the memory because of the lacy appearance of the background material as well as the remembrances of roses from gardens or wedding bouquets. The small motor skills are stimulated by the act of gluing the rose petals and flowers onto the background, and the cognitive level is awakened by the decision of the arrangement of flowers or choice of colors of rose petals used.

I have used pink foam paper, trimmed in lace for the lower functioning groups, and they love the "pinkness" for Valentines Day. This product is also much easier to glue onto than the crochet items and, thereby, eliminates frustration with the procedure.

The higher functioning groups like the dainty look of the crocheted heart background and many have used this as their door decoration for the month of February.

BACKGROUND INFORMATION: There are more than one hundred species of roses and each one is loved! The rose is our national flower. Depending on the color, it can signify passionate love or just a great friendship. Red signifies love, yellow means joy and friendship, and the white rose indicates purity, innocence and beauty. In the Victorian era, the yellow rose was a symbol of jealousy.

The rose can be placed in one of the following general categories:

1. The hybrid tea rose is a single flower on one single stem.
2. The floribunda rose produces many flowers on a stem.
3. The climbing rose can be either a floribunda or a tea variety.
4. The grandiflora rose is a tall tea rose.
5. The shrub rose is the hardiest and most disease resistant. The rugosa variety produces tasty hips that are a source of vitamin C. They contain more vitamin C than oranges and are also rich in vitamins A and B.
6. The miniature rose varieties grow just six-to-ten inches tall and require a lot of water.
7. The wild rose has a brief flowering period and is a source of nutrients for wildlife.

Roses provide excellent shelter and protection for the birds. The prickly stems provide great nesting sites for the smaller birds. Cats will think twice before sticking their paws into a thorn-covered bramble. Roses are also a valuable winter food source for birds.

The rose has been cultivated since biblical times. It was a symbol of all things pleasurable to the ancient Romans and Greeks.

The first roses were in Persia. The Hanging Gardens of Babylon had over three hundred varieties of roses and were a remarkable sight. The Elizabethans sat in rose gardens to induce a quiet and calm mood, and Cleopatra slept on pillows filled with fresh rose petals.

To this day, you can purchase rose oil and rose scented room fresheners to try to capture that same feeling of calmness.

Studies have shown that rose oil can lift depression, calm the heart and soothe irritability, grief and anger.

The colonists used roses for dyes, medicines, pomanders, oils, confections and in wine making. Petals and rose hips steeped into a tea can bring down fevers and clear toxins out of the body. Rose syrup can be taken to relieve sore throats, and rose water placed on the temples can help end a headache. Rose water washes help tighten sagging skin and rose cream can be used to keep the skin baby-smooth.

The Damask Rose is the oldest of all varieties, dating back to 2000 B.C. and is grown for its essential oil, known as attar of roses. This is the variety that is desirable for making perfumes. While hybrids will live thirty to forty years, antique varieties can live up to one hundred and fifty years or more. As a result, the fragrances from antique roses are more potent and their healing properties more effective.

And you thought that the rose was just beautiful to look at!

MATERIALS REQUIRED:

- One heart shaped item as the background for each participant. If using the pink foam paper, glue lace around the edges and make a pink ribbon loop at the top for hanging purposes. If using the crocheted form, it is a less frustrating project if you line the well with white tissue paper. This step makes the gluing process much easier. Have this much completed prior to the session.

- Fresh roses in a vase to stimulate the sense of smell
- Dried rose petals of various colors and/or other small dried flowers (e.g. dried carnations, sweetheart roses, statice, baby's breath, etc.)
- White glue for everyone
- Handy wipes for cleaning sticky fingers
- Plastic bags to work on so that the glue doesn't make a mess on the working surface (optional)
- A finished sample for demonstration purposes
- Pictures of rose varieties from mail order catalogues

Rose petals drying are beautiful in themselves.

HANDS-ON INSTRUCTIONS:

1. Pass around the sample for everyone's observation and reaction. There will probably be shared memories already at this point in the session.
2. Spread out the dried rose petals, or other dried flowers, on the table and encourage the participants to feel the dried petals as well as to smell the fresh roses in a vase, if you have them.
3. Distribute the plastic bags, if you are using them, the glue and the wet cloths at this time. The cognitive skills go to work with the decision making process of types of petals or flowers to use.
4. Once the petals are in place, advise them to allow the project to remain flat until the glue dries completely.

SPECIAL INSTRUCTIONS: Be advised that in the lower functioning groups, the dried yellow rose petals may resemble potato chips and will want to be sampled!

RESPONSES TO THIS SESSION (or to any that utilizes roses):

A gentleman who didn't want to participate, told us that he was an award winning rose grower and also raised show dogs. He went into great length to tell us the care that was required to grow roses. The activity director was impressed that he was sharing any information with us because he rarely, if ever, participated in any discussions. This same man came back for my session the next month.

A very uncommunicative Alzheimer resident began talking about her beautiful rose garden. The activity director noted, "She hasn't spoken about anything coherently in weeks and here she is talking about beautiful roses!" That resident even helped with the clean up when we finished working on the project. She was happy for that hour.

SESSION TITLE: Mardi Gras Masks

PROGRAM DESCRIPTION: This is a session that causes a lot of laughter and fun as the participants create their own floral masks and then model them for each other. Depending on the level of ability of the participant, the masks will be color coordinated and detailed in design or just colorful. Any ability level seems to enjoy this program and as simple as it seems, there is ample opportunity for small muscle development and strengthening, as well as eye-hand coordination and cognitive skills. The social interaction is obvious when they model their finished creations.

BACKGROUND INFORMATION: The Mardi Gras celebration came to this country by a group of homesick French explorers in 1699. It took place at the mouth of the Mississippi River as they toasted the King of France, in remembrance of the holiday being celebrated back home. It took one hundred years though, before settlers were able to make Mardi Gras a major part of their culture. It now occupies many weeks each spring and has months of preparation going into it. While Mardi Gras and New Orleans seem to be synonymous, Mobile, Alabama's celebration claims to be older, as well as more family-oriented. Mobile claims to have been the first Mardi Gras celebration! Celebrations there begin about four weeks before Fat Tuesday, and there may be as many as thirty-five parades before it draws to a close.

"Mardi Gras" is a French phrase translated to mean "Tuesday Fat" and was observed on the eve before Ash Wednesday, the beginning of the Lenten Season. You could eat, drink and be merry on that evening because the next day Lent began, a time of fasting, abstinence and penance for Christians. "Shrove Tuesday" is the Olde English terminology for that same night. "Shrove" translates into "repent." Shrovetide was celebrated for the three days preceding Ash Wednesday. It was interesting to see how many participants identified with Mardi Gras, Fat Tuesday or the Shrove Tuesday terminology.

It also initiated remembrances and conversations about their past trips to New Orleans and/or their specific Mardi Gras festivities.

The holiday actually had its origin in ancient Greece and Rome as a pagan spring ritual. Since Christian leaders found it impossible to remove the practice from the population, they decided to incorporate it as part of the feast day before Lent. Truly a case of, if you can't beat them, join them!

There are specific colors to Mardi Gras. They are green, purple and gold and have specific meanings. The green color signifies faith, the purple is for justice and the gold colors indicate power. In Fairhope, Alabama, a town with floral displays throughout the year in its downtown area, Mardi Gras brings hundreds of yellow daffodils, purple and yellow pansies and purple hyacinths to the main streets, much to the delight of the visitors.

Another carnival tradition is the King Cake. Inside the cake is a small toy doll, and the person who gets that slice has to buy the next cake.

There are some varieties of flowers with "Mardi Gras" in their name. A few of them are: Helenium 'Mardi Gras" (Helen's flower), a perennial that produces a riot of multicolored blooms for six-to-eight weeks in the summer, from late June to early August. They have yellow petals lavishly splashed with orange-red color. Hemerocallis "Mardi Gras Ball," is a gorgeous lavender day lily with a burgundy colored eye. The entire edge appears to have been dipped in brilliant gold paint. Hemerocallis "Mardi Gras Parade" is a beautiful rose and wine colored day lily. Mardi Gras Spray Asters are purple, among other colors, and are a very sturdy, bushy plant whose flowers will stay fresh in a vase for two weeks.

Heuchera "Mardi Gras," (Coral Bells), has huge leaves that reflect a changing palette of variegation from coral to orange to green to gray.

MATERIALS REQUIRED:

- a purple, green or gold plastic mask for each participant
- dried flowers and petals

- clear drying glue
- sample masks
- wet paper towels or wipes for hands
- purple, green and gold Mardi Gras beads (to wear as part of your outfit… If possible have a strand for each participant as well.)

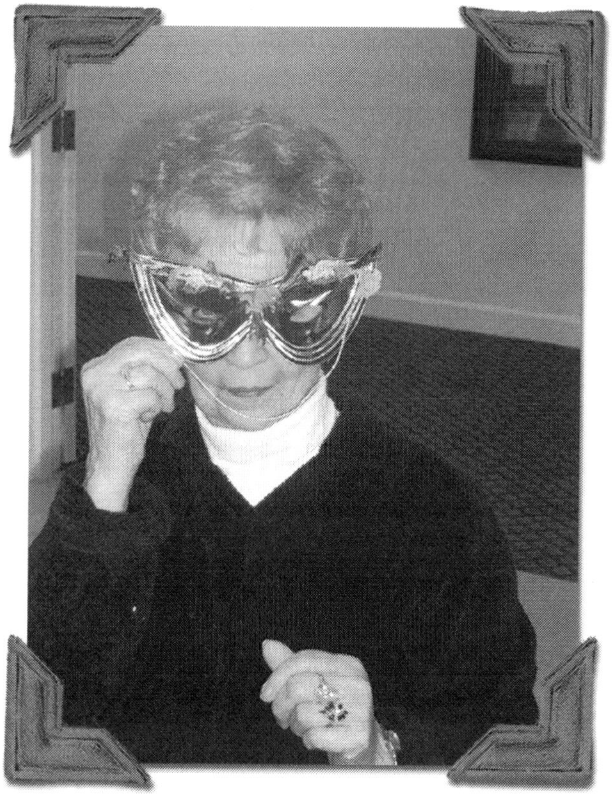

HANDS-ON INSTRUCTIONS:

1. Give everyone the choice of colored beads and a mask.
2. Show the sample masks.
3. Show the container of dried petals and let them smell the floral fragrances.
4. Spread the dried petals out in the center of the table and see if they can identify any of the petals and flowers as to those that they grew in their own gardens.
5. Pass out the individual glue containers, if your group is high functioning.
6. Explain that there is no right or wrong way to decorate their mask. Some may completely cover the mask with petals; others may do individual designs, or eyelashes, with their petals.

7. Pass out the paper towels to remove the glue from hands and then suggest that they either hold them up or if the glue has dried, model their work of art. Be prepared for the laughter to begin!

NOTES: This session is adaptable to low functioning groups as well. You will have to spread the glue on the masks for them, but allow the participant to pick up the petals and put them in the glue. You may be surprised at the creativity displayed.

~~ MARCH ~~

* *

Sweet peas sown on St. Patrick's Day are said to produce larger, more fragrant blooms

- Olde English words of wisdom

* *

Spring is officially here this month! Did it come in like a lion or a lamb? Even if the weather doesn't seem any different from January, it feels better to know that "spring has sprung."

It might be windy, rainy and chilly but "March winds and April showers bring forth May flowers!" Spirits are lifted as high as the kites that soar on the wind.

There is a plethora of spring flowers in my yard creating a virtual palate of pastel colors. I have planted hundreds of bulbs in my yard and in my woods and Mother Nature has added to my efforts with her wonderful wildflowers. My woods are a carpet of spring beauties; trillium, bloodroot, squirrel corn, Dutchman's breeches and eight hundred yellow daffodils and crocus! This wooded area is very dry and heavily shaded and the springtime is the only time that there is magnificent color in it. Once the trees have leafed out, my pleasure from the woods comes in the form of shade and coolness and a feeling of tranquility as I listen to the owls and tree frogs converse at night. I also enjoy the serenade of the songbirds during the daylight hours. I always think that I like this season the best of all...until the next season's beauty arrives!

The program possibilities seem endless for this month. Read further and see how shamrocks, pansies, heirloom gardens and red clover hold the interest and provide horticultural therapy for the residents this month.

SESSION TITLE: Red Clover

PROGRAM DESCRIPTION: This is a "play in the dirt" kind of session that will stimulate small muscle development and motor skills, as well as reminiscent conversation. This session has the participants learning about the benefits of the red clover blossom to man, insect and farm animal. The participants will plant red clover seeds and have the pot to take with them to care for. If they give it good care, perhaps they will be able to harvest a handful of the blossoms for their own cup of tea.

BACKGROUND INFORMATION: The red clover is also known as purple clover or meadow trefoil because of its three leaves. Less than a generation ago, it was the main ingredient in homemade spring tonics because of its reputation as an all-around wellness herb and blood-purifying agent.

The Chinese revered red clover sap as a remedy for colds and influenza. It was a popular healing plant in Europe and came to this country with the colonists. It grows wild today but is still considered a healing herb. The blossoms contain hormone like substances called estrogenic plant sterols, as well as important minerals, including calcium, magnesium, potassium and vitamins B and C. At the turn of the century, this herb was brewed into a strong tea to halt spasmodic coughing, and Mennonite communities still rely on it to ease whooping cough and croup.

Also known as a sweet herb, butterflies feed on its blossom. Its use also extends to the farmers who plant it for soil improvement and for forage and wild life feed. It can be traced to prehistoric times when it was also used as an agricultural crop.

The red clover is the most popular and widely grown clover variety. There are three different types, depending on its flowering season. It grows best in the northeastern states where the summers are cooler and there is sufficient moisture during the growing season. Since 1894, this clover has been adapted as the state flower of Vermont.

In the southeast, it grows as a winter annual.

The red clover is a honeybee's gourmet meal. The large blossoms are very sweet tasting and smell like honey. When you buy "clover honey," there is usually some red clover in the finished product, for the sweetening agent.

The smaller white clover variety is also an important pasture crop that grows best in humid, hot areas. Sadly, for the butterflies and bees, most people try to rid their lawns of this invasive plant because of the bees that it attracts.

The common clover gained celebrity status during the days when St. Patrick roamed around Ireland using it to demonstrate the unity of the Trinity to his listeners. He did this in a land where people easily believed in mythical beings such as elves, fairies, goblins and leprechauns. Clover was considered a good luck symbol as well as a protector of love and heroism. The clover was adapted by the Greeks and Romans to mark festive occasions and as garlands to grace their banquet halls.

Today, we recognize the red clover as an important herb which has many varied uses, such as a general tonic, a good muscle relaxant , an excellent blood purifier, an expectorant and a tasty tea used for getting a good night's sleep. It is also used to make a poultice to treat skin eczema and to soothe burns and sores. It has also been used to treat indigestion, urinary tract infections, muscle cramps and arthritis! Because of its popularity, it can be easily purchased at vitamin stores in capsule form, which is the most concentrated form. You can also buy it in a tincture form that can be added to water and used as a gargle for coughs, bronchitis, sore throats and, as reported in Victoriana times, for "weak lungs."

The tea form is easily found in stores, or you can make your own! Pick wild clover from unsprayed locations on a dry day, choosing blossoms that are fresh and colorful--a bright, rosy purple. Thoroughly wash and dry before using. Use one handful of fresh blossoms and a few leaves into a two-cup teapot. Fill with boiling water, cover and infuse for five to ten minutes on low heat. Strain into a hot cup, add a twist of lemon and sweeten with honey if desired. You can also add a sprig of fresh mint to give it added flavor.

Red clover flowers can be dried for later use in tea. Dry them in the sun, in a single layer. Use less of the dried flowers, than the fresh, when making tea. Approximately one, to one and a half teaspoons of dried clover per cup of water makes a good cup of tea. Enjoy!

Besides using the flowers for making a tea, you can also use them to make vinegar, a sweet butter, as an omelet additive or in Irish Clover Bread. Of course, a red clover wine has also been popular! Recipes for these can be found in a book entitled, "The Forgotten Art of Flower Cookery," by Leona Woodring Smith.

MATERIALS REQUIRED:

1. Take a sample pot of previously planted seeds for show and tell purposes
2. Have a purchased red clover tea bag for each participant
3. Potting soil
4. Spoon "shovels"
5. Plastic bags to work on
6. Red clover seeds
7. Small watering can
8. Cups or flower pots and saucers
9. Gravel, if using a container without a drainage hole
10. Quart sized sandwich bag
11. Handy wipes for cleaning of hands when finished
12. Plastic gloves (optional)

HANDS-ON INSTRUCTIONS:

1. Distribute the plastic bags, pots (cups and gravel if using these) and the shovel spoons.
2. Have them fill their containers to within an inch of the top, with potting soil.
3. Instruct them to take a pinch of the tiny red clover seeds and sprinkle them on top of the soil.
4. Cover with a thin layer of dirt, pat down gently and water.
5. Put the sandwich bag over the cup, like a tent, to help in the germination process and to keep an even moisture until the first leaves appear.

Participants will be able to see the beads of moisture form on the inside of the bag. It should take about ten days to germinate. Once the first set of leaves has appeared, the bag can be removed and frequent watering will be necessary. Keep in a sunny window. If the participants are tea drinkers, give them a purchased red clover tea bag to enjoy at their next meal.

SPECIAL INSTRUCTIONS: This can be a very good session to use in conjunction with St. Patrick's Day on March 17th. You may also want to ask the participants if they know any songs with the word clover in them. "Put on your old grey bonnet with the blue ribbon on it...," and "I'm looking over a four-leafed clover...," will most certainly get a song fest started!

RESPONSES HEARD DURING THIS SESSION:

One participant was writing a children's book about forgotten games and she was glad to remember making clover chains when she was a little girl herself. That pastime was now to be added to her book!

Another resident told us, "I'm a farm girl and I know all about red clover. My Dad used it to feed the livestock, to keep them healthy."

It seems as if there is never a session where someone does not share a childhood memory. That is also horticultural therapy!

<u>SESSION TITLE: Seed Art</u>

The pig and the cow are made entirely from different types of beans and seeds.

PROGRAM DESCRIPTION: This colorful, creative, hands-on program can develop the eye-hand coordination skills as well as the small motor skills. It focuses on springtime in the dead of winter and the colorful seed packets are cheerful and uplifting. The discussion centers on the structure of seeds. With the help of a large poster board display, showing the various sizes and shapes of seeds, an appreciation of the wonders of Mother Nature is again discussed. This session can be used and enjoyed by any level of ability. The results will be more perfect and complex with the higher functioning groups, however.

BACKGROUND INFORMATION: The length and detail of the discussion depends on the level of the group participating. The higher functioning the group, the more scientific the presentation. The lower functioning groups need little information but more time given to the actual project itself and the reminiscences that will ensue.

A seed is a plant-survival capsule. It contains a minute embryonic plant surrounded by a food store. Both are protected by a tough seed coat, allowing some seeds to remain dormant in the soil for decades or even centuries.

The uptake of water, through the minute sized pores in the seed coat, triggers germination of the seed. The cells inside then expand generating pressure on the rigid seed coat which then ruptures. Proteins, carbohydrates and fats, in the unfurling leavers sustain the early growth of the root and shoot. These are some of the same nutrients that we humans also require for our development.

All seeds have a seed coat. It can be tough and leathery, brittle , porous or even water proof (like the coconut seed), or smooth or hairy. No matter what its shape, size or texture, all seeds have a little scar at the point where the seed breaks free from its stalk. When you see the first tiny leaf sprout, this is called the seed cotyledon. Now you know that your plant is on its way to becoming an adult. The next thing you see is the first true leaf pair. It has germinated and is now an independent plant. The miracle of life has begun!

Seeds travel many ways from one place to another. These methods of dispersal allow the species to survive and spread out to new areas.

Coconuts have the largest seeds surrounded by a thick fibrous husk and they are water-proof, which is why they float in seawater and germinate many miles from where they might have originated. The waves wash them ashore and eventually that beach will have a new palm tree. Some seeds, such as those of the orchid, are as small as dust particles.

Some seeds are hooked and become entangled in the fur of animals and the feathers of birds and can be carried long distances from their origin.

Wild cherry trees and the rose hips from the wild roses varieties, as well as many garden flowers, provide food for the birds and are deposited great distances away in the bird's droppings. That is how flowers pop up unexpectedly in your garden and give pleasure in their blooms without the effort of you planting them. Other plants, like the dandelion, milkweed and butterfly weed, form seeds that are carried on plumes by air currents and can go as far as the wind takes them. Maple trees produce a multitude of seeds that children call helicopters, and they also twirl and soar on the air currents. If they land on fertile ground, another maple tree begins. That is how the forests are born.

The woodland animals help with this re-forestation too. Squirrels carry acorns and pinecones away from the parent tree and store them for winter. If they forget where they buried them, that acorn or pinecone will sprout and the mighty oak or pine tree has begun.

An exploding type of seed process disperses some seeds, like the touch-me-nots, peas and beans. They have succulent fruit walls which develops an enormous tension as they dry out. Their seeds hurl away from the parent plant when the pod splits open. Plant breeders eliminate this dispersal mechanism for crops so that the seeds can be harvested before they are exploded.

An interesting fact about seeds is that the large seeds, which are produced in smaller number, are generally long-lived, while the tiny seeds that are produced in enormous numbers are often short-lived.

Plants didn't always produce seeds. Millions of years ago, when the world was mostly water or swamp, spore producers, like the ferns and mosses, were supreme because they used the water to reproduce. Once the landmasses formed, the earth's climate changed and the seasons were born. Seed bearing plants were one adaptation to the drier conditions.

Not only do squirrels and other animals of the forest eat seeds. Seeds also form a larger part of man's diet than any other part of the plant. About ninety percent of all plants cultivated for their seeds are cereal grains, like wheat, corn, rice and oats.

The second major source of food for both man and animals are seeds of the legume family, such as peas and beans. Soybeans and peanuts are also part of this family, which supply half of the world's edible oils.

MATERIALS REQUIRED:

- colored construction paper
- a variety of seed packets or flower photos from seed catalogues
- clear drying glue
- handy wipes
- plastic bags to protect working surface
- large sunflower seeds
- sample of finished product
- seed packet poster
- samples of various seed pods such as lotus pods, milkweed pods, coconut seed, pinecone, peas, helicopters, etc.
- various photos, if available, of flowers blooming before the seed pod is formed
- scalloped edged scissors for trimming the paper
- black marker for signing the artwork
- any variety of seeds from your kitchen: mustard seeds, sesame seed, poppy seeds, caraway seeds, etc.

HANDS-ON INSTRUCTIONS:

1. Distribute the glue and plastic bags.
2. Show the finished sample so that participants can feel the seeds and understand what they are to do.
3. Give each participant the choice of the seed packet (or picture) and the construction paper.
4. Carefully open the seed packet and empty out the seeds. The participants may want to incorporate those seeds into their design.
5. Give each one a handful of the large sunflower seeds.
6. Demonstrate how to glue the packet or picture in the center of the colored construction paper.
7. Use the large seeds to trim the packet or to create a seed frame. See photo for placement ideas.

When their artwork is completed, trim the edges of the paper with a fancy edged scissors and initial the finished masterpiece. It is now time for show and tell!

SPECIAL INSTRUCTIONS: This session incorporates a lot of sensory stimulation, and even though it is difficult for the visually impaired to participate, they can still enjoy it because of the touching of the various seeds. One such resident decided she could do the actual placement of seeds around the packet, if I would just put the glue where she directed me. She did it very successfully by feeling where the glue was and then dropping the seed onto it. The handy wipes were a constant necessity to avoid the frustration of the seeds sticking to her fingers, but she was most pleased with herself upon completion of the project.

The accompanying photos and colors of the seed packets and construction paper were described in great detail to her and she felt a part of the group.

RESPONSES TO THIS SESSION:

The seed packets themselves triggered fond memories for one participant, whose family had been involved in a seed packing house. Unbelievably, another woman in that same group told us that her father had been the foreman at The Burpee Seed packaging operation. What was the chance of that happening! That experience verified the fact that horticultural therapy has many forms and you just never know what is going to trigger the conversation and memories.

<u>SESSION TITLE: Everybody is Irish</u>

PROGRAM DESCRIPTION: Here are two ideas for low functioning groups that involve smelling, smiling and probably singing!

In the first project, they are asked to glue dried, crushed, green herbs, such as mints or parsley, onto a large shamrock shape. The herbs are fragrant and eye-hand coordination and small motor skills are stimulated by the crushing and gluing motions.

The second project is a more passive one for even lower functioning participants. An Irish spoon doll is whimsical and as the individuals' names develop as a smile on the spoon face, a smile is also inadvertently formed on their own faces as well. Usually by the end of this session, you can hear the words of "When Irish Eyes Are Smiling" being sung by everyone, because in March everyone is Irish.

BACKGROUND INFORMATION: The first written reference in the English language of the shamrock was in 1571. It was called St. Patrick's cabbage. It is actually native to Spain but was found growing in Ireland as well. As St. Patrick walked and preached over the Irish countryside, he picked the tiny clover and used it to explain the concept of the Trinity. Surprisingly, the shamrock is not the national emblem of Ireland, as we all think. The harp has that distinction. The Gaelic word for shamrock is "seamrog" and is pronounced "shamrog," meaning, "a summer plant, or "little clover."

Since parsley is used in both of these projects, it is interesting to note that it is a member of the celery family and has been known for two thousand years as a medicinal herb. Its leaves are a good source of iron as well as a good source of vitamins A and C. In medieval times, parsley wine was thought to improve circulation and to help those suffering from heart conditions. It was also used as a digestive aid. Parsley has a reputation for dispelling black and blue marks, and parsley ice cubes have a two-fold purpose. The ice prevents swelling, and the parsley lessens the black and blue discoloration. An instant remedy that is stored in the freezer! To make one, blend the parsley with water to make a slush and freeze in ice cube trays. If you don't need it for the bruising remedy, you can use it in cooking!

The ancient Romans wore curly-leaved parsley garlands in their hair. Not only were they attractive, but it was also believed that nibbling on parsley sprigs would allow one to drink more wine without becoming drunk! They also fed parsley to their horses because they thought it made them swifter.

FOR THE SHAMROCK PROJECT

MATERIALS REQUIRED :

- one, large shamrock shape per participant
- glue and Popsicle sticks for spreading
- plastic bags to work on
- herbs of choice to be crushed
- a shamrock plant if available (optional)
- Bells of Ireland, if available (optional)

- marker for identifying project
- finished sample to show

HANDS-ON INSTRUCTIONS:

1. Let everyone look at the plants and/or fresh flowers that you have brought. Encourage conversation about green flowers and the shamrock and point out that the shamrock leaves will close down as they are in artificial light.
2. Distribute the dried herbs and instruct and show how to crush them.
3. Distribute the glue and have them (or you), cover the surface of the shamrock, using the Popsicle stick.
4. Sprinkle the herbs onto the glue, covering completely the shamrock's surface.
5. Tie green ribbon through a hole at the top, so that it can be used as a door decoration for the month.
6. Have the participants smell the herbal fragrance on their hands.
7. See how many participants can sing an Irish song.

FOR THE SPOON DOLLS PROJECT

MATERIALS REQUIRED:

- the same plants and green flowers as above, for discussion stimulation
- one flesh colored spoon per participant
- a bunch of fresh, curly-leaved parsley
- green ribbon

- shamrock designed mini muffin liners for the bodice
- marker to give the spoon face features
- green pipe cleaners for the shoulders and arms
- finished sample
- handy wipes or paper towels for clean-up

HANDS-ON INSTRUCTIONS:

1. Affix the green pipe cleaners around the neck of the spoon, forming shoulders and arms.
2. Using a small bunch of parsley, affix the stems to the neck with a piece of ribbon.
3. Cut a small slice in the muffin liner and drape liner over the shoulders, forming the bodice.
4. Apply a drop of glue to hold it into place, if necessary.
5. Add an additional few sprigs of parsley, short stems down, at the neck, and secure with ribbon, to form the lacy collar.
6. Glue a few sprigs and a loop of ribbon to the inside of the spoon, to give your doll some hair.
7. Using the marker, add two dots on the back of the spoon for the eyes, and use the participant's name to form a smile.
8. Watch their reaction with a smile in return!

* *This is a project that you will have to make, with their assistance in holding the spoon.*

SESSION TITLE: Pansies Mean Contentment

PROGRAM DESCRIPTION: This hands-on session brings the joy and feel of potting soil to the participant. There is a great deal of visual stimulation due to the colorful nature of the pansies, as well as a great deal of memories being shared because of the old-fashioned nature of this beloved flower. The sense of smell is also awakened because of the sweetness produced by a flat of pansies. The small muscle stimulation and development of motor skills is a great benefit of this activity. The participant will be doing the actual planting, watering, and caring for the finished product. This therapeutic benefit last for weeks due to the daily observation of the little "pansy face."

BACKGROUND INFORMATION: The pansy and the viola are part of the violet family and are one of the earliest blooming spring flowers because snow does not harm them.

We've read about pansies in Shakespeare's, "A Midsummer's Night Dream," and they used to be considered a love potion. These tiny flowers have been used to communicate messages ever since the Victorian times, when talking about emotions wasn't proper. In this time of "the language of flowers," pansies conveyed the meaning of contentment or think of me. This was a nice message to receive through a beautiful flower.

The old-fashioned pansies weren't like our big colorful "faces" that are so popular today. Instead, they were the smaller ones that we know as violas or "Johnny-jump-ups." Often these Johnny-jump-ups combine three colors, violet, lavender and yellow in their flower, thus the name "tricolor viola."

It wasn't until after 1800 that the British growers made big faces synonymous with the favorite pansy that we know and love today.

They are one of the most popular garden flowers to show their cheerful faces in late February or early March. Perhaps that is because by that time, everyone is anxious to have winter finished and these little blossoms give us hope that spring can't be too far behind.

They are cool weather plants and do not appreciate hot, humid summer days. However, they have bloomed profusely in my Cincinnati summer garden on those rare occasions when we have a cool season with few days of high humidity. Even if that isn't the case and I have to pull them up in their straggly, wilted look by June, I still love them. By that time, they have already given me three-to-four months of vibrant color and sweet fragrance. I am satisfied with that. They are also available to plant in the fall gardens and that oftentimes gives pansy "contentment" into December or January in our climate.

Pansies are edible flowers and are fun to use for cake decorations or as salad garnishes. For cooking purposes, you want to use only the blooms that haven't been sprayed with insecticides.

Pansies require a sunny spot to bloom profusely and require deadheading to keep those blossoms continuing. Deadheading is simply pinching off the spent bloom at the stem so it doesn't go to seed. If the plant is allowed to go to seed then that is a signal for the plant to cease making flowers. They like to grow in moist soil but not soggy soil. People kill more plants by over watering them then by not giving them enough water.

MATERIALS REQUIRED:

- One four-inch flower pot with a drain hole per person
- One saucer per person
- One beautiful pansy per person (use the small ones in a cell pack)

- One tablespoon, alias "shovel," per person
- One bag of good potting soil
- Plastic bags to work on
- A small sprinkling can
- Handy wipes and paper towels for clean-up time
- A marker for identification purposes (optional)

HANDS-ON INSTRUCTIONS:

1. The first thing that the participants will want to do is to have a close-up look at the flowers. Be sure to pass them around, especially to demonstrate their subtle fragrance. Most people do not realize that there is a sweetness to pansies.
2. Distribute the flowerpots, "shovels" and bags to each person.
3. Dump a small amount of the dirt on their bags and encourage them to shovel it into their pots. It should fill the pots half way at this time. If the group is more advanced, it can scoop its own dirt from the bag.
4. Now the fun begins! Let each one choose a pansy. This decision-making process is sometimes lengthy!

5. Before planting the pansy, instruct participants how to loosen the roots if they are tightly interwoven. If these roots are not loosened, the plant will not thrive because the roots will continue to wrap themselves around each other instead of growing outward into the soil.
6. Once the pansy is placed into the pot, have the participant shovel more dirt around the root system until the pot is filled almost to the top. (Allow about a quarter of an inch space at the top of the dirt, to allow for watering).
7. Instruct them on how to gently pat the dirt around the plant to give it some support. If there are any wilted flowers, show them how to deadhead at this time and emphasize the importance of checking the blossoms daily for spent ones.
8. It is now time to water the plant to get it established into its new surroundings. The act of watering with a small watering can is good small muscle therapy, and also points out that this plant is dependent on them for its very survival.
9. Time for clean up!

SPECIAL INSTRUCTIONS: You may also want to offer the participants disposable gloves to wear before working in the soil. Most of the time they will refuse them. Then the true gardener has been exposed to the group!

Often they will want to plant more than one pansy in their small pots. This is not advisable because as the pansies grow, neither one will thrive because of crowding conditions. These plants WILL spread out and grow taller if they are cared for properly.

Instead of using a flowerpot, you may choose to use tall, colorful, plastic cups. This will allow the participants to have their choice of cup color to coordinate with pansy color and a lot of laughter sometimes follows their choices. These cups do not need to have a hole punched into them for drainage. You can use small gravel (about one to two inches deep) for the drainage system. By putting the gravel into their cups, an added therapeutic tool has been added to this activity. They then place the dirt on top of this gravel layer, not mixing it in, but rather maintaining the two distinct layers. Any excess water will then stand in this gravel layer instead of in the soil, eliminating soggy roots and a rotting plant.

* *

Pansies are edible, and are fun to use as garnishes.

* *

RESPONSES HEARD DURING THIS SESSION:

"I just love the smell of dirt." "I always used to grow pansies at home and I never thought I'd be doing it after I came here! Thank you for bringing them to us." "It's a good day for us when you come!"

-- APRIL --

* *

The first spring-blown anemone,

She in his doublet wove,

To keep him safe from pestilence

Wherever he should rove.

- An Olde English Ballad

* *

The maple and oak and buckeye trees have begun their greening. The flowering trees are creating a pastel painting in my front yard. The walkway is edged with dainty, fairy-like, purple grape hyacinths and there is sweetness everywhere. It seems as if all of a sudden, the world has awakened and everything is rested and alive and filled with energy and ready to fill the senses with its natural beauty. My soul sings!! Some days are teasingly mild and I'm called outside to survey and plan, re-organize, and start the projects that I thought about in the bleakness of January. Do I dare remove the winter mulch? Better not, since our frost date is May 15th. I am impatient to begin but know that you can't hurry Mother Nature; so I take the time to enjoy the moment and the sweet smells that she has given us. The lilies –of-the-valley are among the things that I search for each spring and breathe a sigh of relief when I see the little pips making their appearance through the soil. It seems like just a short while later their beautifully shaped leaves unfurl and the delicate stem of tiny bells impart their powerful identifying aroma. I am relieved. They made it through another winter. These aren't just ordinary lilies of the valley. These plants came from my grandmother's garden to my garden almost forty years ago. She had them in her garden when my Father was a youth and they were his favorite. I have lived in three houses since my husband left the Army, and each of those yards has smelled like lilies of the valley in the springtime. I just keep moving clumps of my lily bed with me as we change residences, and now my daughters also have some clumps of Grandma's lilies-of-the-valley in their yards. These little "fairy ladders" are truly heirloom plants!

Springtime can mean different things to different people. To some it is synonymous with spring housecleaning while to others, a new Easter bonnet is anticipated. But the child in all of us says Easter eggs and Easter grass. Mother Nature can provide help in all of those areas and that is no April Fool's joke! Read the modules that follow to see how she accomplishes that and how horticultural therapy fits into spring chores.

SESSION TITLE: Easter Grass

PROGRAM DESCRIPTION: This is a very tactile program whereby the participants will feel the sample pot of lush grass and remember the feeling of walking barefoot in it as a child or sitting in the cool grass on a warm summer's day. They will also be able to participate in conversation concerning various kinds of grasses and their uses, before actually planting a pot of grass seed to care for. This session stimulates many remembrances from playing in the grass to mowing it, or to using it as farm animal feed. Because it is Easter Grass, we will incorporate a marshmallow bunny into it.

BACKGROUND INFORMATION: Grass is the common name for most members of a large family of plants with fibrous roots and jointed, hollow stems. The grass family is a large one with eight thousand species of plants in it. This family includes corn, rye, oats, rice and other cereal grains. For thousands of years the fruit of some member of that large family has been a staple in man's diet.

Rice was cultivated in prehistoric Asia. In some parts of the world, the members of the grass family make up seventy-five percent of the population's daily food intake.

All of the following plants fall into the Grass family: 1.) sugar cane; 2.) cereal grains; 3.) grazing grasses which are necessary for livestock (timothy grass and red top grass are two such varieties); 4.) hay, which is cured grass; 5.) silage, which is chopped, fermented grass used for feed; 6.) sorghums, used for making molasses for human consumption and also used in broom making; 7.) bent grass varieties which are used on golf courses; 8.) blue grass is used on athletic fields because of its durability; 9.) Fescue is one of the recommended varieties for Ohio lawns; 10.) Rye grass is drought tolerant and is a fast growing cover; 11.) Zoysia grass is used primarily in southern regions because cool temperatures cause it to become dormant in the fall.

Before 1850 there were few lawns as we know them today. "Launde,",an obsolete European word, meant merely a woodland glade, a place void of trees. By the eighteenth century European lawns had come to mean a plot of grass to be closely mown by gardeners with scythes or by grazing animals. When the lawnmower was developed in the nineteenth century, the lawn addiction began, and by the twentieth century, we had power mowers and the sound of a weekend morning would never be the same. The "mow-a-maniac" was born! Interestingly, the grasslands were the cave man's preferred habitat. He loved tall grasses! How far we have come from that mind set!

Running your fingers through soft grass is soothing. Adults are finding that a pot of green, growing grass (and I don't mean marijuana) to run your fingers through is a stress reliever and a calming thing to do while sitting at your office desk or watching TV.

MATERIALS REQUIRED:

- a six-inch deep, clear container for each participant
- potting soil and a scoop
- grass seed
- spoon "shovels"
- plastic bags or paper to work on

- marker for identifying each person's project
- scissors
- hand wipes or wet paper towels
- "Peeps" and tooth picks or other bunnies
- tiny dried flowers on stems (optional)
- spray bottle for watering
- sample for demonstration purposes

HANDS-ON INSTRUCTIONS:

1. Distribute the plastic bags, spoons, and containers.
2. Show and pass around the growing sample and encourage them to touch it and feel how cool and soft it is. If possible, demonstrate how you "mow" it with a scissors!
3. Put a scoop of dirt on their bags and have them spoon it into the containers.
4. Have them take the grass seed from their bags and "sow" their container.
5. They must pat down the soil firmly, not tightly, so that there is good contact with the seed. Some may want to scratch it into the soil and that is all right.
6. Have them spoon a very thin layer of dirt over the top of the seeds and pat into place with their hands or the back of the spoon.
7. Water lightly with the spray mister.
8. Insert a toothpick into the marshmallow bunny and stick it in the dirt.
9. "Plant" a few of the dried flowers (optional).
10. Give growing instructions: keep the dirt moist but not soggy, and place the container in a bright place. An option for self-sufficient people is to put the container inside a clear plastic bag that acts as a greenhouse. That has to be watched

carefully so that mildew doesn't form. Germination is speeded up with this technique.

11. Now is their chance to sit around and watch the grass grow…all around the dried flowers and the bunny. Within a week they should see the grass sprouting and within 3 weeks they will be "mowing" their lawns with a scissors!

12. This is a good time to talk about grass sayings: "The grass is always greener on the other side," or "Getting down to grass roots," or " Don't let the grass grow under your feet!"

SPECIAL NOTES: This is a program to avoid if your participants have a tendency to put the dirt in their mouths or if they would want to remove the marshmallow bunny from the "lawn" and eat it! Perhaps a rabbit sticker on the Popsicle stick is a better choice for those participants.

This session is not limited to an Easter project. You can use it at any time with dried flowers or birds inserted into it instead of the bunny.

RESPONSES TO THIS SESSION:

"I never thought I'd have to cut grass again!"

"It does feel so good. I had forgotten how good."

SESSION TITLE: Put On Your Easter Bonnet

PROGRAM DESCRIPTION: This is a very simple and colorful project that appeals to all levels of participants. The finished bonnet can be used for a door decoration or as spring hats for teddy bears and dolls that always sit on their beds. The visual stimulation and decision-making are the primary therapies for this session. Minimal gluing is required. Maximum enjoyment is inevitable!

BACKGROUND INFORMATION: There is very little information that is necessary to get started with this project. I use any fresh flowers that are available at the time. Field daisies and miniature rose buds are favorites. Ground ivy provides the green background. Pansies, daffodils and lilac blossoms have all been used successfully and their fragrances have been enjoyed and remembered from times long past. If fresh flowers aren't available, dried carnations and other flowers can be used.

MATERIALS REQUIRED:

- A small straw hat per person
- Ribbon for making the loop hanger (do this in advance with a hot glue gun)
- White glue for everyone
- Plastic bags and wet paper towels for everyone
- A variety of fresh or dried flowers and ivy leaves
- The finished sample for show and tell

HANDS-ON INSTRUCTIONS:

1. Go through each of the flowers that you are using and identify them. Ask if anyone has grown such a variety. Does it have any fragrance? If you are using

daisies, invariably someone in the group will start with "He loves me, he loves me not."

2. Distribute the hat, plastic bags for the working surface and a small bottle of white glue to each participant.
3. It is imperative to give each one a damp paper towel to eliminate the frustration of having the flowers stick to their fingers.
4. Give them the choice of which flowers to use for their bonnets.
5. Glue them onto the hats. It is easier to apply the glue directly to the straw brim and then to drop the individual flowers on to it.
6. Advise them to allow the glue to dry thoroughly before they pick them up and hang them on their wall or door.

RESPONSES HEARD DURING THIS SESSION:

"My Mom had a hat shaped just like this one when she was young."

One participant was a past president of a garden club and had judged flower arranging competitions for fifty years. Her bonnet was done with artistry and she put it on her doll's head as part of her Easter outfit. "You always make us feel good when you come here," she said. That made ME feel good!

ADDITIONAL NOTES:

This same idea using fresh or dried flowers can create many different projects depending on the background used for the flowers. For instance, a straw fan or a wicker basket rim can also be trimmed. Remind them that the fresh flowers will shrink as they dry, so they must take that into consideration when they place them on the hat rim, straw broom or basket rim. If trimming the basket rim, glue Spanish moss on the rim prior to the session. This provides a wider surface to glue on, as well as a surface that the flowers adhere to easily.

SESSION TITLE: Spring Housecleaning with Mother Nature

PROGRAM DESCRIPTION: This program points out all of the natural herbal products that can be used for housecleaning chores. It initiates many reminiscences about the "good old days." The hands-on project can be accomplished by any functioning-level participant. The completed dryer bags can be utilized as such, for those participants who still do their own laundry, or the bags can be used as sachets for those who have no need for the drying purpose as they have a pleasing scent. The crushing of the lavender and the pinching together of the edges of the coffee filter provide great sensory stimulation as well as fine motor skill involvement.

BACKGROUND INFORMATION: In times gone by, a woman kept a domestic diary. It was a ledger of herbal recipes for everything from making soap to getting rid of ants, from removing stains in fine linens to keeping a porcelain sink gleaming white.

These diaries passed down from mother to daughter for generations. Even though most women today have time only to purchase a ready made product from the grocery shelf, it is interesting to learn how some household chores were accomplished a few generations ago.

Lemon balm leaves were not only used to make a tasty, calming tea to drink, but when wrapped in cheesecloth they were used as an excellent wood furniture polish. The furniture was left smelling clean and fresh and lustrous, and the scent of the herbal oils kept cats off the furniture.

Instead of using the toxic oven cleaners, our grandmothers used straight herbal vinegar. It was easy to make using white vinegar and a handful of herbs from the garden. The herbs gave a pleasing fragrance to the vinegar, which did the actual cleaning. That same herbal vinegar was used as a most effective glass cleaner when diluted with water.

Fresh sorrel leaves kept the shine on Grandma's copper pots. She just dampened the pot and rubbed the moist sorrel leaves over its surface.

That musty or smoky, stale odor in carpets disappeared after she had sprinkled baking soda mixed with dried mint or lemon verbena leaves, over the carpets 20 minutes before vacuuming.

Instead of buying dryer sheets, lavender dryer bags make good "scents." The word lavender is derived from the Latin word, "lavare," which means to wash, thereby giving us our word lavatory. This "washing herb" can go to work for you in the dryer. It will lend a soft summer scent to all of the laundry. Just toss it in with your wet clothes and enjoy the fragrance. It can be used many times over.

Indoor air quality is becoming a serious concern for many people. Toxins are brought into the home through carpets, paints, wood and even in cleaning products. Since most newer homes are airtight and have central heating and cooling systems, often there is no fresh air being brought in from the outside and toxins can build up in the home. Plants absorb these toxic air pollutants through their leaves and roots and that helps to purify the air as well. Philodendrons, spider plants, golden pathos, gerbera daisies, mother-in-law's tongues, chrysanthemums and peace lilies work very well in absorbing benzene, and formaldehyde molecules from the air.

MATERIALS REQUIRED FOR MAKING LAVENDER DRYER BAGS:

- Coffee filters for each participant
- Dried lavender flowers
- Glue stick
- Completed sample to pass around
- Lavender plant, if available, for passing around
- Fresh lemon balm leaves, if available, for smelling and discussing

HANDS-ON INSTRUCTIONS:

1. Distribute a coffee filter to each person.
2. Pass around the dried lavender sprigs and instruct on stripping the flowers from the stems and placing them into the center of the filter paper.

3. Use approximately one cup dried material per bag.
4. Have the participants smell their fingers after stripping the flowers from the stems. Wonderful!!!
5. Using the glue stick, secure the edges of the filter paper and have them press it together.
6. The more the bag is touched and shaken, the more fragrance is released.

SPECIAL NOTES: These bags are great as sachets as well. They can be used multiple times in the dryer.

~~ MAY ~~

* *

First April, she with mellow showers,

Opens the way for early flowers:

Then after her comes smiling May

In a more rich and sweet array.

- Robert Herrick

* *

Our month of May, in the Ohio River Valley, sometimes means working in the rain and mud and chilliness if you want to be able to see the blossoms through the weeds! While most non-gardeners grumble about that kind of weather, I personally find it perfect for all of my transplanting, weeding, and redesigning projects that I thought out in January. Of course, sometimes I can barely lift my feet due to the weight of the mud-caked shoes, but the weeds come out with long roots intact. That makes the soggy working conditions all worthwhile.

The month of May brings to my mind a childhood remembrance of May crowning processions at school. Many of the children brought the beautiful bearded iris, or "flags" as I had heard them referred to, from their homes, to carry in this procession throughout the school grounds. I now have many varieties of that showy flower in my garden and the variegated species is one of my favorites. The foliage is stunning even after the bloom has faded, and I think of May crowning processions of long ago and simpler times.

My lamppost is smothered in huge purple and white clematis blossoms as it welcomes visitors to our front door. The miniature roses are in full bloom and the feathery pink and white plumes of the Astilbe and the dainty Coral Bells, seem to be extending an invitation for a fairy visit. I am sure that invitation has been accepted on moonlit nights.

By the end of this month, my woods are carpeted with the huge leaves of the May Apple. My grandchildren and I have fun looking for the ones with the pretty, white flowers hiding in between the stems. These are certainly wonderful fairy umbrellas for the spring rains.

The oxeye daisies look wonderful mixed in with the purple spikes of the Liatris, and the butterflies have found my garden again this year.

My horticultural therapy programs this month usually center on projects and discussions concerning different types of gardens. We have made fairy gardens, water gardens and butterfly gardens, All of these can be accomplished as container gardens so read on and learn how to do it.

SESSION TITLE: Heirloom Gardens

PROGRAM DESCRIPTION: This is a hands-on program that is informative on the subject of heirloom plants, and where the participant can either plant such a flower or create an heirloom garden collage depending on the level of participant ability. There is a therapeutic value in caring for a plant as well as fine tuning motor skills. This session seems to promote a lot of conversation, reminiscences and social interaction.

BACKGROUND INFORMATION: An heirloom seed is not an old seed. In fact, because seeds are alive, they must be grown nearly every year or they will no longer be viable. What is old about an heirloom seed is the genes inside that seed that make it different from other varieties. In other words, the variety is old even though the seed is not. For example, Tom Thumb lettuce was grown in gardens in the 1700s and that variety is still available for us to plant, three hundred years later.

Seeds have always been among the treasures passed along through families. That was always the case until the ability to purchase seeds from stores or catalogues became so easy.

People used to rely on their gardens for their food and would save only the seeds for the next year's garden. These seeds were the best producers, had the best flavor, or generally grew best in their gardens for whatever purpose they needed. There was no point in saving seeds that were marginal in their productivity or beauty. Therefore, varieties that have been saved for many years by gardeners are usually the "cream of the crop."

As our civilization progressed and we were able to purchase seeds from catalogues and stores, the seed suppliers began an educational campaign aimed at redirecting gardeners' thinking. The "new and improved" varieties were the featured ones. There were two reasons why the suppliers made this push away from the old varieties. If you didn't save your seeds, you then had to buy seeds from them every year. Home gardeners make up only a small portion of a seed company's business. The large-scale farmers are the ones to cater to and hybrids are helpful for that large farm market. Hybrids allow for mechanical harvesting and long hauls across the country without loss of quality.

For the last fifty years, gardeners have been told that hybrids are superior in every way, and we all bought into this concept. People now realize that the heirloom garden varieties are tastier as well as hardier in the home garden. There is an interesting diversity in the plants. A blight can wipe out an entire field of hybrid varieties because they're all exactly the same!

We've come full circle now. Old-fashioned plants have become increasingly popular in the last few years. Maybe that is because many of our fondest garden memories are of the flowers that our mothers and grandmothers grew; the ones that we grew up with in family gardens.

There are now "Heirloom Garden" catalogues from which to order seeds and plants. In order to qualify as "heirloom," a vegetable must have been in existence prior to 1940, when commercial growers planted the first hybrids. An heirloom rose variety must have been in existence prior to 1867, which was when the first hybrid tea rose appeared. Fruit trees, berries and grapes must have been in existence before 1900 in order for them to be considered as an heirloom plant.

If You Are Planting

MATERIALS REQUIRED:

- A flower pot, spoon "shovel", and plastic bag per participant
- A flower per person to be planted , e.g.: pansy, dianthus, viola, or primrose can be used successfully
- A bag of good potting soil
- Small watering can
- Handy wipes and paper towels for clean up time
- A marker to identify each person's project
- A catalogue page showing pictures of heirloom varieties that are available (to encourage remembrances of their gardens, or their mothers' gardens)

HANDS-ON INSTRUCTIONS

1. Distribute the pots, shovels and plastic bags for the working surface.
2. Pass around the flowers to be planted so that their fragrance may be enjoyed.
3. Let each participant choose a flower to be planted.
4. Put a pot of dirt on each participant's plastic bag and encourage him or her to shovel it into his or her pots. Fill the pots about half way with the dirt. Give assistance if needed.
5. Show them how to loosen, not tear off, the fine roots if they are root bound. Explain that this must be done in order to keep the plant from choking itself and to give it the ability to grow well.

6. Place the plant into the dirt and shovel additional dirt to within one-half inch of the top of the pot.
7. Firm the dirt around the plant to give it stability and to help it make good root contact.
8. Let each participant gently water around the plant. If using a pot with a hole in it, be sure to have a saucer under it or make one with Aluminum foil.
9. Encourage conversation concerning gardens the participants remember.

If Your Group Is Making the Collage

MATERIALS REQUIRED:

- A bouquet of fresh flowers, for discussion purposes
- Pictures of flowers already cut from catalogues
- Colored construction paper
- Spray Adhesive (purchased in craft stores)
- Marker for labeling their "gardens"
- Colorful, bee or butterfly sticker

HANDS-ON INSTRUCTION:

1. Pass around the sample bouquet of flowers. Invite everyone to "take time to smell the flowers." Initiate conversation by asking the participants if they recognize the flowers. Have ever grown them or seen them in their mothers' gardens? Do they know any songs with flowers in the titles? For example: "Rosemarie" or "Second Hand Rose" or "Lili Marlene" or "The Yellow Rose of Texas".

2. Have a variety of flower pictures torn from flower catalogues from which they can choose their favorites.
3. Let them chose their favorite color paper for the background.
4. Spray the glue on that paper and instruct them on how to "plant" their garden with the pictures by just pressing them in place.
5. With the marker, write their name on it as their garden (e.g., Jan's Garden).
6. Because every garden has a bee or butterfly, let them choose a sticker to position in their garden.

SPECIAL NOTES: If you choose not to use a pot with a hole in the bottom, a deep, colorful plastic cup will work well. Use either gravel or non-soluble Styrofoam packing material as the drainage system. One fourth of the cup should be for drainage.

RESPONSES HEARD DURING THIS SESSION:

"I like all kinds of flowers, but I sure do like the garden flowers the best!"

"Gardening is such fun and I've missed it so."

"My mother is smiling from heaven. She knows I could never garden well!"

There were also good responses from the lower functioning groups in response to their collage:

"I was just gardening and didn't get dirty."

"This looks like my mother's rose garden."

SESSION TITLE: Fairy Gardens

PROGRAM DESCRIPTION:

This hands-on session allows the participants to "play in the dirt" as well as be creative and imaginative. You will be describing the whimsical art of fairy gardening and describing the flowers, trees and other things that attract fairies to the garden. This program brings out the child in all of us as well as being a light-hearted topic that still includes the therapeutic tools to improve social interaction, cognitive abilities and fine motor skills. It is whimsical horticultural therapy at its finest!

I had made a fairy house and took it with me for the program, just to set the tone for inviting fairies to the garden. Everyone thoroughly enjoyed seeing it and it achieved its purpose. It is an optional tool that I personally recommend after seeing the reaction of the participants. A picture of my fairy house, and one that my grandchildren constructed on their own, is included so that you may see how simple, or complex a fairy house might become.

BACKGROUND INFORMATION: Since the beginning of time, every culture has had nature spirits, or sprites, or gnomes, or elves that stories have evolved around. That belief in fairies, pixies and elves has captured the imagination of children of all ages throughout history. Is there a child or grown-up who doesn't like the story of "Peter Pan?" I still clap for Tinkerbell! I personally feel that we all need a little magic in our lives and working in the garden can lead to that. There are the little seedlings that come up in odd places. Perhaps a fairy, not a bird, planted it there! Dew drops glistening on spider webs in the morning light seem enchanted and delicate, just like a fairy necklace. A little imagination can place a fairy napping on the soft pine needles or using the giant leaves of the Mayapple as an umbrella. Seed pod bath tubs, soft lambs ear comforters, acorn cap bowls and hollyhock blossom skirts with snapdragon hats, do not go unnoticed by the attentive, imaginative gardener! Magic in the garden keeps us young and the problems are put aside for that short time.

Fairies don't like to be seen by humans so you have to have a steady gaze or you may miss them with the blink of an eye. Was that a firefly's light blinking or a fairy lantern lighting the way back to a woodland home?

There are certain enticements that have been known to attract even the shyest little folk. They are especially fond of things that glitter in the moonlight and certain fragrances, such as thyme and rosemary. Fairies especially like the little Johnny-jump-ups (violas), clover, lilies–of-the-valley, buttercups and primroses. The white garden flowers that reflect the moonlight are also among their favorites. Fairies enjoy dancing in the moonlight reflected off such plants, you know! A small pond or waterfall will also attract these friends to your garden because they like hearing the splashing sounds and watching the ripples on the water's surface made by insects. If you plant bluebells in your garden, you may be able to hear the fairies ringing them on a midsummer's night when there is a full moon. That is how they summon all the garden fairies to their meetings!

A small part of the garden should be left a bit wild and not too perfectly cultivated. They like the carefree feeling of such an area, and will feel welcomed there. Create a garden that is conducive to all life. Fairies like to be in places where there are beautiful birds and butterflies.

There are many fairy legends that can be told. Here is one of them: The foxglove plant has much to do with fairies. It has several other names including fairy caps, fairy petticoats and fairy thimbles. According to legend, fairies used to give the blossoms of the flower to their fox friends to wear as gloves so they would not get caught raiding the chicken coop. It is very likely that the name "foxglove" came from this legend.

MATERIALS REQUIRED:

- A container of your choice per participant
- Spoons for a shovel
- Hand wipes or wet paper towels
- Plastic bags to cover working area
- A small sprinkling can
- A soil-less mix that contains perlite instead of heavy, dark top soil

- Your choice of small plants, such as lobelia, alyssum, violets, mosses or grass seed
- Short, pre-cut twigs to be used as fencing
- Gravel for pathway
- Plastic thimbles or pods for a pond and/or bathtub
- Fairy stickers and Popsicle sticks
- A fairy house for show and tell (optional)
- Any fresh fairy flowers that are blooming in your garden, for show and tell (optional).

HANDS-ON INSTRUCTIONS:

1. If you have a fairy house or fresh fairy flowers, now is the time to discuss them and start the imaginative process! Set the whimsical tone by telling the foxglove legend and by talking about Peter Pan and Tinkerbell.
2. Distribute the spoon shovels, containers and bags.
3. Have the participants place dirt into their containers and then do the landscaping!
4. Give them enough twig fencing, pathway gravel and pond material to create their garden.

5. Let them choose their plant material and instruct them on the proper planting techniques. Perhaps they will want to add grass seed for a soft fairy lawn instead of using more flowers.
6. When their garden is completed, give them the choice of a fairy sticker and put it onto the Popsicle stick. Let them place their fairy in their garden.

Be sure to instruct them on the proper light and watering requirements depending on the type of plants that you've provided. Be sure to remind them to watch for signs of a fairy visit, especially when the moon is full!

SPECIAL NOTES: If you are working with a lower functioning group, give them step-by-step directions on the fence building, the pathway placement, etc.

The whimsical nature of this program is enjoyed even by the lower functioning groups. Everyone responds to a magical fairy tale!

RESPONSES TO THIS SESSION:

"This has been so much fun, thinking like a kid again!"

SESSION TITLE: Seeds of Sunshine

PROGRAM DESCRIPTION: This very simple session is geared towards instilling an interest in planting seeds, yet gives the participants something colorful to display on their doors or bulletin boards for the springtime. This works very well with those groups who do not want a lot of information, but enjoy "playing in the dirt." I used a colorful piece of sunshine notepaper as the background for gluing on sunflower seeds. These are large seeds, and therefore easily manipulated by stiff fingers. The second part of this program involves planting the dwarf sunflower seeds in containers that will eventually be planted in larger containers for a patio or courtyard garden, if available.

BACKGROUND INFORMATION: Seed information is in the session titled "Seed Art." Choose the amount necessary for your group's interest level.

The Sunflower is part of the genus Helianthus. It is derived from two Greek words, "helios," meaning "sun," and "anthos," translated as "flower." That name is certainly appropriate when you look at the disc shaped flowers with their sunny yellow petals!

Sunflowers are native to the Americas, and have played an important part in the life of a variety of American cultures. In Peru, the Incas worshipped that flower as a symbol of the sun. Their priests wore golden medallions fashioned in the sun's image.

That cheerful flower was introduced in the United States in the sixteenth century, and not only was it beautiful, but it also provided food for people as well as their animals.

There was a superstition connected to it also. The pioneers felt that if they planted the sunflower close to their homes, it would offer protection against malaria.

MATERIALS REQUIRED:

- Sunshine notepaper or hand drawn picture of Mr. Sun
- Mammoth sunflower seeds
- Clear glue
- Handy wipes or wet paper towels for sticky fingers and clean-up

- Peat pots or other seed starting containers (four-to-six per participant)
- Seed starting soil
- Tablespoons for shovels
- Plastic bags or paper to cover the working area
- Sprinkling can
- A seed packet of a dwarf sunflower variety, or other fast growing, showy flower of your choice
- Ziploc bags
- Completed sample of Mr. Sun
- Popsicle sticks for each participant to identify his or her containers
- A marker for identifying the pictures and seed containers

HANDS-ON INSTRUCTIONS:

1. Talk about seeds to the extent that you feel your group requires.
2. Distribute the notepaper/picture, glue and a handful of seeds to each participant.
3. Have each cover the center with seeds, as in the photo. The finished picture appears to be a big sunflower with the seeds in the center as in the real flower.
4. Set the picture aside and prepare to plant the individual seeds in the containers.
5. Pass out the plastic bags for each person to work on.
6. Distribute the containers, Popsicle stick and spoon/shovels.

7. Put a small pile of dirt on the bags and instruct them to fill the container almost to the top with the soil. This activity is good for exercising small muscle groups.
8. Show them how to make a depression in the soil, either with their fingertips or with the Popsicle stick.
9. Plant the seed to the appropriate depth as stated on the back of the seed pack.
10. Cover over lightly with additional soil, pat down gently and sprinkle with water.
11. Place the seed containers into a Ziploc bag and close. This will hasten germination.
12. Using the Popsicle stick and marker, identify each participant's container. That way they will know which ones they need to care for and observe on a daily basis. It is exciting to watch for the germination! Some groups make it into a race to see whose seeds will sprout first!
13. Place in a sunny spot and make sure that there is not an excessive amount of moisture formed inside the bag. This will lead to mildew forming.
14. When the seed has sprouted, open the bag.
15. When the seedling has its second set of leaves, transplant it to a bigger container.

NOTES: If possible, repot these seedlings to an outside container. This can make a nice follow-up session. Be sure to harden off the seedlings before moving them to their permanent location outside. This means gradually, a few hours at a time, moving them from inside to outside, in a shady, protected location. Gradually move them to their permanent sunny spot.

SESSION TITLE: Lilacs, the Mother of Memory

PROGRAM DESCRIPTION: In this session, you will make a potpourri using the fragrance of lilacs as the predominant fragrance. Because lilacs are such an old-fashioned flowering shrub, this session stimulates many reminiscences and conversation among the participants. A brief history of the use of potpourri and the necessary ingredients that must be a part of a finished potpourri is discussed. This is a very tactile and sensory-stimulating session that can be enjoyed by participants of any functioning level.

BACKGROUND INFORMATION: Lilacs are a member of the olive family (Oleacae), and are one of the oldest, hardiest, best known and loved of shrubs. Once it is established, it will defy all that the elements have to throw at it, and emerge victorious each spring with gorgeous flowers and fragrances. The sweet aroma brings with it the gift of recall from May processions to Mother's Day vases filled with blossoms. No wonder it is called "the Mother of Memory."

In the Victorian language of flowers, the lilac is given the meaning of "young love." I have wondered if that has something to do with "in springtime, a young man's fancy turns to love," just as our noses turn to the fragrance of the lilac.

The late springtime is the time of year when our noses and eyes are directed to the beauty and fragrances of these wonderful shrubs. They offer the gardener a large variety of sizes and flower colors. The parade of lilac flowers begins in late April and early May and continues through mid June. There are many lilac festivals throughout the country during this time of year.

Hybridizers have worked extensively with the common lilac resulting in over one thousand different varieties. Some varieties can grow ten to twenty-five feet tall and six to twelve feet wide while others, such as the dwarf Korean Lilac, rarely grow over five feet tall and spreads a maximum of five to seven feet. The shapes of the species are as varied as the sizes. They can be upright or spreading, or dense or airy. The colors are as varied as an artist's palette, and you can have blooms from early spring until two months later, depending on the varieties that you plant. Colors of the blossoms can be any shade of purple, pink, or blue and now there are even yellow, white, orange and red varieties to choose from. The earliest to bloom is the Korean variety (S. oblate), and the latest is a Japanese tree lilac (S. reticulate). There are always new varieties being developed that give us greater resistance to powdery mildew and more colors to choose from. In my mind, I don't care about the color as much as I do the magnificent aroma!

The common lilac (Syringa vulgaris) was seen growing in Turkish gardens in the early 1500's. From there it found its way to Austria in 1562 and became the favorite in European gardens. The enjoyment derived from lilacs was so renowned that it was the first flowering shrub, after the rose, to be imported to the New World in the 1600's. Within four hundred years it has become a crowning shrub in American spring gardens. All over America, early settlers planted lilac bushes in their yards and by their doorways. So long-lived are they that you'll often find one growing on the site of a home now long gone. Because they are so hardy, sociologists use them to track human migration patterns westward across the continent. Long after the house and garden have disappeared, the resilient lilac often lingers, a final testimony to a once-flourishing, fragrant homestead.

While no lilac makes a great cut flower, because they wilt within two days in a vase, those two days are filled with a heavenly fragrance!

"Potpourri" is a French word translated to literally mean "rotten pot." The term was originally used as a culinary term meaning a stock pot of vegetables and meat. Now it means a pot of fragrant plant material.

Humans have always enjoyed perfumes. The caveman burned scented woods and their caves were "perfumed" by fragrant smoke. The Latin word "perfumin," means "through smoke," and that is the origin of our word "perfume". The Egyptians used sweet smelling oils to appease the gods and to anoint the body. Perfumes were an important part of the lives of the ancient Greeks and Romans. They used fragrances for religious celebrations and ceremonies. Four hundred years ago, mixes of scented flowers were perfuming the Victorian homes, and two hundred years ago the term "potpourri" came into common usage. To have the fragrance of a bowl of potpourri in your house is like bringing a flower garden indoors. It is uplifting on a dreary day to be able to smell the spring garden from inside.

There are many different things that can be added to create a potpourri but there are five types of ingredients that are an absolute necessity:

1) Scented, and dried whole flowers, petals or other botanicals such as dried orange slices, pinecones or berries

2) Herbs such as rosemary, lavender, thyme, mints, scented geraniums, etc.
3) Spices, such as nutmeg, vanilla, cloves and cinnamon
4) A fixative that absorbs and retains the oils and fragrances added. If you omit this one ingredient the potpourri will quickly lose its aroma. You can use cat litter (unused, please!) or vermiculite to do the job.
5) Essential oils of your choosing, such as lavender, rose, vanilla, citrus, etc. We rely on these much more than did our ancestors because of our method of making the potpourri.

MATERIALS REQUIRED

To make a Spring scented potpourri, use:

- Dried flower petals, predominately lilacs, daffodils, hyacinths, violets and other spring blooming varieties
- Herbs of your choice, lavender, crumbled sweet bay and mints are my favorites
- Vermiculite as the fixative
- Spices such as vanilla beans and cinnamon
- An essential oil that is light and airy, such as lavender or lilac oil (my favorite for this, if you can find it)
- One Ziploc bag per participant
- Dried orange peel (optional)
- A bouquet of fresh lilacs, daffodils or hyacinths for "show-and-SMELL"
- Completed sample of potpourri in a pretty container for show and tell

HANDS-ON INSTRUCTIONS:

1. After talking about lilacs and the history of potpourri, pass around the vase of flowers and the completed sample of potpourri. Enjoy the looks of pleasure on the participants' faces!
2. Prompt reminiscence stories from the participants.
3. Distribute the Ziploc bag to each person.
4. Measure out about one tablespoon of vermiculite and put into the bags.
5. Add five to ten drops of the essential oil of their choice.
6. Have them close the bag completely and mix those two ingredients together, making sure no oil remains clinging to the side of the bag. You want all of it mixed into the fixative.
7. Add the flowers, herbs and spices, one at a time, mixing well after each added ingredient. If you use the orange peel, break it into small pieces before adding to the bag.
8. Mix again!
9. Smell your hands!

After everything has been added and thoroughly mixed together by inverting and/or shaking the bag, tell them to zip the bag (leaving a little air in it) and not to open it again for one month! They cannot sneak any smells during that time. What they do have to do however, is to shake it at least once every day, if not more often. The longer it stays closed and the more times they shake it, the stronger and fuller the aroma will be when they do open it. At that time, they can pour it into a pretty saucer or container and leave it open on their tables or in their bathroom. The fragrance should remain strong for months. When it does start to fade, add additional oil and once again thoroughly mix into the other ingredients. Enjoy!!

NOTES: It is nice to give them a choice of essential oils. It is a decision-making process and will give individuality to each person's finished product. Use just one oil fragrance per bag. When they take their handfuls of dried flowers, stress the feel and aroma of them. See if they can perhaps identify the types of flowers they have in front of them. If you are using dried stems of the herbs, let them strip the stems of the crunchy leaves. That is good muscle activity and the crushed herbs emit a wonderful aroma. Be sure to encourage them to smell their mixture after each addition to the bag, as well as the individual ingredients. It's interesting to note that the finished product is a blend of all the different fragrances.

If you don't grow your own flowers, try to find a florist who will give you the "too old to sell flowers" that they have available. These bunches can be hung upside down, not in sunlight, or put into a food dehydrator, for drying. The faster the material dries the more color it retains. I think that hanging flowers and herbs are a beautiful display in themselves. It can get out of hand, however! My children's bikes, hung from the garage ceiling, now have every spike and spoke decorated with drying flowers and herbs!

~~ JUNE ~~

* *

There once was a door mouse who lived in a bed

Of delphiniums (blue) and geraniums (red),

And all the day long he'd a wonderful view

Of geraniums (red) and delphiniums (blue)

- A. A. Milne

* *

During this month, summer becomes official. I walk through my garden path in between the colorful and aromatic day lilies and watch the butterflies land on the purple cone flower and see the milkweed pod ready to burst with it's delicate cluster of pink flowers. I know without a doubt that summer is my favorite season of the year! Fortunately, heat and humidity are not my enemies. I seem to thrive in the warmth of the sun and always choose to be outside rather than in air conditioning. In my circle of friends and co-workers, I have always been in the minority on that issue. I do feel sorry for those gardeners who wilt with the heat.

This month's garden stroll always presents me with the wonderfully, strong fragrance of the white lily that we recognize as the Easter Lily. It took me years before I realized that this wonderful Easter gift from my family could be planted outside and would survive our winters and bloom for years to come. Its unforced bloom in June, however, always makes me stop and smile. We are so programmed to think of it in a beautifully foil-wrapped container, blooming in March or April. The butterflies and bumblebees appreciate it now as much as I do.

Not only do I enjoy the wide variety of flowers in my gardens but I also enjoy working around, and using the fresh herbs that I have planted in and amongst my flowers. Since my front yard exposure is my only full sun area, I have parsley, sage, rosemary and thyme, plus other favorites, in that part of the yard. At least I am not growing corn stalks in the front! My neighbors are thankful.

This month all of the varieties of mint seem to be at their fullest flavor. I love blending some of the varieties together in a teapot for a "specialty of the house" variety. Orange and apple mints blend well together, and lemon with peppermint is another refreshing combination that we enjoy all summer long. Spearmint water is refreshing in itself but it's doubly nice when used in making lemonade. Of course, I dry all of these varieties as well, for use in horticultural therapy projects and for tea in the winter, but somehow, the freshly picked sprigs in a tea pot or in a salad are special. Maybe that's because it means summertime!

Two of the programs that seem to be favorites during this month, or any summer month, involve fresh and dried blossoms from my yard. The following modules will inspire the artists among your residents and be a source of laughter for those who think they are not creative. Horticultural therapy wears many hats!

SESSION TITLE: Butterfly Gardening

PROGRAM DESCRIPTION: This program can be adapted for any level of participant, from the lowest functioning dementia patient to the most alert, self-sufficient resident. The activities connected with this topic are determined by the functioning and comprehension level of the participants. This topic can lend itself to merely a show and tell type activity, or as one that can encompass actual planting of either a dish garden or outside gardens by the residents. It is highly stimulating since the beauty of butterflies is obvious, and the plants that attract them are fragrant. You can make this session as tactile and as informative as your participant level dictates.

BACKGROUND INFORMATION: Did you know that scientists have estimated that fifteen thousand species of butterflies and two hundred and fifty thousand varieties of moths are flying around in our world? A few characteristics differentiate a butterfly from a moth. Butterflies do not spin silk as the moths do. The butterfly rests with its wings closed above their body while a moth rests with its wings open on either side of their body. Butterflies are active during the day and moths fly around at night. Butterflies are brightly colored, and are very obvious. Moths have dull coloration that acts as a camouflage. The butterfly's antennae are very long and thread-like in structure while the moth's are feathery. The immature butterfly is in a chrysalis while the moth forms inside a cocoon. More than one hundred and forty different kinds of butterflies have been recorded in Ohio and people are really becoming interested in butterfly watching, just as they like bird-watching. Some of the most common species found in Ohio gardens are the Black Swallowtail, the Cabbage White, the Painted Lady, the variegated Fritillary and the brilliant Monarch.

Centuries ago, in Britain, there was a common yellow insect that people first referred to as a "butter-colored fly." Over time, it became shortened into "butterfly."

The average life span of the adult is two to three weeks but some varieties only live three to four days. The Monarch however, may live as long as six months.

Butterflies don't really eat. They drink their meals to maintain their water balance and their energy stores. Butterflies can find their favorite plants from miles away. They will travel miles to savor the nectar of their favorite flowers and shrubs. Favorite flowers of butterflies are: lavender, asters, daisies, yellow marigolds, milkweed, Queen Anne's lace, lilac bushes, black-eyed Susan, purple coneflower, zinnias, alyssum, verbena, lantana, phlox, yarrow, coreopsis and mints. These flowers are all sweet, and will bring the adult butterfly to the garden. Butterflies love flowers that are yellow, purple and red as well as being sweet! However, you also need to have some flowers in your garden that will act as the host plant for the caterpillars to eat so that they will develop into the beautiful butterflies. The milkweeds, the parsley family (dill, parsley and carrots), violets, viburnum, snapdragons, clover and sunflowers are some of the favorite host plants. The host plant is where the female lays her eggs and that plant then feeds the caterpillar.

Because of insecticides, and building developments in open fields, there are fewer butterflies then ten years ago. In fact, many species are added to the endangered species list. By creating a butterfly garden you are helping preserve the butterfly species as well as creating a place of beauty and enjoyment in your garden space. Butterflies will also come to container gardens and hanging baskets on patios and balconies if you've provided their favorite things!

Aside from providing favorite nectar and host plants, an outdoor butterfly garden should also have some dark stones for warming their wings when they are at rest. There should also be a water source and/or a small mud puddle or wet sand available. Mud is important for the male butterfly as a source of needed amino acids and salt. The water source can be a shallow dish with pebbles around it. Butterflies are cold-blooded and seek warm air. They are sun lovers and use the sun to navigate. The sun raises their body temperature so that they can fly. The more sun your garden has, the more butterflies will be attracted to it. Of course, you won't want to use any insecticides or herbicides in your garden space.

It's nice to know you're doing something beneficial for nature!

MATERIALS REQUIRED: If this session is going to be used as a sensory session for the lower functioning population, then a beautiful bouquet of garden flowers taken from the above list, can be used. Container gardens can be planted according to the hands-on instructions found in the "Pansies Mean Contentment" program in the March section of this book. Use the nectar flowers from the above list and include a dark rock. The plants listed are sun loving, and so are the butterflies!

HANDS-ON INSTRUCTIONS:

1. If you are using the bouquet of flowers only, then be sure you include those that are highly fragrant as well as those with good texture, such as the black-eyed Susan. Their hard, dark center is a good tactile tool, and can also be described as the butterfly's landing pad!
2. If possible, also include photographs or pictures of butterflies enjoying some of the flowers in an outdoor garden.
3. Ask how many of the flowers grew in their own gardens, or their mothers' gardens. You will be surprised at how this opens the door for social interaction.
4. If you are planting a container garden, be sure you have plastic to cover the working surface, spoon shovels, good potting soil, containers with a drainage hole and a saucer, a small watering can, appropriate plants or seeds and handy-wipes for cleaning hands afterwards. You can also use a marker to identify each participant's garden if this isn't a group effort.

SPECIAL NOTES: Those residents who have planted container gardens for their balconies or patios have come back for the succeeding sessions with progress reports. They have enjoyed reporting not only on how well their plants have grown, but also on how many and which kinds of butterflies they have noticed. At one facility, it almost became a competitive thing!

SESSION TITLE: Water Gardens

PROGRAM DESCRIPTION: This session is suitable only for independent living participants or a high functioning group where there is an outdoor patio available. I say this only because five hours of sunlight are needed for the water plants to thrive, and there must be an area big enough to accommodate a large, deep container. It would become a messy project to have in a health care facility. It is doubtful that the nursing staff would be pleased with you!

The participants will learn about different water plants and will take one home to put into a suitable container.

BACKGROUND INFORMATION: Everyone seems to relax around bodies of water. Watching the ripples and the reflections of clouds drifting across a mirrored surface of a still pond is soothing. Watching fish glide through the water is tranquilizing and spellbinding. The sound of rippling water is hypnotic. Water watching brings us to a blood pressure-reducing state of calm. Water gardens do not have to be in or around, huge ponds, however. You can use large ceramic planters, old washtubs or deep clay pots. Any water tight, large container can be used to add a touch of interest to a patio or garden area. There are some aquatic plants that only require a few inches of water and others that require a depth of up to five feet to survive. A still pool or container is better to use than one with a water fall spilling into it or a fountain splashing in it.

In the world of water plants there are those that are considered to be oxygenating, bog plants or floating aquatic plants. There are also tropical marginal plants.

The oxygenating plants are those that are submerged and are essential to maintain a proper balance in the pool. They add oxygen to the water and serve as a filter by absorbing dissolved nutrients and competing with the algae. These kinds of plants are essential for pools with fish. Not only do they help establish a natural balance in the pool, they also serve as a food source, spawning mats and a hiding place for baby fish. Oxygenating plants should be potted using any good heavy soil. Do not use soil-less mixes or commercial potting mixes. After planting these plants, cover the pots with a light layer of gravel or sand to avoid muddying the water. Place oxygenating plants in their own containers, since they will compete with other plants when they are mixed.

Bog plants are those taller plants that give a lush attractive look to a pond garden. They usually grow in shallow water or soggy areas at the edges of ponds and streams.

The tropical marginal plants are very useful and add beautiful blooms throughout the summer. The foliage of these plants is often uniquely spectacular. The vivid colors of the flowers and the distinctive foliage of these aquatic plants add to the lush look in the water garden. They are sensitive to cold weather, however, and should be protected from frost. In many cases, they are treated as tropical household foliage plants and wintered indoors as long as they have sufficient light and moisture. The beautiful water lilies fall into this category.

The floating aquatic plants are interesting and very simple to grow. They are considered annuals in all but the most southern zones of the USA. Their extensive root system serves as a spawning pad and hiding places for fish and tadpoles. These plants are extremely useful in helping to maintain a balanced pool. Their floating foliage provides shade cover that helps stabilize water temperatures while the root system provides oxygen through photosynthesis. The foliage also blocks the sun, which algae need for their survival. These plants compete with algae for nutrients in the water and they will win that battle, thus starving out the algae. The water hyacinth and water lettuce are great examples of the floating plants. The purple blooming water hyacinth (Eichhornia crassipes) has air filled bulbs that keep it afloat and its bright green leaves act as sails, moving it across the container or pond. It is a vigorous grower and needs regular harvesting, but should never be turned loose in the rivers or lakes. In the southern states it is the scourge of commercial fisherman and boaters since it will clog the waterways very quickly. The water lettuce (Pistia stratiotes) is also a vigorous grower that has hairy, soft green foliage and is lettuce-like in its formation. It may get tiny greenish flowers but it is not grown for its flower production: it is for its interesting foliage and texture.

Water lilies were enormously popular in the Victorian times. Crowds gathered to see the giant Amazonian water saucer, when it was first established at the Kew Gardens. These saucers are so strong that one can support the weight of a small child, and can grow two feet in diameter. The heady scent of the lotus blossoms became part of the romantic image of the Far East.

The leaves of the water lily were used to reduce fevers, and the syrup of the flowers induced sleep and calmed "distracted patients." Some varieties need only a few inches of water while others need a depth of up to five feet. They all produce impressive flowers that only last about four or five days.

Cattails (Typha latifolia), are one of the most recognized water garden plants with their decorative, cylindrical, dark brown seed heads.

Water gardening is no more demanding than an herb or perennial bed, possibly even easier. Once it is established, not even dandelions will invade! There is no watering chore either. The only maintenance is to fertilize, remove the yellow foliage, and share with a friend. These plants are relatively free of disease and parasites. If aphids attack, hose off the leaves and shake the foliage underwater where goldfish will gobble up those aphids in a minute.

Water gardening can be very elaborate or as simple as plunking a water lettuce or water hyacinth in a deep container. Simplicity is the name of this session!

MATERIALS REQUIRED:

- A deep five-gallon bucket, if you are doing the actual planting there, or a Ziploc bag for transporting the plant back to a residence
- One water plant per participant (I like to use the water hyacinth or water lettuce since they grow vigorously.)
- Take pictures of various water lily blooms and other blooming aquatics for show and tell
- Take lotus pods or cattails (also for show and tell - They have great textures)

HANDS-ON INSTRUCTIONS:

1. Pass around the show and tell samples and ask if they recognize them or have collected or grown them.

2. Depending on the group, present the background information.
3. Examine the two varieties of samples and give them their choice with which they would like to experiment.
4. Be sure they fill a water tight container with water and let it sit out for a few days before adding their plant to it.

NOTES: A water garden in a container is an easy and magical addition to any garden or patio and is the perfect answer for the gardener with no time to water. This session works well as a high functioning group project. Many can enjoy one single, large water garden, if placed in a common, sunny area. As the plants spread and fill their container, divide them and place in new containers for other areas of the patio or garden.

-- JULY --

* *

Cut thistles in May, they grow in a day

Cut them in June, and that is too soon

Cut them in July, then they die.

- Olde English words of wisdom

* *

My gardens are brilliant with color, fragrance, butterflies and hummingbirds! The cottage garden seems to change color predominance weekly and it is a sheer delight to observe and photograph its subtle metamorphosis from delicate and dainty Columbine and Astilbe to the bold, brilliantly colored Asiatic, Day Lilies, Zinnias and stately Hollyhocks. As I amble along the path that leads through tese flowers in the front yard, to the shaded, cool looking back yard, the purple, white and pink Phlox stand tall and their sweetness floats in the air and beckons to the butterflies, providing me with sensory overload. How I love this stroll to the driveway to pick up the morning newspaper. What a wonderful way to start a day! The oval marker in my garden says it all, "The kiss of the sun for pardon, the song of the birds for mirth, One is nearer God's heart in a garden, then anywhere else on earth."

This is the month for patriotism, and red, white and blue flowers. I have occasionally planted containers containing just those colored flowers but I recently noticed that I also have one tiny area of the garden that is perennially patriotic, quite by accident. The flowers of the red and white dianthus and the delicate blue Nigella (love- in- a- mist) have spread into each other and since they have the same blooming time, a patriotic splash of color has been created by Mother Nature for my enjoyment.

The Hostas are in full bloom, and the vibrant orange of the Butterfly Weed and the fragrance of the now blooming Milk Weed and Sweet Peas are part of the butterfly buffet table. The tube shaped petals of the red Bergamot also bring the hummingbirds to this floral feast.

I know that in a few weeks, the leaves of the Milkweed will be chewed to pieces and look unsightly, but that is a good thing. If I look closely I will find the culprit—the big green caterpillar that will eventually become a beautiful monarch butterfly. I think of "The Hungry Caterpillar" book that I read to my grandchildren and delight in the unsightly foliage. I dug this "weed" from the side of the road many years ago and transplanted it into my garden because I knew it was not only food for the adult monarchs, but it also acted as a host plant. I feel I'm doing my little part in maintaining the butterfly population. Every little bit helps in this age of pesticides and subdivision development. An added bonus is the beautiful pod, which will form, that can be utilized in many horticultural therapy projects later in the year. So we all benefit from this "weed."

The next modules will show how patriotism, mint and wild flowers add to the enjoyment of the horticultural therapy provided in the course of a year.

SESSION TITLE: Bug Repellant Plants

PROGRAM DESCRIPTION: A discussion of, and visual stimulation by, those herbs that are considered to be bug repellant in nature, is the basis of this session. The hands-on activity accompanying this topic is the making of a bug repellant sachet. All levels of participants, in some form or other, can successfully accomplish this session and have a pleasant smelling sachet to keep.

BACKGROUND INFORMATION: There is a variety of plant material that bugs just do not like to be around. Fleas stay away from Lavender, Eucalyptus, Pennyroyal; Rue and Winter Savory. Lavender, Sweet Woodruff, Santolina, Tansy, rosemary and the Artemisia varieties repel moths. Aphids stay away from the odor of Lavender, Costmary and Chives. Ants don't like Wild Marjoram, and mosquitoes are adverse to the citronella plant (a Pelargonium species). Lice are repelled by Pennyroyal, Southernwood and the seeds of the Columbine, while the weevil avoids Sweet Bay.

Lavender - Down through the ages, migraine headaches, insomnia and fevers have all been treated with this fragrant shrub. In ancient Rome the public baths were strewn with the flowers and lavender oil. In the sixteenth and seventeenth centuries it was used as a strewing herb for floors and even in the public streets to sweeten the rancid air. In early England, charcoal and Lavender had been mixed together and used as a tooth cleanser.

During World War I, English nurses used sphagnum moss sprinkled with lavender oil when they ran short of bandages and antiseptics.

In pioneer days, lavender was included in the bedding, not only for its fresh and calming fragrance, but also to keep the bedbugs away.

You can see that lavender has certainly proven itself as a very versatile herb.

Scented Geraniums (Pelargonium sp.) - The citronella variety of this species protects a fifteen foot radius from mosquitoes. Rub the leaves of the plant in order to release the fragrance and stay within that radius. You can also rub the leaves on your skin for several hours of protection.

Chives (Allium sp.) - It is the onion smell that acts as the repellant in this case. The flowers are edible as garnishes. Did you know that chives, if grown near roses, will enhance the fragrance of the rose?

Sweet Woodruff (Gallium sp.) - When dried, the leaves smell like newly mown hay, honey or vanilla. I find it a very pleasant fragrance but then, I'm not a moth! It was used to repel moths and insects among stored linens in earlier times. Its common name, bedstraw, dates from the Middle Ages, when it was used as a fragrant strewing herb and mattress filling. It was also hung in churches as a symbol of humility.

Aremeisia Species - One variety, Southernwood, was used to expel worms as well as to treat bronchitis and colds. It was a moth repellant for cabbage moths, fruit tree moths and it also dispelled beetles. It was grown near hen houses to protect the hens against lice.

Tansy - This is a very Old World herb brought here by early settlers. Its camphor-like odor repels moths and flies, thereby giving it the common name of "Stinking Willie". I've never been able to find out who Willie was.

The leaves have been rubbed on raw meat to keep off the flies. I have seen that practice in some rural parts of Greece. The fern-leaf tansy was used as a healing herb in Victorian England. The tea was used as a tonic but an overdose resulted in death! No thank you for that remedy! It has also been used as a wash to treat sprains and bruises.

MATERIAL REQUIRED:

- An 18" piece of narrow ribbon for each participant
- A 13" x 13" piece of netting for each participant
- Dried lavender leaves and flowers to equal 1/8 cup per participant
- Cedar chips to equal approximately 3/8 cup / participant
- Paper towels for the working surface
- A 1/8 cup scoop
- Samples of bug repellant herbs (dried or fresh) for bruising and smelling
- The sample of the finished sachet to pass around

HANDS-ON INSTRUCTIONS:

1. Distribute a paper towel for everyone to work on.
2. Pass around the bag of cedar chips for distribution and SMELLING!
3. Pass around the lavender flowers and leaves for distribution and SMELLING!
4. Have them mix the two ingredients together on the paper towel and SMELL the new fragrance created.
5. Give a pre-cut net square and a piece of ribbon to each participant.
6. Place the mixture from the paper towel onto the center of the netting.
7. Pull the edges together and tie the ends with ribbon. SMELL the finished sachet and be glad you're not a bug!

SPECIAL NOTES:

These fragrant and practical sachets can be put into the pockets of stored coats or in sweater drawers to repel moths. They also have been used as gifts for the participants' family members. If possible, it is helpful to have samples of all of the different bug repellant herbs for a show and tell and smell period of time beforehand. Interesting comments may be heard at that point in this session.

BUG REPELLANT PLANTS

For Fleas and Ticks:	lavender	winter savory
	eucalyptus	rosemary
	pennyroyal	basil
For Moths:	perilla	sweet woodruff
	lavender	santolina
	lemon basil	tansy
	rosemary	bay leaves
	artemisia varieties	
For Aphids:	mints	lavender
	chives	coriander
	fennel	castor bean
	marigolds	nasturtium

For Ants:	marjoram	peppermint
	tansy	spearmint
	wormwood (an Artemisia variety)	
For Mosquitoes:	citronella	mountain mint
For Chiggers:	lemon grass	catnip
	santolina	basil
	pennyroyal	
For Cabbage Worm:	dill	nasturtium
	garlic	onion
	sage	thyme

* *

A Recipe for a liquid bug repellant:

- One part each of the following dried plants: rosemary, wormwood, lavender, sage and mint
- Place in a jar and cover with vinegar; let stand for 7 days
- This can be used on clothing or on exposed skin to repel ticks, fleas and chiggers.

SESSION TITLE: Patriotic Petals

PROGRAM DESCRIPTION: This hands-on topic was born in the aftermath of September 11, 2001. I needed horticultural therapy myself at that time and I found myself not wanting to do anything if it didn't have a patriotic feeling to it. Most activities, music, books, radio and TV programs seemed frivolous and meaningless to me and so this session topic was developed. I found that all of my participants also enjoyed doing something with a patriotic overtone at this time.

The concern for our country and the horrific nature of the attack seemed to be dealt with a little better while working with flowers. Perhaps it was the sweetness and beauty of nature that transported us into a peaceful, gentle frame of mind, at least for that hour.

The photos below will show you a variety of tactile, sometimes fragrant as well as colorful sessions. They have even caused the participants to break forth into song on a few occasions. To have heard a group of participants singing "America the Beautiful," upon completion of the petal flag project, was an overwhelming experience for me. That is a song that I find difficult to get through under normal circumstances so this spontaneous singing of it as they held their petal flags, was awesome!

Some of the project ideas included, are a little more detailed but I'm sure you will find one that accommodates any functioning level that you are working with at the time. I have used these projects beginning with Memorial Day and continuing through July 4th. Most of the projects involve glue so if that is a problem, be forewarned.

BACKGROUND INFORMATION: In the first spring/summer growing season following the September 11th attack, I was one of the many gardeners that turned to a patriotic theme for my home garden designs. Any annual that I put into the ground or into a container, had to be a red, white and blue flower. There were many varieties to choose from, in both annuals and perennials, but the biggest challenge was finding a true blue blossom. Even if the identifying tag said that it was a blue flower, it was usually more of a purple color in reality.

However the Heavenly Blue Morning Glories, are just that...a heavenly blue color!

Some Salvia and Ageratum varieties and especially Lobelia provide a good blue color for the annual choice. Catmint, Delphiniums, Nigella and some Veronica varieties are in the blue-ish perennial list.

There are many red and white annuals and perennials to choose from, and the only challenge in your patriotic scheme will be to decide on the "bluish" flower. Petunias, Verbena, Impatience and Geraniums all work well in a summer annual display. Obviously it is easier to do such a color scheme using annuals since they bloom continuously throughout the season.

A beautiful summer shade garden combination is one featuring red impatients, white begonias and blue lobelia.

I have tried a patriotic trellis as well, in a sunny location, using a mixture of red, white and blue morning glories. It was very pretty but since they bloom in late summer in my area, and then only in the morning, I had to have other patriotic flowers in my gardens for an earlier and more continual display.

For the Petal Flag Project

MATERIALS REQUIRED:

- one foam paper or heavy white cardboard flag per participant
- fresh red carnations or red rose petals (either dried or fresh will work)
- tiny dried white flowers to be used for the stars
- fresh or dried blue flowers (optional)
- glue and handi-wipes
- plastic bags on which to work
- one wooden craft stick per participant
- a marker to use for identifying each participant's

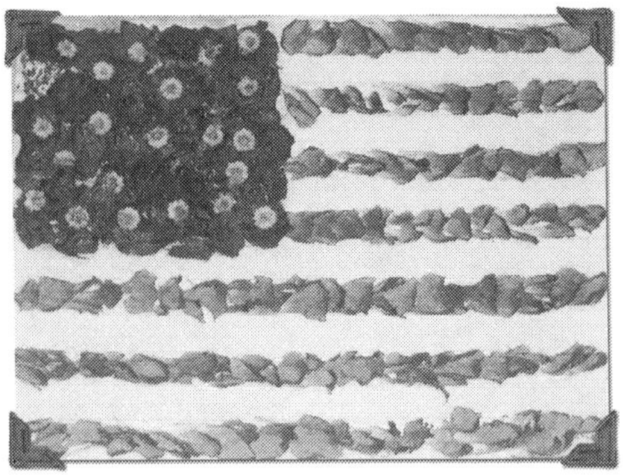

finished flag

- blue spray paint
- a completed sample for show and tell

PREPARING THE FLAG FORM:

1. The flag forms are best prepared prior to the session. The flag can be any size you want to make it. Obviously the larger the flag, the more flowers you are going to need and the longer it will take to complete the project. I've found that flags measuring approximately 6" x 9" are a good size to work with and can be completed within an hour's time.
2. Using a pencil, draw the stripes and the square area for the field of stars on the paper. Be sure you have allowed for seven red stripes and six white ones.
3. The red, fresh or dried petals will be glued down in the first area by the participants and the white paper in between the red petal lines will form the white stripes. If you have a supply of white petals on hand, they can be used for the white stripes instead of leaving that area empty to achieve the white stripe.
4. Spray paint the field of stars area and let it dry overnight. If you'd rather use blue spray painted petals instead of spraying the field of stars area, that is also an option.

HANDS-ON INSTRUCTIONS:

1. Distribute the prepared flag forms to the participants and mark their name on the back.
2. Show them the completed project and talk about, and encourage discussion regarding the types of flowers that will be used in this project.

3. Distribute the glue, plastic bags and craft sticks to everyone.
4. Now it's time to do the unthinkable…rip the fresh flowers apart! This will always be accompanied with gasps and groans but soon everyone will see the beauty that a ruined flower can still provide.
5. Instruct them in applying the glue and spreading it thin with the craft stick.
6. Show them how to gently press each individual petal onto the pre-marked stripe. When all of the stripes have been completed, give them the white flowers to be used for the stars. I only used approximately thirteen white flowers (stars), depending on their size, to glue into the field of blue. Fifty stars will never fit on a 6" x 9" flag.
7. Be sure to distribute the handi-wipes for fingers that get sticky. There is nothing more frustrating than trying to glue a petal on a stripe when you own finger is full of glue!
8. When everyone has completed their flag, encourage them to hold them up for all to admire…and then wait for the song to begin!

*These flags are easily displayed on bulletin boards or can be used as a door decoration.

For the Straw Hat and Crocheted Fan Project

MATERIALS REQUIRED:

- a purchased straw hat or fan for each participant
- fresh daisies, ivy leaves, and red and blue dried flowers
- narrow ribbon to make a hanger for the hat or to trim the fan
- glue and handi-wipes
- plastic bags to cover the working surface
- the finished sample for show and tell

HANDS-ON INSTRUCTIONS:

The pictured hat project has been created using fresh ivy leaves, field daisies, dried red mini carnations and blue Statice to accomplish the red, white and blue motif. Any red, white or blue flower can be used. A narrow ribbon loop is glued to the back of the hat in order for this project to be hung, and should be completed prior to the session.

1. Distribute the plastic bags, glue, hats and fresh flowers.
2. Show them the finished sample to give them the trimming idea. However, they can and will come up with unique trimming patterns of their very own. There is no right or wrong way to trim this hat, as long as the patriotic colored flowers are used.
3. Be prepared for a fashion show of sorts, upon this project's completion.

FOR THE PATRIOTIC FLORAL ARRANGEMENT PROJECT

MATERIALS REQUIRED:

- fresh red, white and blue flowers
- flag picks
- small containers containing a piece of oasis (floral foam)
- watering can
- clippers

HANDS-ON INSTRUCTIONS:

1. If you are having your group make their own flower arrangement, be sure to have a piece of oasis foam in their container, prior to distributing. Using the watering can, show them how the water is absorbed into the oasis. It's magic! They've seen the water added to the cup, but where has it gone?
2. Talk about the flowers that you have brought and let them smell the fragrant ones. Ask if they recognize any of them, and did they have them in their gardens at one time.
3. Begin by clipping off a flower stem to the proper length for their containers and demonstrate how to stick it into the softened oasis.
4. Continue to distribute the cut flowers and let them arrange them in the containers. Help them only if necessary.

5. When they are satisfied with their arrangement, give them a flag pick to add to the completed project. They will be happy to have a flower arrangement to take back to their rooms.

SPECIAL NOTES: All but the lowest functioning groups seemed to enjoy working with the fresh petals to create their own flag. Even participants with macular degeneration were able to stick the petals in a straight line for a stripe, once I had applied the glue for them. Their feeling of accomplishment was great at having been able to complete such a colorful project just by being able to feel the glue on their fingers.

Obviously this is not a project for the lower functioning groups that may put the petals in their mouths. For those groups, I used the discussion of the fresh flower arrangement; from the beauty of the red flowers to the fragrance of the finished bouquet.

If your group is able to make their own arrangement, be sure that the flag pick provided won't be used as a weapon!

In some lower functioning units, one large arrangement can be made with everyone's help, and then placed on the nurses' station desk to be enjoyed and admired by everyone passing by that area.

RESPONSES TO THIS SESSION:

After making the petal flag with a group of Alzheimer residents, a single participant started singing "America the Beautiful" and one by one, the other participants joined in with the singing. It was an overwhelming experience for me, and a very meaningful, yet fun experience for them.

There always seems to be at least one participant who is very adept at flower arranging and has been in a garden club, or has decorated her church altar with fresh flowers. Most of the time the flowers will remind the Alzheimer residents of their mothers' gardens instead of their own gardens and that makes them happy in their reminiscences.

I've also learned from residents, that "red and yellow flowers catch a fellow and red and blue will catch two!" I love learning from them.

One lady told me that,"working with fresh flowers just makes you feel cheerful." I have to agree with her!

SESSION TITLE: Colorful Coleus

PROGRAM DESCRIPTION: This session describes the popularity of the colorful Coleus varieties as well as its simple propagation, and care of beautiful foliage house plants in general. These types of plants are grown strictly for the beauty of their leaves, rather than for their flowers. You can create a beautiful outdoor garden or windowsill display using only interesting foliage. Flowering plants beware!

If your participants are high functioning, this will be a "play in the dirt" kind of hour. If you do that, the motor skills and small muscles are stimulated. If you'd rather not have the hands- on experience, then a strictly show and tell session is still visually stimulating and promotes cognitive skills and socializing. I've taken various types of both indoor and outdoor foliage plants for observation and discussion, and the participants' interaction was not only informative and lively but humorous as well. Their childhood gardens are always remembered with fondness.

BACKGROUND INFORMATION: An old Victorian parlor plant makes a twenty-first century comeback. The Coleus is enjoying a new popularity with colorful hybrids and sun tolerant landscape varieties. Leaves ranging from one inch across to eight inches across, make this plant easy to use in any situation. They are easy to grow and propagate and are inexpensive to purchase. There are so many beautiful leaf varieties to choose from that it could become mind boggling if you don't have a plan. I find myself saying, "Oh I'll take two of these and three of these and I just have to have this one, and oh look at that gorgeous combination...."

The Coleus have square stems, which make them a part of the mint family, Lamiaceae. This large family of plants has many interesting members, such as Sage, Monarda Oregano and Lavender, to mention just a few.

The name Coleus, is derived from the Greek word "Koleos" meaning "sheath". This describes the male portion of the flower, the stamen, which are fused into a sheath-like structure.

During the 1800's these plants enjoyed a frenzy of popularity in Victorian England as parlor plants, providing great indoor color during the bleakness of wintertime. Now, hundreds of years later, actual societies have been formed to study over a thousand different varieties of this colorful foliage plant.

It lost its popularity in the early 1900's but by 1920 it was once again popular and new varieties began making their appearances in nurseries.

It is really a tropical plant and is grown as an annual in most of our country's zones. However, if you visit a tropical or subtropical zone, these wonderful plants look like giants compared to the ones growing in my southern Ohio garden. They prefer 60 degrees or warmer, morning sun or dappled shade and are very forgiving plants. They are heat tolerant and they'll let you know when they're thirsty by the drooping leaves. However, they perk up right away after a good watering. They prefer moist conditions but don't like to have "wet feet". They do produce a spiky, non-descript flower which is to be cut off, thereby promoting branching out of the plant and also height control for container gardening. The best thing about pruning these plants is the fact that you can just put the cut off stem in a pot of dirt, water and voila! You have just propagated another plant.

I'm including an abbreviated list of some of the imaginative names given to the Coleus varieties since they do promote conversation and laughter among the participants.

- Coleus Furnace (they have a deep red color to their leaves, naturally!)
- Coleus Black marble
- Coleus Pineapple Queen
- Coleus Fishnet Stockings
- Coleus Kong (the new huge variety)
- Coleus Purple Passion
- Coleus Alabama (since my son and his family lived there, I had to have this one!)
- Coleus Blackberry Waffle
- Coleus Blonde Bombshell
- Coleus Flamingo (you can guess this one's beautiful coloration)
- Coleus Inky Fingers
- Coleus Mr. Wonderful

If you have decided to make this a "play in the dirt" session then the following information concerning planting and care of houseplants can be shared.

Most plants, whether indoor house plants or outside container gardens, are killed by too much love (watering!) Some indoor plants need more water at different times of the year taking into consideration their dormancy period, if they have one. In winter watering, don't use cold tap water because it's a shock to the plant's root system. Would you like to be doused in frigid water in the winter? Instead use tepid water for both watering and spraying the leaves, if necessary. Know if your plant shouldn't have water droplets on the leaves, such as African Violets. If you are misting the leaves, avoid hard water since the chemicals present will clog the pores of the leaf. Test for soil dryness with your finger inserted knuckle deep into the dirt or use a knife blade. If it comes out clean, then it's time to water. It's the cake tester theory! Never let your plant stand in water accumulated in the saucer for longer than 15 minutes. If you can, the plunging technique works great. Plunge your plant (to just cover the rim of the pot) in a bucket or sink, filled with water for approximately fifteen minutes, until the air bubbles cease. This is a great, thorough watering technique.

Some gardeners take the time to clean the leaves of their plants on a regular basis by using a feather duster, spraying with soft water (not done in the sunlight though) or by using a damp cloth. This removes dust as well as red spider mites. I'm ashamed to say that I'm not one of those gardeners who do that on a regular basis. Sometimes I'm lucky to find the time to dust my furniture! My Mother would do this for me when she came to my house to baby-sit because she felt so sorry for the plants in the window sill garden!

If you purchase a leaf cleaning spray be sure to read the directions, since some of these can damage the plant if used too often. Of course that wouldn't be my situation!

Some foliage plants require high humidity levels. If you group a cluster of plants together, they will create their own atmosphere. It is also beneficial to spray a mist of water on those humidity-loving leaves. As I have mentioned before, avoid doing this in sunlight. Another way to improve humidity for your house plants is to place their containers on pebbles in a dish. Add enough water to the pebbles to just half cover them. You don't want the flower pot touching the water because that will cause root rot. The water vapor rises from damp pebbles creating humidity under the thirsty leaves.

Sometimes you can give your houseplants all the TLC possible and still they may be vulnerable to insects such as mealy bugs, scale, red spider mites, aphids or whiteflies.

If one has become infected, move it away from the others....put it in isolation! You certainly don't want an epidemic on your windowsill. Some infections, such as the mealy bug, may even be hiding in the soil of the plant's pot.

There are three different types of insecticides that you could choose from: concentrated liquids, aerosols or systemic spikes. Any spraying should be done outside or in a well ventilated area. Never mix different types of liquids together or keep a solution more than a day.

It is always my choice to use an organic insecticide, thus eliminating the possible deadly chemicals found in the other products. Insecticidal soaps are such a solution, or denatured alcohol applied on a cotton tipped swab, can also be used to remove the insects causing a scale problem. Red spider mites can often simply be prevented by improving the humidity that is surrounding the plants.

Another thing the indoor gardener needs to check, is the repotting of the plants periodically. If the roots have filled the pot and only a little soil remains, your plant is not receiving the nutrition it needs. Weak growth is a good indication that repotting is necessary. Don't bother to replant unhealthy plants. The shock to its root system may kill it altogether. Repotting is usually done in March and April since most plants are beginning their spring growth with the increase of daylight. Don't forget the drainage system when you repot! Use pots with a hole in the bottom or if you have to use a closed container, be sure to have a layer of gravel in the bottom.

Once you have repotted your plant don't give it water for two to three days. The roots will spread out in the new soil, searching for water, thus giving it a strong root base. Don't forget, more plants are killed by over watering than by anything else!

Sometimes the choice of soils can make a big difference in the happiness of your plants. Just like the people caring for them, they don't all like living in the same situations!

A general purpose soil can be used for most plants as long as you pay attention to the watering of the plant. However some plants such as the African Violet, Begonia, Azalea and Philodendron prefer soil high in humus whereas the cactus and succulents like just the opposite. The beautiful orchids and other air plants, (epiphytes) prefer a soil-less growing medium. Luckily for us, these various soil preferences can be purchased at any garden center.

Earlier I had mentioned that the Coleus plant is easily propagated by taking cuttings. This is the most common form of plant propagation. These cuttings should contain a growing tip and two pair of leaves. In the case of the Coleus, these cuttings can be stuck directly in the soil or rooted directly in water and then planted in soil. Other more fastidious plants prefer to have their stem dipped in a hormonal rooting powder before being planted in their soil. Within just a few weeks the root structure is formed and you have a new viable plant baby!

Another way of increasing the plants in your garden is by the technique called "layering". This is a great way for trailing plants to be propagated. Make a slit in the lower part of the stem and have that slit directly touching the soil. The new roots will grow from that point. When the new plant is healthy and strong, it can be removed from its mother plant if desired, and given its own pot to continue growing.

Last, but not least, pruning plants is also a beneficial step in their care. The removal of dead leaves, as close to the stem as possible, results in new leaf development. Pruning back in the springtime encourages new shoots to form thereby creating a bushier, fuller, more compact look to your plant. In general, cut back the stems by half, just above a leaf or side shoot, to maintain a nicely shaped, healthy plant.

MATERIALS REQUIRED: Before presenting this session, I already root enough coleus cuttings in water so that each participant can have one. It's nice if you can take more than one variety of these colorful coleus leaves, providing a decision making opportunity for everyone involved.

If you are working with a high functioning group you may also want to take a mature coleus plant with you to demonstrate the art of pruning and propagating directly into the soil.

- a 5 inch pot and saucer
- potting soil
- coleus plant and/or cuttings
- a spoon-shovel for everyone
- plastic bags to cover their working surfaces
- show and tell coleus varieties and/or pictures
- small watering can
- handy-wipes for clean-up
- a black marker for identifying each person's flower pot

- a pruning shears if you are demonstrating the technique of pruning and planting directly into the soil

HANDS-ON INSTRUCTIONS:

1. Share the pictures of various Coleus and have fun with the variety of names given to the individual varieties. This activity stimulates the cognitive and reminiscence aspect of the program. Socialization also comes into play here as the participants share their stories with the group.
2. Distribute the plastic bags, spoon shovels and pots to each participant.
3. Scoop out the soil for each participant, placing it on their bag.
4. Have them shovel it into their individual pots to the half-filled capacity.
5. The decision making time has come! Which of the colorful cuttings would they want to plant and take care of?
6. Demonstrate how they can use the other end of the spoon to make an indention in the soil for their cutting.
7. Show the delicate root structure and tell them to carefully insert the stem into the pre-formed hole.
8. Once that is accomplished, fill in with more soil, patting it gently around the stem. A little watering, not too much, is appropriate at this time to compact the soil so that the roots make good contact and resume growing in their new homes.

RESPONSES TO THIS SESSION:

One of the foliage plants that I took for show and tell, was a pink freckle face plant (Hypoestes species). A lady started laughing and said she looked like that when she had too much sun.

SESSION TITLE: Petal Painting

PROGRAM DESCRIPTION: This is a loud, fun and educational activity that can be adapted to most levels of participation. It can be thought of as an individual project or even as a group activity. It can even be just a show and tell program if your group is not a hands-on-type of group. It is so much fun to be creative with a hammer! Motor skills, strength building, creativity and sensory stimulation are all part of this energizing session.

Beautiful, abstract designs are easy to create and every one registers surprise at how the color of a flower or leaf can be transferred to paper or to a piece of fabric. Designs develop right before your eyes and because they are so abstract, no one needs to feel that they can't do it because of "no talent." That will not be an acceptable reason for not participating in this activity!

BACKGROUND INFORMATION: Since any flower or leaf is a candidate for becoming an important source of color or design for this project, I like to start this session by taking a bouquet of mixed flowers with their foliage, to the working area. We observe and talk about the colors and textures, variety and familiarity of each plant. I point out the differences of the sides of the different leaves. Some have prominent veining on the backside of the leaf or flower petal. Some petals and leaves are much more moist and "juicy" than are others. The participants begin to notice details about the parts of the plant that may have gone unnoticed prior to this session.

Their observing skills are becoming tuned into Mother Nature's beauty. Isn't it strange that a flower that appears to be pink, when pounded actually produces a blue dye?

Grasses can also be used and many times they produce a surprise color because of unnoticed pigments or oils. Any plant has dyeing possibilities and it is fun to experiment with whatever you happen to have on hand. I like to use sprigs of fresh herbs, especially any of the mints, because not only is the room filled with the noise of hammering and laughter, but it is also filled with the fragrance of the mint when their oil sacs are bruised. Actually "bruised" is an understatement!

This activity will not only stimulate personal creativity but will also increase gross motor skills of the participants as well as increase exercise to their upper bodies.

If white or a light colored fabric is being used, avoid using white flowers since they will go unnoticed, unless you put them over a darker color. Plants with waxy surfaces are also to be avoided since their wax actually keeps their color encased. The leaves from the rose bush give a very nice shade of green, as do the stems of the chive plant. You'll find that the chive stems require very little pressure to release their color and are a good choice for the frail participant to work with for achieving a bright shade of green.

The petals of the yellow coreopsis produce the most beautiful, vivid shade of yellow of any flower that I've used. Because the individual petals are small, the entire shape as well as the color, was able to be reproduced on to the background material with success.

Impatience varieties are great to use for vivid pink, red and purple colors. Rose petals produce rich colors and Alstromeria petals show good "freckled" designs. Marigolds, pansies, ferns and parsley are also good choices for your palette. You will begin to look at foliage and flowers in an altogether different light. You'll begin to think, "How will this hammer out?"

Have fun with the practice flowers and samples. Experiment! Don't say you have "no talent". This is abstract art and is foolproof!

MATERIALS REQUIRED:

- the fabric or paper to be used as the background material (Little canvas tote bags can also be used for variety)
- cardboard or a foam backed placemat for each participant to work on, (to eliminate damage to the working surface and to help muffle the sound of hammering)
- a sheet of wax paper for each participant
- steel hammers, not rubber of soft ones
- fresh flower petals and leaves
- colorful mats for framing the completed project. I use a 5 x 7 mat for each person
- scissors and scotch tape
- green or black markers for adding stems, if done on paper, or for the artists' signature on the matting
- completed samples for show and tell
- fresh bouquet of flowers

HANDS-ON INSTRUCTIONS:

1. Discuss the flowers making up the bouquet and ask for participants' reminiscences of any of the flowers. Did they have their own gardens? Do they recognize any of these that are in the bouquet? Which one is their favorite? Can they pick up the fragrances of the herbs or flower petals? The perfection and variety of the various flowers can be noted at this time.
2. Show them the finished sample and point out that flowers can produce beauty even when hammered!

3. Distribute the placemats or cardboard to each participant and distribute a piece of wax paper the size of the fabric, to each person.
4. Pass out the fabric or paper to each one and lay it on top of the cardboard.

5. Distribute the hammers and demonstrate the following technique: Choose a flower petal, place it on top of the fabric or paper. Cover over it with the piece of wax paper. While holding the wax paper in place, pound firmly on the petal and then peel off the wax paper. Remove the squashed petal from the fabric. Voila! The color has been transferred, producing the first stroke of your masterpiece.
6. Repeat the procedure as often as you like, working with just one petal or leaf at a time until the design is as you like it.

Note that the harder that you pound with the hammer, the more intense the color will be. If you use just the edge of the hammer head, little lines will transfer, while if you use the back of a ball peen hammer, little circles will be the end result. That is a fun way to add polka-dots and squiggles to your artwork.

To get the complete image transferred, you must pound with the head of the hammer, eventually touching the complete surface of the leaf or petal.

When the picture is completely "painted", give your participants their choice of framing mats. If you offer a variety of colors, their decision making skills will be noted. Which color better enhances the artwork? Do they want to pick up a color in their design or would they rather pick out their favorite color mat?

Trim the paper or fabric to fit inside the mat and scotch tape it into place on the back of the matting. If you've used paper, now is the time to draw stems or butterflies with the markers. Don't forget the artist's signature!

Give everyone the opportunity to show their project to the entire group for approval. Notice how different each one is. They are just as different as the individuals, but each one beautiful and worthy of framing. Self esteem runs high by the end of this session.

SPECIAL NOTES: Since this is a loud session, advise the staff and activity personnel ahead of time. They may not want someone with sensitive ears or jumpy nerves attending this program.

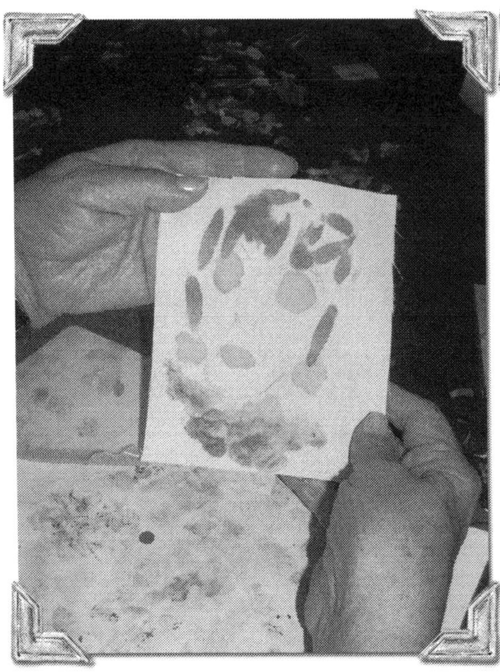

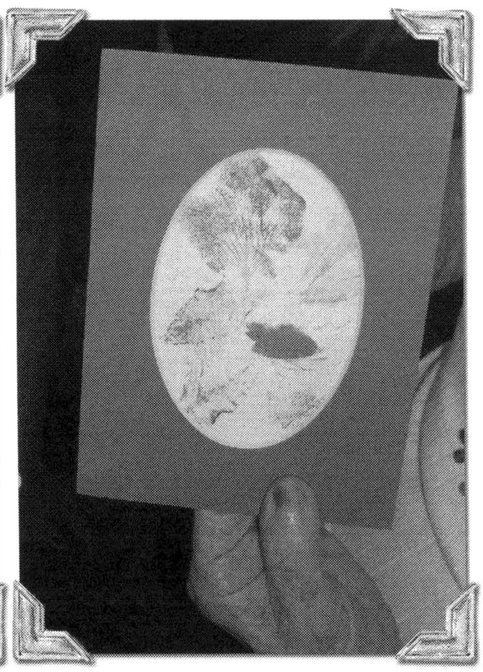

You can also easily make this into a show and tell session if you yourself, make a picture and let everyone see the design unfold in front of their eyes.

This program can also be used as one large project, with everyone adding their personal touch to a banner sized piece of paper or fabric. That kind of project encourages the feeling of working together to create a beautiful end result that can be signed by everyone and displayed in a community room for many to enjoy.

RESPONSES TO THIS SESSION: A man who was part of a group declared that he would help any lady present who didn't know how to use a hammer. That offer was met with quite a variety of comments and laughter from the ladies present. He probably wished that he had never made that comment.

A few participants broke out into singing the song, "If I had a hammer, I'd hammer in the morning...."

After using the hammer, one frail-looking lady announced, "I didn't realize that I was so strong!" Other comments I heard were:

"My daughter teaches art history in her school. Now I'll show her that I am the real artist."

"I'll think of something that I don't like while I hammer."

"Look, I did something by myself...and it's beautiful."

"Well I SHOULD be good with a hammer. You can't miss the mark when you shoe horses!"

In one group of participants there was a mother-adult son pair working on the project. He was mentally challenged and living with his mother, who was physically challenged.

When the project was completed she whispered to him, "Oh, your Daddy would be so proud of you for painting a picture, wouldn't he." She then told me that his father had been a professional artist. The pride and delight in both of their faces was quite evident.

Responses such as these warm my heart and not only make my day, but hammer home the fact that horticultural therapy really does work and is an important therapeutic tool.

SESSION TITLE: Wildflowers

PROGRAM DESCRIPTION: This session involves the Wild Carrot, or Queen Anne's Lace, in all of its roadside beauty. There are two projects described below. A suncatcher using dried and pressed flower heads for this regal sounding "roadside weed," as well as a "Lace Mosaic" using fresh flower heads will be described below.

If desired, you can also talk about the other wildflowers found alongside the road, such as Thistle, Chicory (blue), Jewelweed, (yellow or orange), and even the common yellow Dandelions. This is a session that participants of all functioning levels can enjoy and feel proud of their completed project. Cognitive skills, some upper body strengthening, small motor skills as well as visual and olfactory stimulation are utilized in this program, not to mention reminiscences about the various wildflowers picked for mothers' bouquets long ago.

BACKGROUND INFORMATION: According to folklore, the beautiful wild carrot is named for the rather homely Anne of Bohemia, who married England's Richard II in 1382. Anne challenged her ladies-in-waiting to a contest to see who could create an embroidery (tatting) pattern most similar to the delicate wildflower.

Another version of the naming of this wild flower was that it was named for St. Anne, "Queen of Heaven" and the Mother of Mary, Grandmother to Jesus. Appropriately Saint Anne is the patron saint of all lace makers.

Yet another story surrounding the naming of this beautiful wildflower, describes the occasion of Queen Anne of England (1655-1714) pricking her finger while making lace, thereby staining the lace with a drop of blood. If you look closely, you'll notice that each large flower has a reddish/purple dot in the middle. This is actually the seed, not a bug as some of my participants thought!

The flower was first brought to America by Virginia colonists for use in their formal flower gardens. It was not thought of as a weed then.

When the flowers are older and are ready to finish their blooming season, they curl up in a "bird's nest" shape, which make very interesting dried flowers and is the reason that another name for this wildflower is "Bird's Nest Weed". Caution must be taken by the inexperienced when picking this flower. Both the flower and the foliage closely resemble that of the poison hemlock and fools parsley, both of which can be deadly if ingested. A simple way of knowing that you have Queen Anne's Lace is simply to rub the leaves between your fingers and smell! Also, if you pull out Queen Anne's Lace from the ground by its very long tap root, and scratch that root, you will be able to smell the very distinctive aroma of carrots, thus it's name of Wild Carrot. The fern-like leaves and stems smell like carrots when bruised. That distinctive carrot smell will set you straight in its identification.

These delicate, lacey, snowflake-like flowers can also be tinted colors by using food coloring in a vase with a small amount of water. Add the desired color to the water before adding a freshly cut stem of Queen Anne's Lace. In a matter of hours you can see the results of the osmotic action of the colored water tinting the white lacey flowerets.

Beauty is at the country roadsides if we just peek through the grasses and look for the color!

* *

Many eyes go through the meadow, but few see the flowers in it.

- Ralph Waldo Emerson

* *

THE SUNCATCHER PROJECT

MATERIALS REQUIRED:

- two pieces of 5" x 6" self-laminating paper / participant
- narrow ribbons of various colors
- one pair of scissors
- dried and pressed Queen Anne's Lace flowers
- one wooden craft stick / participant
- the completed sample for show and tell
- a vase of tinted Queen Anne's Lace of many hues, as well as a vase of white ones
- the long tap root of the flower for scratching and sniffing the carrot smell
- samples of other wildflowers that are in season
- scotch tape
- a hole punch
- tiny suction cup hooks for each participant (optional)

HANDS-ON INSTRUCTIONS:

1. Discuss the various wildflowers that you've brought with you.
2. Show the vase of fresh white and tinted flowers. Sometimes it is fun to fool Mother Nature!
3. Show the completed project to give them ideas for their own design.

4. Display the pressed flowers on the work space and have everyone notice the flattened beauty of this wildflower. Notice the intricacies of its lacey formation.
5. Distribute the laminating paper and wooden stick to each participant
6. Give them their choice of colored ribbon that will be used as the framing edges
7. Give them their choice of pressed flowers to place inside that ribbon framing. Perhaps they would like just one large flower instead of multiple smaller ones. Don't overlap the flowers since this will keep the top laminating sheet from lying flat and will cause air bubbles.
8. Peel off the protective sheet from the first piece of paper. If necessary, put the ribbon choice on the paper, about an inch from the edges, for them. This is sometimes necessary to avoid frustration.
9. Demonstrate how to take the stick and firmly flatten the ribbon on the sticky paper, while keeping fingers off the sticky surface. Every fingerprint will show on the finished project!
10. Advise them to know what kind of arrangement they'd like to have BEFORE sticking the flowers on the paper. The flowers will not easily come loose from the stickiness if a change needs to be made.
11. Once they have their arrangement in place show them how to GENTLY touch each part of the delicate flower with the stick, in order to flatten it on the paper.
12. Peel off the protective paper from the second piece of laminating paper and starting from the top, cover over the design.
13. Show the participants how to press the paper in place to squeeze out any air bubbles that may have formed.

14. Trim the edges of the finished project if necessary. Sometimes the top paper will be slightly larger or smaller than the bottom piece. That is why you never put the ribbon close to the edge! Give yourself a little leeway!
15. Put scotch tape across the top edge so they can hang their sun catcher in their window or on a mirror. Instead of using tape, you can also punch a hole through the top edge of the laminating paper and make a ribbon loop at the top, if you've provided the suction cup hangers for everyone.
16. Now it's time for show and tell and to graciously accept the compliments from the other participants!

SPECIAL NOTES: There are a lot of decisions that need to be made in completing this project, from ribbon color to flower choices, to placement of flowers on the paper. There is no right or wrong way to design this sun catcher. Mother Nature will take care of providing a beautiful work of art. Stress the importance of tapping down (not rubbing) the ribbon and flowers with the wooden stick as well as the smoothing action of the top sheet of laminating paper.

RESPONSES TO THIS SESSION:

"I'll certainly look at the roadside differently now when we take a drive, thanks to you!"

"I'm going to think of this as my summer snowflake".

The Lace Mosaic Project

MATERIALS REQUIRED:

- Ziploc bags of various colors of crushed chalk
- a vase filled with freshly picked Queen Anne's Lace
- 1 container / participant containing oasis foam
- scissors for trimming stems
- paper towels to cover work surface
- sample project
- a tap root (optional)
- watering can
- handi-wipes for clean-up

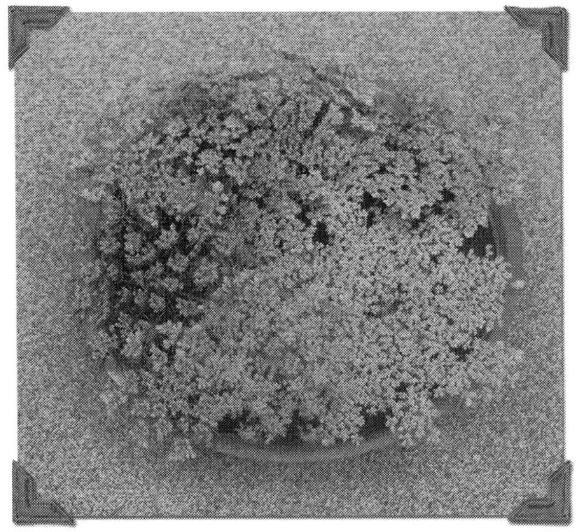

HANDS-ON INSTRUCTIONS:

1. Let everyone see and smell the vase of cut flowers. Can you smell the carrots?
2. Point out the reddish-brown spot in the center of the flower and talk about the naming folk lore attached to this wildflower.
3. Do any of the participants remember picking or seeing this flower along the roadside or in fields when they were children?
4. Pass around the tap root and have them scratch

and sniff. Can you smell the carrots?

5. Distribute the paper towels to cover the working surface.
6. Distribute the containers to be used to everyone and have them wet the oasis with; the watering can. You can have fun with this step too as you pour water into the container, and tip it over with no spillage. The oasis soaks it up magically… to a point!
7. Using a short stemmed flower, demonstrate the art of "painting" the flowers by dipping it into the bag of colored chalk, closing the top and gently inverting the bag so that the flower is completely covered in the chalk dust. Open the bag and gently tap the flower to the inside of the bag to remove the extra chalk. Place the flower in the oasis.
8. Distribute the short-stemmed flowers to the participants and allow them to "paint" their flowers with various colors of chalk dust.
9. Stick each finished flower into the oasis and fill the container with flowers creating the lacey mosaic. Encourage them to place the flowers close together and to completely fill their containers. The flowers will shrink as they dry but will retain their color and remain as a pretty arrangement.
10. When their masterpieces are completed allow them to add a little more water to the containers to ensure the complete wetness of the oasis foam.

SESSION TITLE: The Grass Is Not Always Greener

PROGRAM DESCRIPTION: This is an informative session on the ornamental grasses, which ends with the hands-on activity of either arranging dried grasses and everlastings in a seasonal container or creating a dried grass and everlasting wall plaque as pictured.

BACKGROUND INFORMATION: Depending on where you live in this country, a reference to "pampas grass" could mean one of several totally different grasses. If you live in the Southern US, Cortaderia selloana is pampas grass. In the upper Midwest, Miscanthus sacchariflorus is pampas grass. By any name, ornamental grasses are becoming one of the most popular additions to gardens and landscape design all over the country.

One of the most commonly held misconceptions about grasses is that they all look alike. Some grasses are blue, some are burgundy, and some are variegated. Some grasses are short, some reach heights to eight feet. Some have pink plumage; some are silvery white in color. Even their growth form is varied. Some have a weeping form while others are erect or even vase-shaped. Some varieties will take over an area while others, like the Fescues, are more contained in their growth habit. The one thing they all have in common, however, is their low maintenance. They ask only that you cut back last year's growth to three inches in the early Spring. They all prefer full sun and seem to do well in any type of garden soil. Ornamental grasses add texture and movement to gardens. They are an interesting addition to the Winter garden with their decorative plumage and there is no more soothing sound than that of the wind rustling through their foliage at any season.

MATERIALS REQUIRED:

- A variety of grasses and plumes for show and tell
- Clear-drying glue and wooden craft sticks
- Scissors
- Narrow ribbon
- One painted wooden plaque with a hole drilled in the top / participant or seasonal containers can also be used for a variation of this topic
- A variety of globe amaranths or other everlastings

HANDS-ON INSTRUCTIONS:

1. Distribute the plaques or containers.
2. Let the participants choose their grasses and everlastings.
3. Distribute the glue as well as the ribbon for the loop and the bunches of plant material if you are doing plaque project.
4. Show them the sample and encourage them to exhibit their own creativity.

SPECIAL NOTES: This session can be as complicated or as simple as the participants' ability will allow. In either case, everyone will enjoy the textures. The discussion and show and tell will be fun.

RESPONSES TO THIS SESSION:

"I remember holding these kinds of plumes between my thumb and index finger and squeezing so that a worm-like creature would pop out!"

"Everybody had that tall Pampas grass in their yards. It was a great, but itchy hiding place."

~~ AUGUST ~~

* *

If lavender grows well in the garden,

the girls of the house will never marry.

- Olde English folklore

* *

I'm sure that my daughters are grateful that I had no lavender growing in our yard before they became betrothed!

It's hard to believe that summer is coming to an end. Now is the time when the gardens seem to need a pick-me-up. The lilies are cut back, most of the flowers look as if they long for a cold front to move in to help them become revitalized, and the gardener has been on vacation…but the weeds have not! Just when I feel like the peak has past for the cottage garden's beauty, lo and behold the wonderful "magic lilies" and the "naked ladies" make their appearance. Even though I knew they were there due to the spring foliage, I always seem to forget about them until one August morning when I notice their stalks shooting up in between the other plant foliage. It seems as if they go from stalk to spectacular in a matter of hours! Their delicate pink color and wonderful fragrance once again reminds me that there are still a lot of gardening weeks ahead. I am happy!

This is also the month that honors St. Fiacre, the patron saint of gardeners, especially those who grow vegetables. He is a saint whose aid may be implored in clearing weeds and brush and stones from the garden, and if he does not help with the digging and the heavy lifting, he can at least grant patience and persistence in labor that is never finished. He deserves a horticultural therapy program in his honor. You will find one in the modules below.

There can't be a summer season without bugs to swat at, while weeding. So it seems appropriate to have a program designated to those bug repellent herbs that our forefathers depended on, since they couldn't run to the store and buy a can of "Off."

All of my herbs are full grown and have been snipped for weeks now, to add flavor to summer meals. There is just nothing more pleasing than identifying herbs by their individual aromas as they are bruised in weeding, or mowing. The nose knows and that is the basis for another program which is described below.

SESSION TITLE: "Scent-sational" Geraniums

PROGRAM DESCRIPTION: This is a hands-on session that involves all five senses the subject matter revolves around the Scented Geranium (Pelargonium), plant. It begins with hearing a description of that species, then feeling the many different textured leaves of that species, then seeing the delicate flowers and different growth patterns of that species. We continue by smelling the wonderful fragrances from rubbing the leaves of this species and finally tasting in mini-cakes, the sweet, subtle flavor of the different varieties of scented geraniums. Be sure to clear this tasting session with the Activity Director or nursing staff prior to presentation.

Scented Geraniums are really "scent-sational," and a wonderful part of my garden.

BACKGROUND INFORMATION: To know scented geraniums is to appreciate an olfactory pleasure unlike any other offered by nature! The fragrant wonder is hidden in their leaves. The scent is contained in small beads of oil produced in glands at the base of tiny leaf hairs. Bruising the leaf breaks the beads and releases wonderful

fragrances. There are approximately two hundred and fifty different species of the Pelargonium native to South Africa. Their scented leaves are a natural deterrent against grazing animals. Most of the scents are the result of hybridization between species or other hybrids. In South Africa these plants are perennial and can live and flower for many years there. Sadly in my Ohio climate they need to be treated as an annual in the garden or as a container plant which can be wintered indoors. They are truly a living potpourri for the home in the wintertime. I always have a bowl of their leaves somewhere in the house for touching as I pass by. The fragrance lingers in the air and my fingers smell wonderful!

These plants, unlike the common garden variety of geranium, are not grown for their flowers. They do produce flowers but not the showy blossoms that are usually associated with geraniums. The blooms are delicate and don't over-shadow the beauty of the leaves, but rather emphasizes them.

The leaves of each plant variety are different from one another. Some are oak leaf shaped, some are fern-like, some are tiny, and some are rounded. Even the color of the leaves varies. They can be anything from light green to dark green to grey-green. Their textures can be as interesting as their fragrances. Some are rough, some feel like velvet, some are hairy. Their flowers have several common characteristics, however. They are always grouped in umbels (clusters) of five to ten flowers, and most flowers have five petals and all of the flowers appear delicate and fragile.

Scented geraniums add wonder to any garden area. Just by brushing against their leaves while weeding can transform that mundane chore into a sheer delight for the nostrils. The fragrances are powerful and are released easily into the air all around you.

These geraniums grow best in a soil-less mix since ordinary garden soil packs down and drains too slowly. They also like slightly acidic growing conditions. They can be propagated by cuttings placed in the soil-less mixture. They will not root in water. They prefer to dry out in between watering times.

In the Victorian language of flowers, geraniums in general signify gentility. An oak leafed scented geranium means true friendship while a rose scented one signifies preference. All scented geraniums are rich in vitamin C. The flowers can be used as garnishes and the leaves can be eaten!

There are many uses for these wonderfully fragrant plants. Aside from flavoring food such as butters, cakes and sugars, you can also use them in potpourris and cosmetics. Perhaps the best usage of scented geraniums is the sheer delight of working around them! They are "scent-sational" plants to be around and to work with.

MATERIALS REQUIRED:

- An ordinary garden variety of geranium
- A pot of scented geraniums (for show and tell and comparison)
- Have a picture or laminated sample of the different kinds of blossoms produced by the scented varieties
- Provide a tray of prepared mini-cakes, muffins and/or teas for the taste test portion of this session
- Take paper plates, napkins and cups
- Serve fruit punch for those less adventurous residents

HANDS-ON INSTRUCTION:

1. The session begins with the show and tell information about geraniums, both the garden varieties and the scented Pelargoniums.
2. Give the residents an opportunity to feel and smell the leaves, and their fingers, after personally rubbing the leaves of these plants.
3. Finally enjoy the taste test portion and distribute napkins and drinks.
4. Once again show them the specific plant, e.g. rose scented geranium, and then offer a rose scented mini-cake for tasting. Don't distribute all of the cakes at

once. Emphasize the comparison between the smells and the tastes.

SPECIAL NOTES: This is a great session for all levels of capabilities. You can elaborate on the horticultural information to match the interest of the participants. The sight-impaired residents can also enjoy all of the textures, smells and tastes of this program. Be sure you have checked with the activity director or nursing station before you present any taste-test program. There may be dietary restrictions.

CULINARY USAGE: Not all scented Pelargoniums have tastes that complement cookery. I've successfully used the rose, lemon, nutmeg, mint and orange varieties for cakes and teas. Most often their flavors are infused into the dish and the leaves are removed and discarded before serving. Fresh leaves can be used as a decorative garnish.

Be sure you avoid using pesticides on plants that are destined for the kitchen.

Scented geraniums are best used in sweet dishes. Rose varieties add a delicate flavor to granulated sugar, which is then used in baked goods and icings, or to sweeten teas and cereal. It certainly seems gourmet-like when I sprinkle rose scented geranium sugar on my Wheaties in the morning! To make the flavored sugars, stack clean, dry, and bruised leaves in a canister between 1-inch layers of granulated sugar. Place the canister in a warm spot for 2-4 weeks and then sift out the leaves.

In making mini-cakes, I finely chop the fresh leaves (approximately 3 tablespoons / white or yellow cake mix) and gently fold them into the prepared mix right before baking.

SESSION TITLE: The Language of Flowers

PROGRAM DESCRIPTION: This informative session goes into the discussion of floriography, which is the art of sending messages through the use of flowers. It is defined as "the language of flowers" and is a sentiment from the past. All flowers don't have a positive connotation however! Insults were also given through flowers in the Victorian times when it was considered rude to actually speak insulting words. For example, the beautiful Morning Glory's meaning was "Affectation".

The amount of information concerning the symbolic meaning of the various types of flowers will be dependent upon the cognitive levels of the participants. We will be making either a tussie-mussie, which some may know as a nosegay, or just a simple bouquet of flowers tied with a dainty ribbon.

This session can be hands-on for most levels of participants, but if necessary, it can easily be made into a show and tell activity. Everyone will enjoy the nostalgic and the sentimental quality of the tussie-mussie and the Victorian history behind it.

BACKGROUND INFORMATION: The language of flowers came to England in the 1700's but actually originated in the Middle East where the Turks sent one another fruit and floral greetings as part of their custom. This very romantic, indirect communication and elaborate custom reached its peak in the Victorian era. In the seventeenth century it was suggested to use herbs to make a delicate tussie-mussie for both sight and scent. The origin of the name "tussie-mussie" remains a mystery but it soon became a necessary part of every Victorian woman's wardrobe.

Some flowers have held traditional meanings for centuries, such as a red rose associated with true love. The symbolic meanings of flowers were known to many people in Elizabethan times, and Shakespeare scattered meaningful references to flowers throughout his plays. However, the Victorians coded these meanings into an elegant language without words.

In Medieval times the custom of carrying a tussie-mussie was more of a necessity than of a wardrobe accessory. Before good sanitation practices, fresh air wasn't very fresh and was in fact, thought to be unhealthy. Fragrant herbs and flowers were held to the nose to counteract the not-so-pleasant aromas of an area. They became a breath of fresh air, a refreshing necessity. These then became known as "nosegays."

To take it a step further, the strewing herbs and those with medicinal fragrances were used to combat germs and even the plague. Doctors were known to carry one on the end of their walking sticks to ward off disease as they made their house calls.

Tussie-mussies are making a delightful comeback today. They recall a time when gifts were handmade and given from the heart. They are a very personal gift.

By the nineteenth century, there were floral dictionaries to be had and you knew exactly which flowers and herbs to incorporate into your little bouquet, in order to convey your desired message for the recipient. They are a talking gift and the Victorians had no trouble understanding their messages. Nowadays, if you give someone a tussie-mussie, you'll need to write out the flowers used, and their meanings, and include that little note with your floral gift.

The shy, demure Victorian woman would have blushed to the roots of her hair had a young man blurted out his true feelings for her delicate ears to hear. However, she knew exactly what his feelings were if he handed her a dainty tussie-mussie at her garden gate. If the nosegay included a red Rose with a sprig of Lavender, a Daisy and a piece of Sage, she would interpret it as follows: "He loves me passionately (the red rose) and is devoted to me (lavender). He's hopeful (the daisy) about our relationship and wishes me the best of good health (sage)." That is a powerful message given and understood, without a word being spoken. The language of flowers is definitely a forgotten art. Somehow a text message doesn't have the same romance to it!

The flower symbolizing the most important sentiment is placed in the center of the tiny bouquet. The young woman may have been disappointed or relieved, as the case may have been, if the red rose had been a yellow one instead. That shift in color indicates that her young man wishes her only as a friend, and nothing more. If the flower had been turned upside down in the bouquet, that indicates the opposite meaning of the color of the rose. That message could cause the blushing girl to run and cry, or at best, throw it on the ground and stomp on it with her dainty foot. Of course she could also send him a tussie-mussie in reply…sort of having the "last flower" so to speak. She could send back a piece of Larkspur indicating his fickleness. He'd be well off to reply with a bouquet including white Violets for innocence or one containing a large amount of Rue signifying his repentance.

If there was a ribbon in the nosegay, its placement also had a meaning. If it were on the left side of the arrangement, it meant that the flowers' meanings were in regard to the sender and if the right side was adorned with the piece of ribbon, the recipient had to look to herself for the interpretation. I've always hoped that both the giver and the recipient had the same dictionary and that neither was dyslectic!

In the Victorian era, these tussie-mussies were carried in elegant silver holders and both men and women used them. Today you can purchase dainty, small lapel pin tussie-mussie holders. They have even become collectibles now.

These sweet little conveyors of messages can be made from fresh flowers and herbs or from the dried ones. The scent of the dried ones can be preserved or refreshed by sprinkling Orris root and/or an essential oil on the dried leaves.

We've always known about body language and its pitfalls and now the language of flowers has to be reckoned with. With that said, be forewarned about what you might unknowingly be communicating when you present someone with a tiny nosegay!

The next time you walk in a garden, keep in mind all of the messages that are there for you to hear!

MATERIALS REQUIRED:

If each one is making a tussie-mussie of their own you will need:

- a 6" doily / person
- green floral tape
- scotch tape
- an assortment of fresh or dried flowers and herbs
- completed sample for show and tell
- pruning shears
- narrow, colored ribbon

HANDS-ON INSTRUCTIONS:

1. Distribute the doilies.
2. Go through the symbolic meanings of the flowers that you have with you.
3. Give the participants their choice of the center flower.
4. Work each layer around the center flower until it's approximately 4 inches in diameter. The ending circle of greenery could be ivy, or other attractive foliage like lambs ears or folded ribbon grass to be the framing.
5. Bunch the stems together and with the pruning shears, clip all stems to be the same length, approximately 3-4 inches long.

6. Pass out the floral tape and demonstrate the wrapping technique to keep the stems secured. Make a cut in the doily so that it fits up to the base of the flowers and scotch tape it in place.
7. Tie the colored ribbon under the doily to secure it and tie one or two "love knots" in the middle of the streamer of ribbon. These knots would have been significant in Victorian times but today, they are just for decorative purposes. Of course we all "love" having our own tussie mussie and we can all enjoy our own "breath of fresh air."

If fresh flowers have been used, they can be kept fresh by standing the nosegay in a dainty vase of water to enjoy a while longer. After 4-5 days, remove them from the water and hang upside down to dry and to be permanently enjoyed, as thoughts of Victorian times dance through our heads.

SPECIAL NOTES: For a low functioning group, the language of flowers can still be discussed and the flowers enjoyed. Instead of each participant making a tussie-mussie, a small bunch of dried flowers, minus the doily and floral tape, can be tied with a ribbon and distributed to everyone participating. Everyone will enjoy these delightful "talking gifts" once they understand the message.

RESPONSES TO THIS SESSION:

"I've never heard of a tussie-mussie before. I like learning about new things. I feel so old fashioned now with my own little nosegay."

A SAMPLE GLOSSARY OF SOME FLOWERS AND HERBS:

Artemisia, Silver King ~ Power, Dignity, Sentimental recollections

Baby's Breath ~ A pure heart

Calla Lily ~ Magnificent beauty

Carnation ~ Fascination, Admiration

Chrysanthemums ~ Cheerfulness, Optimism

Clover ~ Luck

Coreopsis ~ Always cheerful

Daffodil ~ Regard, Respect, Goodness, Chivalry

Dusty Miller ~ Delicacy

Fern ~ Fascination, Sincerity

Freesia ~ Innocence

Forget-me-not ~ Remember me

Globe Amoranth ~ Undying affection

Ivy ~ Fidelity, Wedded love, Trustfulness

Lamb's Ear ~ Support

Lavender ~ Devotion

Lemon Balm ~ Sympathy

Lilac ~ Beauty, First emotions of love

Lily-of-the-Valley ~ Return of happiness, Peace

Marigolds ~ Joy, Remembrance, Happiness

Marjoram ~ Joy, Happiness

Mint ~ Warmth of feeling

Morning Glory ~ Affectation

Orchid ~ Luxury, Love, Nobility

Pineapple mint ~ Welcome

Pansies ~ Contentment

Rosemary ~ Remembrance

Rose (red) ~ Congratulations, Deep love, Beauty

Rose (yellow) ~ Friendship, Highest mark of distinction

Rose (white) ~ Purity

Sage ~ Good health, Long life

Scented Geranium leaves ~ Comfort, Eagerness

Sunflower ~ Haughtiness

Sweet Basil ~ Good wishes

Tarragon ~ Lasting involvement

Thyme ~ Courage, Strength

Tulips ~ Fame, Charity, The perfect lover

Violets ~ Faithfulness, Sweetness, Loyalty, Innocence

Zinnia ~ Thoughts of absent friends

This poem is in a book written by Margaret Pickston

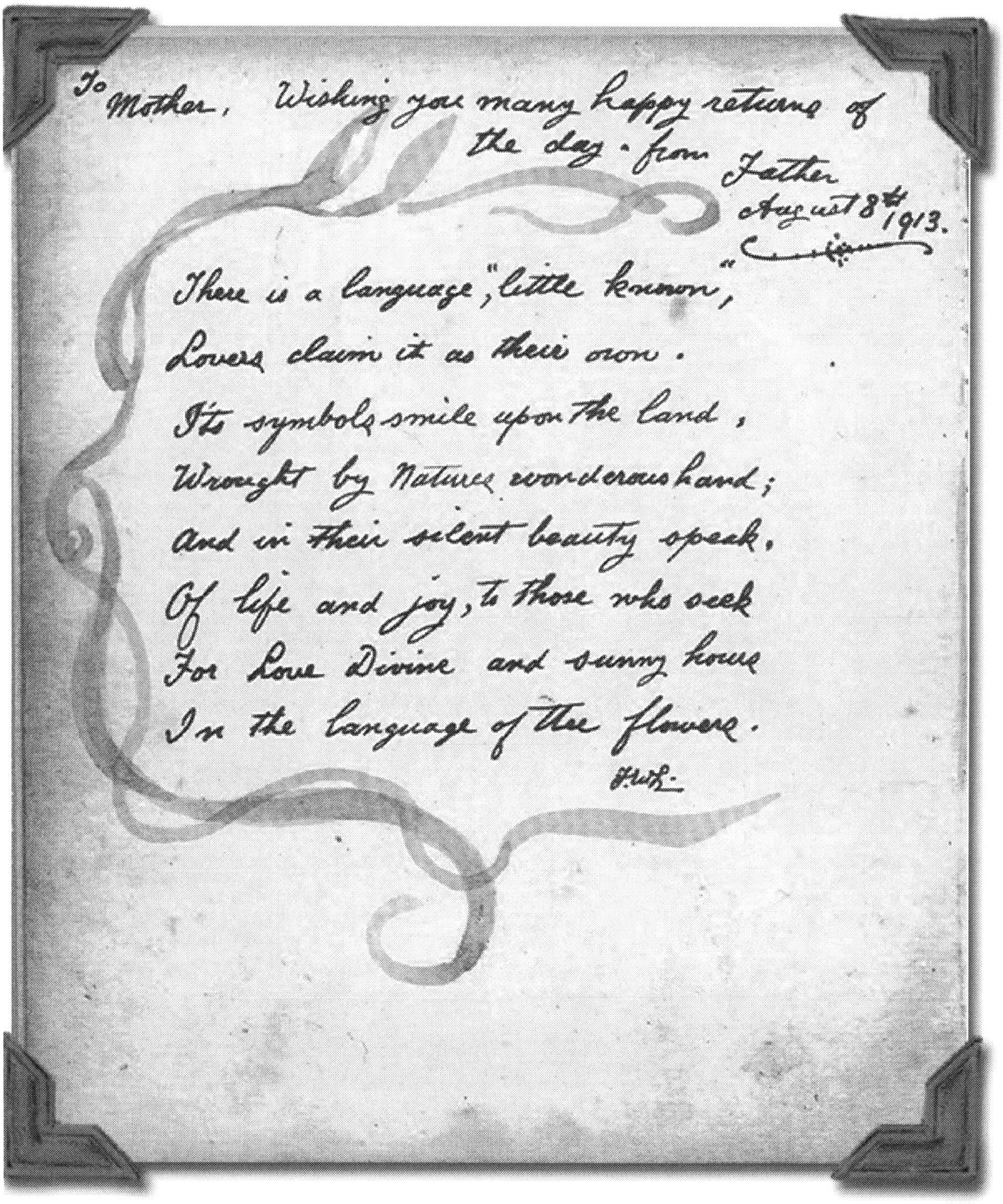

To Mother, Wishing you many happy returns of the day - from Father
August 8th 1913.

There is a language, "little known",
Lovers claim it as their own.
It's symbols smile upon the land,
Wrought by Natures wonderous hand;
And in their silent beauty speak,
Of life and joy, to those who seek
For Love Divine and sunny hours
In the language of the flowers.

F.W.L.

SESSION TITLE: Ferns and Frames

PROGRAM DESCRIPTION: The information in this session is all about the many and varied types of ferns found in both nature and garden centers.

The activity is a simple one which entails only the gluing of dried fern fronds onto a frame matting that can later be used in decorating a favorite personal photo.

This session is adaptable for any functioning level depending on the amount of information you want to share regarding the fern population and history.

BACKGROUND INFORMATION: Ferns are ancient plants that colonized the earth two hundred million years before any flowering plants made their appearance. They formed much of the forest where the dinosaurs roamed. These plants can be just a few inches long or twenty feet tall. The latter are called tree ferns, and varieties of these are still beautifying the hillsides in rain forests today.

There are approximately one hundred different kinds of ferns in the Northeast and Midwestern states, as compared to the thousands of different kinds of flowering plants we see in those same areas.

Many fern varieties are grown easily as potted houseplants and therefore can be appreciated indoors all winter long in all parts of our country. There are wonderful shapes to choose from and interesting nomenclature to spark your imagination. I personally love the Rabbit's Foot Fern (Polypodium aureum) and the Bird's-Nest Fern

(Asplenium nidus) varieties as house plants. Ferns are not winter hardy and so I've been known to bring into my house many large potted ferns for those cold months. I enjoy the tropical feeling they lend to my space when I look out onto a snowy landscape!

The fern is an interesting plant since it reproduces by spores rather than by seeds. If you turn over the frond (leaf) of the fern, you will see a very distinctive pattern of spores. They resemble little brown patches or dots and the patterns formed are used in their identification. If these spores happen to land on a moist surface, they will germinate. This alone, makes for an interesting show and tell exhibit.

Ferns are most common in the tropics or temperate regions that are moist and shaded, however some varieties will also grow on cliffs or in lava fields and in meadows. Some varieties prefer to cling to a tree trunk and this variety is known as an epiphyte, which defines any plant that grows on another plant for its support system, but not for its nutrients. Orchids are also epiphytes.

As was mentioned above, ferns have descriptive, fun sounding names. A few of the outdoor varieties are Ostrich Fern, Royal Fern, Hay-scented Fern, Cinnamon Fern, Interrupted Fern, Maidenhair Fern, Christmas Fern, and the Resurrection Fern. Once they are happily established in your garden you will enjoy them forever. They add interesting texture and detail to a shade garden. The Painted Japanese Fern also adds a beautiful pink-burgundy color to an area for an added interest.

The fern has been the subject of botanical art since Victorian times. They offer an inviting link back to the prehistoric world. The Victorians loved giving meaning to plants and flowers and there are entire books written on the language of flowers. Symmetry, sincerity and fascination are the more common meanings given to the fern.

I love working among great stands of lush, tall Ostrich Ferns. My imagination goes into high gear as I weed and think of prehistoric times. Is that a dinosaur lurking between the giant fronds watching me?

MATERIALS RERQUIRED:

- Glue and Scotch tape
- one 5" x 7" framing mat in a variety of shapes and colors / participant
- wooden draft sticks
- scissors
- handi-wipes for sticky finger clean-up
- a can of clear acrylic spray
- dried and pressed ferns
- dried and pressed small flowers
- potted ferns
- completed project
- pictures of fern varieties
- magazine pictures of scenery, butterflies or dinosaurs

HANDS-ON INSTRUCTIONS:

1. After discussing and passing around the various ferns and pictures, show the participants the completed project sample.

2. Show them the choices of mats and let them choose the shape and color that is appealing to them.
3. Distribute the craft sticks and glue and spread the variety of dried flowers and ferns on the table in front of them.
4. Demonstrate how to position a design on the mats, using the dried material. (Emphasize the importance of designing their mat before applying the glue! Only a small drop of glue is necessary. Keep all ferns and petals on the mat's surface).
5. At the end of this session, spray each mat with the clear acrylic spray to keep their finished work permanent and to produce a glazed look to the completed product.

SPECIAL NOTES: If they have a special photo of a family member or friend, it can be taped to the back of their mat. Some may want to put the entire project inside a frame.

If someone mentions that they have no pictures in their room to mat and frame, then you can offer them a picture of a butterfly, dinosaur or other picture that you've brought with you.

RESPONSES TO THIS SESSION:

One of the residents commented, "Seeing these ferns makes me remember all the small ferns that used to grow in a woods by my childhood home." "Me too," added another woman at the table. "My father would just dig them up and plant them on the farm around our house. Nobody cared if you did that back then. You probably couldn't get away with that now."

Another resident mentioned that she had no family or friends left because she was so old and that, "No one knows who I am anymore." She chose a picture of a dinosaur to frame because, "that's how old I am!" That could have been a sad moment but she got the other residents laughing with her comment. I've noticed that all sessions end on a happy note.

SESSION TITLE: Mint Madness

PROGRAM DESCRIPTION: This very fragrant session revolves around a discussion of the many varieties of mints, their distinctive appearances, their individual fragrances and their tasty and aromatic uses. This is a session, which not only stimulates the sense of smell, but also the sense of touch is put to work. Small muscle groups are exercised when doing the crushing or tearing of the leaves, eye-hand coordination is developed and cognitive skills are also stimulated. All of these things are accomplished amidst the invigorating aroma of mint filling the air!

In high functioning groups the project can be the making of tea balls after the sensory and informative part of this program is completed. Different mint teas or waters can be sampled along with mint jelly on a cracker. Have fun! Enjoy a tea party!

If your group is in a health care unit where there are dietary restrictions you can make a mint-blend sachet instead. The smell of peppermint is both invigorating and calming and so it is a good fragrance for anyone to work around.

BACKGROUND INFORMATION: The mints belong to the family Lamiacae, genus menthe. There are eighteen species and thousands of varieties. Sage, Salvia, Lavender, Rosemary and Artemisia are also part of this huge family of plants.

Mint was designated as "Herb of the Year" in 1998 because of its many and varied uses, the ease of its growing habits, its adaptability and wonderful fragrance. Some variety is easily grown, in every region of North America, no matter what the zone. The purple, pink or white flowers are dainty spikes or ball-shaped clusters depending on the variety. The square stem is characteristic of all the plants within this family as well as the fragrance of the leaves, which are arranged opposite of each other on the stem.

Mints originated from sunny climates and are therefore, for the most part, not shade lovers, although some varieties will tolerate more shade than others. Lemon balm, a cousin, is one of these tolerant plants. They will adapt to a variety of soil types, as long as they have occasional watering or a moist root run. Variegated types (pineapple mint) prefer partial sun but the others do best in full sun. Most people have a fear of growing mint because of its invasive reputation. And that it can be. If it's grown in buried containers, or wide garden bowls, its invasiveness is diminished considerably. Most of the mints don't come from seed, but rather are spread by long rhizomes that can find their way under rocks and boulders.

Few pests bother mints but honeybees and butterflies will come for miles to enjoy the sweet nectar!

Mint leaves are at their most aromatic right before they flower and this is the time to enjoy that peppermint tea or a mint julep!

I have many varieties of mint in my garden, including peppermint and spearmint, chocolate mint (pictured above), apple, orange and curly mint. Lemon balm is also a wonderful flavor addition to iced tea. The leaves are great to serve with fish or to chop up in fruit salads during summer months.

Mint is also a nice addition to peas and carrots or in sauces to top ice cream. I personally am a great fan of the mints. I just can't imagine my yard without at least three or four flavors growing in the garden. Aside from the enjoyment of their flavor, I really savor the fragrances as I brush against them while weeding the garden. A spearmint leaf has often times been a little sweet snack while I'm working in the garden too!

I find that a blooming sprig is also a welcomed fragrance added to a bouquet of cut flowers on my kitchen table.

Long before the settlers came to America, the Native Indians used mints extensively as a treatment for many different ailments. There are even references to this wonderful herb in the Bible. It had always been well known in medieval homes, castles and monasteries for its flavor and usefulness in medicine. It's not surprising then, that it was given the designation of Herb of the Year in modern times as well.

Long ago the mints were used as strewing herbs to freshen the floors of log cabins as well as used for medicinal purposes. Both spearmint and peppermint have always been the medicinal varieties, but spearmint has the longer history. It was grown in every convent garden in Europe by the 1800's. It was common knowledge to drink mint water to ease digestive problems. Nowadays, however, peppermint is the most widely used for medicinal purposes. By 1848 it was thought to be especially useful in treating cholera in children.

In ancient times, it was the custom of concluding feasts by chewing a sprig of mint to settle the stomach and to cleanse the breath. Our after-dinner mints have replaced those sprigs on our dinner tables. Today it is still used as a tea for indigestion, nausea, colds, headaches and diarrhea. In 1704 all medical journals touted peppermint as the treatment of "stomach weakness and diarrhea." Today we buy Pepto-Bismol for the same purpose. Guess what "Pepto" stands for!

Menthol is the primary ingredient in its essential oil. The smell and taste of a given mint is determined by the ratio of menthol to the other components in fruit-scented varieties.

By 1850 the U.S.A. had become one of the world's major producers of peppermint oil. There are 100,000 acres of mint growing in Indiana, Michigan, Wisconsin, Idaho, Oregon and Washington. We encounter mint essential oils daily in toothpastes, mouth washes, chewing gum and beverages, to name just a few items.

Peppermint oil is being used to improve memory and concentration, to aid in sinus problems, to provide stress relief, and to help prevent motion and morning sickness. It clears the mind, and is both energizing and soothing.

In the language of flowers, mint means "virtue." Peppermint imparts the meaning of "warm feelings," and in many parts of the world the mints are a symbol of hospitality.

Folklore tells us, "Grow mint in the garden to attract money to your purse." How I wish that were true. I'd be a wealthy woman!

In the middle ages it was said, "If you would at all times be merry, put a mint in all your meat and drink."

MATERIALS REQUIRED:

- two 8" x 8" pieces of white small-mesh netting
- one 12" piece of narrow white ribbon or string / bag
- a measuring spoon (you will be using 2 tablespoons crushed mint / bag)

- a variety of mints, fresh or dried, for tearing or crushing
- wax paper to cover their working surface
- samples of mint to touch, bruise and smell (Include some sprigs that are in bloom, if possible, since different species produce different types of flowers)
- purchased after dinner mints (optional)
- mint flavored water or minted iced tea to sample (optional)
- paper cups
- completed sample
- purchased mint jelly, crackers, napkins and a spreader (optional)
- use a 10" x 10" piece of netting, if the sachets are being made instead of the tea balls (Instead of tying these with string, give the participants their choice of a pretty piece of narrow colored ribbon)

Each participant can make two tea balls. If they are not tea drinkers instruct them on using the tea balls to flavor plain water instead of steeping it with tea. These tea balls could also be used as fragrant sachets instead of in a beverage.

HANDS-ON INSTRUCTIONS: Be sure to give each person ample time to smell and touch the various mint species. Did they ever grow mint in their gardens? Did they or their Moms ever use it for medicinal purposes? Which is their favorite smell of the samples in front of them?

1. Give each participant a piece of wax paper to work on.
2. Distribute the dried or fresh mint sprigs and have them pull off the leaves from the stems and place them on the wax paper. Take in a deep breath of fragrance!

3. Blend and mix with hands until dried mint is coarsely crushed, or fresh mint is torn into smaller pieces. Give them the option of mixing the different varieties together.
4. Continue stripping the stems and crushing the mint until they have approximately two tablespoons / bag. Don't crush the dried material too fine or it will sift through the mesh.
5. Distribute the pieces of netting and ribbon to each participant.
6. Place the crushed mint blend in the center of the net squares.
7. Have each person smell their hands! Everyone seems to love the freshness of the mint aromas.
8. Instruct them on folding up the corners of their tea ball mesh and tying it off with the ribbon. Keep a long end of ribbon so that it can be retrieved easily from the cup after steeping is completed.
9. Commence with the tea party if you have chosen to add this option to the session.
10. Follow the same directions for making the sachets, using the 10" x 10" piece of netting. One sachet / person is sufficient.

SPECIAL NOTES: Be sure to get permission before taking a tea party to a group. There may be dietary restrictions.

Directions for Making Hot Tea by the Cup:

1. Place one tea bag and one mint tea ball in your favorite tea cup.
2. Add boiling water and let steep covered, for 4-6 minutes.
3. Sweeten if you desire. (With mint flavored teas, taste before you sweeten! You may not need it after all.)

Directions for Flavoring Water:

1. Place just the mint tea ball into a cup.
2. Add the boiling water, cover and steep for 6-8 minutes, depending on how strongly flavored you want your water.
3. If you chill this water for a few hours and then serve with a sprig of fresh mint in a tall glass with ice cubes, you will enjoy a very refreshing summer drink. (This chilled water can also be used in making lemonade, giving the finished drink a mint flavor.)

* *

The tea party is a spa for the soul. You leave your cares and work behind. Busy people forget their business. Your stress melts away, your senses awaken…

- Alexandra Stoddard

Take a few minutes and enjoy your own "spa for the soul"!

SESSION TITLE: The Taste of Lemon Without the Pucker

PROGRAM DESCRIPTION: I can be tasted, crunched, and smelled. I can become a tea, a cake, a marinade, a sachet or calm your nerves. I love sunny days. Who am I? I am one of many of the lemon-scented herbs.

There are many of these refreshing, versatile herbs that have the enticing attributes of a fresh lemon minus the pucker. This session identifies some of them and gives a little of their history and folklore. If you have sprigs and sample plants of any of these wonderful aromatic herbs already dried, that will add the "crunch" dimension to this session.

The hands-on portion can be either the simple construction of a refreshing sachet or a delicious taste-testing hour with the participants. That will be dependent on the level of participant that is at your table. Don't forget to get permission to bring food into the area. There may be dietary restrictions that you are unaware of.

BACKGROUND INFORMATION:

Lemon Balm (Melissa officinalis): was a sacred herb in the temple of the Greek goddess Diana. It is part of the mint family and aids in digestion like the other mints. It has a history that dates back to 980 AD and has been recorded as an herb that was used topically to treat ulcers and wounds. In 1695 it was written, "…to be kept in every gentlewoman's house to relieve the weak stomachs and sick bodies of their poor sickly neighbors." It was also said, "It causes the mind and heart to become merry and revives the heart, in faintings and swoonings."

Today there is research being done on the effectiveness of lemon balm as an antioxidant as well as possibly being used for antiviral activity. It is thought to reduce fevers and to help lower blood pressure. It's also used to treat light insomnia. It has historically been associated with improved brain function. No wonder it should, "be kept in every gentlewoman's house."

In 1988, it was selected as Europe's medicinal plant of the year. It is a must for every garden and is an easy to grow perennial.

Until recently Lemon Balm has not been fully appreciated for its culinary merit. It makes a pleasant tasting tea as well as giving a subtle lemony flavoring to fish, vegetables and salads. In cooking, add it at the end of the cooking time to retain the maximum flavor. The addition of citrus or pineapple seems to intensify its lemony flavor.

Lemon Thyme (Thymus citriodorus): It contains the chemical thymal, which is used in many antiseptic mouthwashes. This variety has a more intense lemon flavor than most of the other lemon-scented herbs. Its culinary uses are many, ranging from honey flavoring, sugar cookies, cream cheese spreads and tea.

Lemon Grass (Cymbopogon citrates): This is a native to Southeast Asia. In Indonesia it is used for combating bad moods. In Thailand it is mixed with ginger and is used in sauces and teas. It is becoming one of the trendiest lemon herbs of all. Chefs use it to tie around fish filets before baking or grilling and it is being used as a clever, tasty way to tie many appetizers together as well. After all, presentation is an important part of the culinary art! At its bulbous base, it is rich in vitamin A. It is also a fine addition to potpourri.

Lemon Verbena (Aloysia triphylla): In my personal opinion, this herb is unexcelled for lemony taste and fragrance! It is more difficult to grow and doesn't winter over in my Cincinnati, Ohio garden, (Zone 5) but it is too wonderful not to make the effort to plant it every year. I've had no success in wintering it over inside my home either, so I just have to enjoy it to the fullest during its outside growing season. I love to include it in any recipe calling for a lemon flavor. It is also tasty snipped on new potatoes and carrots.

I love to include it in potpourri mixes. Victorian women used the leaves in finger bowls and the French used it as a tea for its sedative effects. It has also been used as an aid in indigestion as well as a skin toner. There are so many ways this wonderfully aromatic plant can be used other than the olfactory stimulation. It should grace every garden! Surprisingly, this herb went from the New World to the Old World via the Spanish explorers who found it in Argentina and Chili in the seventeenth century. It grows to become a ten to fifteen foot high shrub in the tropics. How I would love to have that quantity of this magnificent herb in my garden!

Lemon Basil (Ocimum citriodorum): This is a very popular culinary herb. It has much lighter green leaves that are narrower than the other basil varieties. When combined with spearmint leaves it becomes a very tasty, refreshing tea. It also gives a tasty zing to salsa recipes and is great in flavoring pasta and seafood.

In most recipes you can rarely use too much of these lemon flavored herbs because they seem to have more fragrance than flavor. Sprigs of these herbs can be frozen in ice cube trays for summer drinks anytime of the year.

MATERIALS REQUIRED

FOR THE SACHET PROJECT:

- A pre-cut piece of netting approximately 8" x 8" (colors are a nice option) / person

- One 8" piece of narrow, colored ribbon / person
- Dried or fresh lemon balm, lemon verbena and apple mint for bruising or crunching and smelling
- Take sprigs of other lemon-scented herbs for show and tell and-smell purposes
- Don't forget your finished, fragrant sachet sample to share

For a Tea Bag Project:

- Have pre-cut pieces of unbleached, sheer muslin. (2-3 / participant) (Don't use colored fabric with this project because of the dye used in it)
- an 8" piece of white ribbon / tea bag
- dried or fresh herbs as above
- show-and-tell-and-smell sprigs as above
- share your finished sample with everyone

For a Tea Party:

- a lemon verbena pound cake (recipe follows)
- a pitcher of lemon balm, lemon verbena / lavender tea or purchased lemonade for
- the non-tea drinker to enjoy
- paper plates, cups and napkins
- a knife for cutting the cake into small sample-sized pieces

HANDS-ON INSTRUCTIONS:

1. For both the sachet and the tea bag projects, begin with everyone smelling and bruising the plants and sprigs that are available. Within a few minutes, the entire area will smell fresh and clean, like "Lemon Pledge"!
2. Distribute the squares of appropriate material and ribbon to each person.
3. Distribute the dried or fresh herbs allowing everyone to smell each one individually as it is received. When all of the herbs are mixed together, the blended fragrance will be completely different than the individual leaves had been.
4. Instruct them to either tear, if fresh, or crumble, if dried, the leaves and place them in the center of their fabric square. Be sure that there are no big stems in the mixture.
5. When the leaves are blended together, show them how to draw up the four corners and tie closed with the ribbon. For the sachet, the ribbon can be tied off with a nice bow. In the case of the tea bag, allow the ribbon to be knotted and remain long so that it can be left hanging out of the cup or teapot while steeping for 10 minutes.

SPECIAL NOTES: If you are going to do a taste test session, be sure it has been approved prior to the session. Dietary restrictions could alter who is brought to the table.

Lemon Verbena Pound Cake Recipe

Use one packaged pound cake mix and add 3 tablespoons of dried and finely crushed lemon verbena leaves to it. Mix thoroughly and bake according to the package directions. When cool, ice with a lemon verbena glaze. Mix the following ingredients together:

1 stick of melted butter

4 tablespoons of lemon juice

1 handful of finely chopped fresh lemon verbena leaves

3 tablespoons of honey

* *

Lemon Verbena / Lavender Tea

1 cup of dried lemon verbena leaves and 3 tablespoons of lavender flowers make the stock. Mix it together thoroughly and mix it every time that you use it since the lavender sifts itself to the bottom of the mix.

Steep 1 teaspoon of the above stock mix / 1 cup of boiling water.

Strain and enjoy the flavor of two of my favorite herbs.

This tea will have a very calming, sedative effect so it is especially helpful if you suffer from insomnia.

RESPONSE TO THE TEA PARTY SESSION:

"I'm feeling so relaxed and sedated…I think I'll have to have another piece of that cake to stay awake."

-- SEPTEMBER --

* *

Fair weather first day of September,
Fair for the month.

- Olde English folklore

* *

This is the month that brings summer to its official end. By now most of the flowers look as if they need a rest. The heat and humidity has sapped their strength and there is mildew on some of the zinnia stalks. These stars have performed beautifully in their roles in the garden for the past months and are now ready to be replaced by the stars for the fall performance of "Jan's Garden." The next group of actors is ready to be recognized. The fall crocus and Saffron Crocus, the field asters and the hybrid asters have taken center front on the garden stage with their whites, pinks, reds and purples and the early blooming mums are ready to add their splash of color to the front yard.

By the end of the month, the roadsides will be dusted with the wild New England asters and bright goldenrod spikes. The ironweed and artichoke hearts continue the parade of color as summer takes its final curtsey. The fall pansy planting time is here and so this gardening color wheel has come full circle. I do love pansies and their smiling faces.

The days are getting shorter and it's earlier when the moonlight reflects off the silver foliage of the dusty miller, Artemisia, and lambs ear in my cottage garden. It's worth the evening walk on the garden path just to enjoy that brightness, and to be on the lookout for any of the moths that are there for a final banquet.

The cooler evenings are a reminder that the harvest is upon us. To our forefathers this was the most important part of the growing season. Their winter survival depended on their harvest.

A couple of the following programs are designed to be tea parties, for those residents without dietary restrictions. I love to harvest the herbs for butters and the scented geraniums for cakes. I must feel as if I'm part of the ancient harvest ritual.

SESSION TITLE: Remarkable Rosemary

PROGRAM DESCRIPTION: In this session we are going to mix together aromatic herbs that are stimulating and invigorating. They counter mental fatigue and encourage activity. We will be making a sachet that includes rosemary, mint and lemon balm. Not only will the blended fragrances be enjoyed, but the finished project will be uplifting and energizing. It has been said that, "Rosemary is to the spirit as lavender is to the soul." Try it for yourself.

Information on Mints and Lemon Balm can be found elsewhere in this book with their corresponding sessions.

BACKGROUND INFORMATION: *Rosmarinus Officinalis* was given the designation of "Herb of the Year for 2000". People are rediscovering herbs as a way to enhance health and general well being, and rosemary, as it's been known as since 1440, certainly fits into that category. It is a multi-purpose plant that is treated as an annual in the Ohio Valley but it grows wild on the sea cliffs of the Mediterranean and freely along banks, sidewalks and hedges in California.

The "dew of the sea," as its Latin name implies, has a strong but pleasant flavor and a potent aroma, which has contributed to its popularity. Not only is it one of the best of the culinary herbs, it has had a reputation through the ages for improving the memory and has been used for many medicinal purposes, one of which is as an effective inhalant and decongestant. It is also good for aching joints and rheumatism in its oil form. It is used in dying wool, producing a pretty, yellow-green hue. Not only can this remarkable herb keep you healthy but it can dress you in a pretty-colored fabric as well!

It is an evergreen shrub that loves sunshine and is drought tolerant. It doesn't grow well in clay soils but rather prefers the light, well drained soils. Adding potash or egg shells will give it the alkalinity that it also likes. Because of its shallow, fibrous root system, it needs good drainage and will die if it is over watered.

Grown outside, it is hardy to 15 degrees and needs to be kept out of winds since its tips are prone to dehydration. Upright forms of rosemary are more difficult to grow than the prostrate forms, which grow faster and bloom more profusely. It is hard to maintain this plant inside and I have tried many times because I love the fragrance so much. I enjoy brushing past the plant's needles on my kitchen counter and having its pine fragrance fill the air. However, I have learned after many unsuccessful attempts that I will just have to enjoy it when it grows outside in my herb garden.

I have been told that it needs a well lit window and if the indoor air is dry to put the pot on a moist gravel bed for a humidity source. Too large of a pot may be keeping the soil too moist, which would be indicated by the brown leaf tips. It's not to be fertilized until late winter, when the new growth begins and the day length has increased enough to allow the plant to utilize the added nutrients. Ventilation is a must! Maybe I'll have to try again with an indoor topiary. They are so pretty and tasty!

Rosemary has square stems, which puts it into the mint family. The undersides are covered with silvery fuzz and it has dainty pink to blue to lavender flowers that are extremely attractive to honeybees, yielding a fine honey from its nectar. The creeping varieties, which grow easily, root as they spread and are good for preventing soil erosion. It is used in both the fresh, dried and oil forms. The oil is used for scalp ailments such as dandruff and psoriasis and supposedly prevents baldness as well. There is also a Rosemary-Mint shampoo that is used as a lice preventative in school age children.

A few drops of the oil in a glass of water will also eliminate bad breath. Greek scholars placed Rosemary wreaths on their heads to stimulate their brains and to aid in memory before taking their school exams. I wonder if that could become a new trend in schools!

Because the leaves are resinous, they were burned in sick rooms to purify the air and during WWII, in France and England, it was burned with juniper branches to fumigate contaminated areas.

In the seventeenth century in France and England, a Rosemary incense was burned in the courtrooms to rid the air of "jail fever" (typhus). During the plague of 1665 doctors carried this herb in handles of walking sticks and in pouches to be sniffed, when they made their rounds into contaminated areas. Because its oil has antifungal and antiviral properties, it is used to relieve acne and eczema. It's easy to understand why this herb was awarded as "The Herb of The Year."

Rosemary has long been regarded as a preserver of youth. Just by smelling the plant it was thought to "keep you youngly."

Rosemary is also a preserver of meats. Centuries ago it was noted that meat that had been wrapped in crushed Rosemary leaves did not spoil. When I traveled to Greece, I noticed huge slabs of meat hanging outside the butcher shops. When I learned that they were wrapped in Rosemary, I wasn't as apprehensive about their freshness.

Rosemary, when used in massage oil, is a strengthening rub for muscles. It also eases muscular aches when massaged into a sore muscle. Because of its volatile oil, a rosemary bath can refresh a tired body.

You can make a steam facial with an infusion of rosemary leaves and if you are a brunette, a rosemary rinse will brighten your hair.

A tea made from those leaves provides headache relief. If you are not a tea drinker, you can soak your feet in it to treat a fever. It causes sweating, opens the pores, and allows the fever heat to escape, thereby, breaking the fever. Now that is a versatile cup of tea!

If you put 1-3 drops of the oil on a cotton ball or handkerchief, and tuck it into your sleeve, it is then one of the best memory clarifying herbs in use. Are you beginning to wonder what Rosemary CAN'T be used for? We haven't even touched on the wonderful culinary uses for remarkable Rosemary. Maybe Rosemary should be the "Herb for Two Years!"

This herb also has a long folk history. It is esteemed as a token of love, loyalty and friendship and was carried at weddings and funerals signifying remembrance. It was also thought to ward off the evil spirits and only grew well in the gardens of the righteous. There is an old adage the says, "Where Rosemary flourishes, the lady of the house dominates." I imagine that caused a few problems in Victorian households.

Another such adage was, "Rosemary will not grow well unless the mistress is the master." That phrase causes laughs now, but it wasn't so funny back in the Victorian times. It was said that many husbands ripped out, or killed in some way, healthy Rosemary plants in the dark of night! They certainly didn't want others to know that they were not the master of their house!

You will also find Rosemary mentioned by Shakespeare in "Hamlet."

In the language of flowers rosemary means "remembrance" and after reading this, I hope you will also remember to use it freely in a variety of different ways.

MATERIALS REQUIRED:

- a pre-sewn muslin bag (3 x 5 inches) for each participant
- ribbon to tie off the finished bag (15" piece)
- scissors
- green stamp and stamp pad for decorating their bags (optional)
- green marker for decorating or identifying the bag
- tablespoons for filling the bags
- paper towels on which to mix the herbs used
- dried herbs to use: Rosemary, Mint and Lemon Balm
- any Rosemary products you have for show and tell; candles, soaps, essential oils, tea, live plant etc.
- completed sample for show and smell

HANDS-ON INSTRUCTIONS:

1. Give each participant one bag, spoon and paper towel mat to work on.
2. Show them how to use the stamp to decorate their bag and to put their initials on it decoratively.
3. Give them the opportunity to smell the individual herbs and give them sprigs of each to use.
4. Instruct them on how to strip the leaves off each stem (run your hand against the growing leaf direction) and then to enjoy the fragrance on their hands.
5. Mix all of the herbs by hand, and blend them on the paper towel, before spooning that mixture into the muslin bags. About three tablespoons of herbs will fill the bag. I

like to add one drop of the essential Rosemary oil to the blend just to give it more of the delightfully pungent Rosemary fragrance.

6. Using the ribbon, close the top of the bag and finish with a bow. Time to inhale the fragrance and feel invigorated!
7. Tell the participants that they should keep the little bags with them, not use them as a drawer sachet, and whenever they feel sluggish or tired and just can't keep their eyelids open, reach for the pretty, uplifting, fragrant bag and breathe deeply!

SPECIAL NOTES: Because this project is simply a matter of picking leaves off strong stems, and mixing them together before filling a bag, any functioning level can benefit from these motions. Cognitive skills can be stimulated as well as the small muscles of the hand. The senses are stimulated and perhaps the alertness of the group will increase as the fragrances float in the air. The more alert and capable your participants are, the more information they can be given to enjoy and discuss, before the actual project is begun.

RESPONSES TO THIS SESSION:

"Rosemary has such a sassy fragrance!"

"This place smells like my kitchen used to."

A resident became very animated when seeing and smelling the Rosemary plant. She excitedly told all of us how she remembered, as a young schoolgirl, spraining her ankle. When she hobbled home for lunchtime, her mother rubbed her leg with a poultice made by steeping Rosemary in boiling water and putting a towel soaked with it on her ankle. The pain disappeared and she had to go back to school that very same day! She remembers being angry with her Mom for that. Later the Activity Director told me that she hadn't heard that woman speak so many connected sentences all at once at any other time! That made my day.

SESSION TITLE: Tasty Tea Party and Fragrant Acorns

Give the same background information as for the previous project. Since this will be a session used only for high functioning levels of participants, all of the information can be presented and discussed. Not only will the sense of smell be stimulated but the taste buds will also be involved in this session.

MATERIALS REQUIRED:

- The show and smell samples that you have on hand
- pre-made Rosemary tea in thermos jugs (use honey to sweeten)
- pre-made Rosemary butter (Mix dried or fresh Rosemary into softened butter or margarine)
- crackers
- paper plates, napkins, cups and a knife for spreading the herbal butter
- wooden acorns purchased at an herbal supply store
- Rosemary oil
- ribbon to tie around the wooden acorn for hanging purposes
- completed acorn sample

HANDS-ON INSTRUCTIONS:

1. After discussing the background information and smelling the plant, candle, or other Rosemary objects that you've brought along, pass out small samples of the tea to be enjoyed. This tea is definitely either immediately liked or disliked. There seems to be no middle ground since it has a very medicinal taste. I think it is an acquired taste and that won't be possible to do in a single tasting. Some participants will find it a very clean, fresh taste, as I do.
2. Pass out samples of crackers spread with the herbal butter. Everyone seems to like the taste of Rosemary used in this way.
3. After the tea party is completed, distribute one wooden acorn / participant and have them add 4 drops of the essential oil to it.
4. Give them the pre-cut ribbon pieces and show them how it can be used in the car or as a lapel pin, or on their walkers, or carried in their pockets as a stimulating fragrance. They will never fall asleep during an activity or resident meeting again!

If they are able to do any cooking in their accommodations, you can give them the following culinary ideas:

Rosemary Green Beans

2 cups of green beans

2 tbsp. Chicken stock

1 tbsp. fresh Rosemary, chopped very fine

Nutmeg and parsley to garnish (optional)

Steam beans for approximately 8-10 minutes, until just tender. While beans are steaming, place stock in a small saucepan and heat over medium setting. Add the Rosemary and stir. Turn heat off and let sauce sit. Arrange steamed beans on a serving plate, all in the same direction. Pour Rosemary sauce over the top, then garnish with nutmeg and parsley, if desired. Serves 4

When using fresh Rosemary, rinse the sprigs to prepare for use. If chopping, chop very finely because the flavor is strong. Whole sprigs may be used in soups, stews, or other dishes, and then removed before serving.

Whole sprigs can also be used as a garnish on meat and vegetable trays.

The woody stems also have a place in the kitchen. Try using them as skewers for chicken and vegetable kabobs!

SESSION TITLE: Forever and Ever Are Everlastings

PROGRAM DESCRIPTION: These are hands-on sessions that discuss the group of plants known as Everlastings. They are called this because their flowers are beautiful and useful even when they are dried and no longer blooming in the garden. They are everlastingly beautiful!

The activity for these sessions varies with the season and is adaptable for all levels of ability.

BACKGROUND INFORMATION: The Everlastings are a group of plants that are grown for their beauty in the garden as well as for their superb drying capabilities. While they are growing in the garden they often times have an already dried, papery feel to their blossoms.

There are approximately one hundred different kinds of plants that fall into the "everlasting" category. There are both perennials and annuals in this category of plants, and they all require sun and well-drained soil.

The classic Everlasting is the Strawflower (Helichrysum sp.) but there are many to chose from when planning an Everlasting garden. I've listed below a few of my favorite plants that I've included in my garden over the years and that I find interesting to use in projects and arrangements:

- Pearly Everlastings (*Anaphalis*) or commonly known as “Pussy toes” because they resemble the soft pads on a cat’s feet.
- Globe Thistle (*Echinops*)
- Globe Amaranth (*Gomphrena*)
- Cockscomb (*Celosia*)
- Statice (*Lemonium*)
- Love-in-a-Mist (*Nigella sp,*) The flower is a delicate blue but it is the rattling pod that is prized as an Everlasting.
- Baby’s breath (*Gypsophila*)
- Bells of Ireland (*Molucella*) aren’t from Ireland!
- Chinese Lanterns (*Physalis*) aren’t from China!
- Astilbe
- Yarrow (*Achillea sp.*) The wild, white variety of this plant is called Sneezeweed because it’s dried roots were ground up and used as snuff.
- The Money/Dollar plant (*Lunaria*) produces blue flowers in the spring, and produces exquisite (once they are peeled!) seed pods in the fall.
- Silver Dollar plant (*Eucalyptus*)
- Black eyed Susan (*Rudbeckia*) The stiff black centers are used for dried arrangements
- Pincushion Flower (*Scabiosa*) The pods are used in dried arrangements

It is probably our age-old desire to preserve what is temporary, precious and beautiful in life or nature that has led people to begin drying and preserving flowers and plants. A beautiful arrangement of Everlastings in the home is like bringing a bit of summertime brightness indoors during our bleak, grey days of wintertime in the Ohio Valley. They are vivid memories of summer's colors, while providing us with the anticipation of another beautiful blooming season in a few months.

The best part about growing this group of plants is that they provide twice the pleasure, once in the garden and then again in a dried arrangement-- forever and ever and ever!

MATERIALS REQUIRED:

- one small purchased form (made from grape vine or wire) / participant
- Narrow width seasonal colored ribbon choices.
- small glue bottle / participant
- a variety of dried or fresh Everlastings
- Handy-wipes for clean-up
- one pair of scissors
- Pictures from seed catalogues showing the many varieties of Everlastings available for planting
- sample of completed project
- samples of other types of Everlastings grown in your garden (optional)

HANDS-ON INSTRUCTIONS:

1. Distribute the plastic bags and forms being used to each participant.

2. Give them a choice of ribbon color for the trim. Some assistance may be required with this step since some stiff fingers can no longer tie bows.
3. Depending on the functioning capabilities of the participant, spread out the varieties of Everlastings in front of them and allow choices to be made for their individual project. Stress the colors and feel of the individual flowers or pods.
4. Distribute the glue bottles (optional). Again, depending on the functioning level of the participants, you may choose to do the actual gluing. These plants are easily glued to the various forms but beware of lifting up or hanging the finished project too soon.
5. Wait until the glue dries thoroughly or the Everlastings will slide off the surface! By holding the finished project level, allow everyone to show their finished project to their friends.

MATERIALS REQUIRED FOR THE FENCE PICTURE PROJECT:

- green foam paper
- your choice of Everlastings (I've used yellow button mums and purple Globe Amaranth for the flowers, Baby's Breath [Gypsophila] for the flowers behind the fence, purple Statice at base of fence, Eucalyptus at base of the tree and dried Euphorbia leaves for the tree leaves. You may have other varieties on hand for your picture. Be creative!)
- Two regular length craft sticks and four shorter sized ones
- Black marker
- Glue for everyone
- A garden type sticker (bee, worm, bird etc.)
- Finished sample

HANDS-ON INSTRUCTION:

1. Before the session, have the craft sticks glued in place for the fence. Have the tree shape drawn in marker, and have flower stems and leaves drawn in the garden space.
2. Spread out the flower choices and colors and allow the residents time to pick out their favorites. Using your sample as an idea, they can go from there.
3. Glue on the tree leaves first, followed by the flowers.
4. Next, give them thin sprigs of Baby's Breath to position behind the fence. Have a variety of Statice if possible, to have on the ground in front of the fence.
5. With the marker, invite them to identify their garden, by writing their names on the fence posts.
6. Last, but not least, since it's another decision making process, give them their choice of a sticker to position in the appropriate area of their picture.

SPECIAL NOTES: As simple as these sessions appear to be, there is a lot being accomplished by the participant. Choices have to be made, (always have that element present in any session!), glue bottles have to be squeezed, and eye hand co-ordination also plays an important part in this activity. The self-esteem and pride is evident when the completed item is held up for all to admire. Self-confidence is on the up swing!

Drying the plants correctly is essential for getting good results. It is important to gather them from the garden in dry weather. They should be picked just after they have opened out since this is when the colors are strongest and the flowers have their best shape. It is important not to squash the plants while gathering. They will retain that squashed shape or be damaged.

Dry them as quickly as possible to avoid fungus and/or mildew. Hang the plants in a dry, warm place, out of the direct sunlight. Don't bunch them together too tightly. They need a little air circulation for the best shape retention.

I find that flowers drying in pretty bunches can also be used as a decorative accent to a room. In my opinion, it is hard to improve on Mother Nature for decorating tips!

RESPONSES TO THIS SESSION:

After completing her project, one participant commented, "This is my kind of gardening. No weeding, no watering, no frostbite."

-- OCTOBER --

* *

Fall, leaves, fall: die, flowers, away;

Lengthen night and shorten day:

Every leaf speaks bliss to me

Fluttering from the autumn tree.

- By Emily Bronte

* *

The arduous task of bringing all of the tender plants into the house has now begun. It's difficult enough making sure they are cleaned off for their re-entry into the indoors for the next eight months, but the greatest challenge that I face each autumn is where are they all going to fit? My house has no windowsills and Santa has never had a greenhouse in his sleigh with my name on it. Since I can't bear to turn my back on plants that have provided me such pleasure during the summer months, I find myself using the bath tub for the overflow. Each year I vow that I can't, and won't, bring as many in out of the cold, and each year the story is the same. I have even started finding a foster home for some of them at my daughters' houses. However, now that they have developed an interest in keeping their own plants warm over the winter, I do have a problem. We all know about the oxygen exchange that plants provide for us, so we will be breathing with less effort in our home, once again this year!

This time of year presents a splendor all of its own. The Ohio River valley has autumn colors that rival those found in the northeast and our yard is no exception. The dark green spruces are accentuated by the brilliant yellows, reds, and golden colors of the maples and oaks in our woods. The dogwoods are brilliant in foliage color with their red fruit. The crab apples are ready for the feasting mockingbirds and jays, and the chrysanthemums are splashy with the pumpkins and gourds arranged with them. I recall that the mums in China signify rest and ease. Soon our gardens will be at rest during their dormancy.

I do love this season in my yard! Is this my favorite time with the pleasant temperatures, lack of humidity and the colorful sweet gum in my front yard? That is such an interesting tree to watch throughout the month. The color variety of the leaves on the same branch, at the same time, really makes for a jewel- like showing of colors ranging from gold to pink to orange to red to burgundy, and every shade in between. This tree has them all. Even those troublesome prickly balls are saved for a session.

My feet are ready for hiking and I love finding the buckeyes (Ohio's state tree) along the road. I was told, by one very old woman that her mother always carried a buckeye or two in her pocket to keep away rheumatism. It must have been common knowledge then, because many of the participants at that session on weeds and seeds, agreed with her. I can learn something new each day!

Present the following modules and see what you can learn from your participants.

SESSION TITLE: Door Greeters and Saint Fiacre

PROGRAM DESCRIPTION: This program makes use of dried flowers or small dried seedpods. The plant material is discussed individually, and then arranged in a small container, which can be of ceramic, wicker, metal or fabric. Let your imagination be your guide. The only requirement for the containers is that they have a handle so that they can be hung from door knobs. This program is suitable for all but the lowest functioning group.

BACKGROUND INFORMATION: St. Fiacre, (fee-ak-ruh), an Irish monk who lived in the seventh century, is the true patron saint of gardening and gardeners, especially those who grow vegetables. He was raised in a monastery where he enjoyed the planting and harvesting of crops and studied the healing properties of herbs. He had an appreciation for all of nature and an earnest desire to serve God. He led the life of a religious monk, feeding the hungry and healing the sick with herbs from his garden.

Like many other Irish Christians of his time, he went off to the continent to do missionary work among the barbarians. He settled among the Franks, not far from Paris. The Bishop of Meaux received him warmly and gave him a piece of land on which to set up his hermitage. This is where his first miracle occurred. So many local people came to him for assistance that his little garden couldn't provide for them all so he asked the bishop for more land to garden.

According to one legend, he was promised all the land that he could enclose with a ditch to be dug in one day. Saint Fiacre spent a day using an ivory cane to draw a line in the dirt around a large plot of ground, and the ditch miraculously dug itself. The monastery that he built within this perimeter sheltered him until his death in August 670. He led a life of prayer, fasting, vigil and the manual labor of the garden. Disciples gathered around him and soon formed a monastery. The vegetables that he grew around this monastery were said to be of superb quality and fed many poor people who came to the monastery in need of food or shelter. Florists and potters also claim him as their patron saint.

After his death, people continued to visit the monastery for centuries, and legend says that in the seventeenth century, his shrine was famous for the many miraculous cures. The carriages hired to take pilgrims from hotels to the shrine became known as "fiacres," and that is why he also became the patron saint of the cab drivers. His relics at Meaux are still believed to have healing powers and many people visit St. Fiacre's shrine even to this day.

His image stands in churches in France, Belgium and the Netherlands. He always holds a spade at his side, and is dressed in the coarse peasant clothing and shoes of that particular region. He often seems to be looking at the ground, where he will commence digging. He is the saint whose help may be implored in clearing weeds and brush and stones from gardens, and even if he does not help with the heavy work, he can at least grant us patience and persistence in our labor that seems to never be completed! He is a saint for lowly things and for increase. His blessings are welcomed by those of us who love springtime, and planting, summer and harvest, the smell of turned earth, the feel of soil through our fingers, and the joy of a flower garden.

To this day, in Pasadena California, there is an annual three-day St. Fiacre Fair, which draws on a long tradition of garden crafts, one of which is the pretty door greeter.

These door decorations date back several centuries in continental Europe as well as England. Jars, baskets and other container types are filled with arrangements of fresh or dried flowers and foliage, and left as a colorful surprise on someone's front door handle. It is especially appreciated by a recipient who is in need of a little cheering up, or as a welcome gift for a new neighbor. Little notes can also be added to the arrangement as a nice personal touch.

MATERIALS REQUIRED:

- a variety of fresh or dried flowers of your choosing
- one container suitable for hanging / participant
- placed floral foam in the bottom of each container, for stability in arranging
- have the completed sample for show and tell
- clippers for trimming

- information about your choice of flowers, foliage and/or seed pods (For example, *in the pictured sample, one of the dried materials used is the seedpod of the Grape Hyacinth. It is good if you can show a picture of that flower in its springtime beauty. The more flowers and pods that you can do this with, the more interesting and participatory this session becomes.*)
- a watering can (if you are using fresh plant material)

HANDS-ON INSTRUCTION:

1. Distribute the containers to each participant and show and describe the variety of plant material that they have to choose from.
2. Be sure that all of the plant material is placed in FRONT on the handle so that it is possible to place the finished container flat against the door.

SPECIAL NOTES: If you are working with a very low functioning group, one container / GROUP can be worked on by everyone. That finished product can then be placed at the nurse's station for all to admire. The feeling of satisfaction at having made something beautiful is still present even if they don't keep it in their own rooms.

RESPONSES TO THIS SESSION:

"I think I'll give mine to my neighbor who is having a bad week." "Everyone will think my whole room must be so cheerful when they visit my door now."

SESSION TITLE: Autumn's Splendor

PROGRAM DESCRIPTION: This hands-on session begins with a discussion of the fall color changes, and progresses to feeling the textures of many varieties of nuts, leaves and fruits of various deciduous trees. The activity accompanying this session is making a leaf sun catcher. All levels of participants, in some way, can successfully accomplish this session.

BACKGROUND INFORMATION: As the days grow shorter towards the end of summer, the stage is set for one of Mother Nature's greatest performances---the beauty of autumn! Contrary to the belief of some, you do not have to travel to the New England states for the most beautiful fall color. We have it right here, in the Ohio Valley! Actually, the show has its beginning with the summer solstice. From this point on, the days become shorter. As the days become shorter and the temperatures become cooler, the process for leaf color changes begins. The summer leaves are green because of the presence of a substance called chlorophyll. However, leaves of certain trees also contain large amounts of the yellow pigment carotin and xanthophyll. The dark green pigment of the chlorophyll hides the yellow colors in the leaves all summer long. With the cooler temperatures though, the chlorophyll production is diminished, and the yellow colors become visible. Other trees also contain large amounts of anthocyanins that are red or tannin, which gives a leaf a brown color when the chlorophyll production has ceased. So all of the beautiful fall colors that we see have been there all summer long. They were just hidden by the green chlorophyll. The fall leaf color is the true color of the leaf! So much for Jack Frost and his paintbrush! Of course, all of the various colored leaves will eventually turn brown and rot and their minerals returned to the soil. Generally, you can expect the following trees to exhibit these colors in their fall leaves: yellow paints the birches, aspens, and tulip poplar; orange-yellow colors the beech and golden-yellow identifies the hickories. These will never produce red leaves. Various shades of red will be produced by dogwood, sumac, sweet gum and red maples.

All of the various shades of color of the deciduous trees, mixed in with evergreens, paint a beautiful October picture in our area. In the animal kingdom, color can be used as a camouflage. In the plant kingdom, the beautiful colors attract pollinators, which are necessary for seed production. The color of fruits is important for attracting birds, who are then responsible for distributing those seeds far and wide. The gorgeous autumn color however, has no specific function in nature except to be pleasing to our eyes and to provide a last splash of color before the winter arrives.

MATERIALS REQUIRED:

- two pieces of 4 1/2" x 12" Laminating paper/participant
- one 31' piece of narrow ribbon of green, gold or orange/participant
- one 15" piece of same colored narrow

ribbon/participant (optional)

- 4 pressed leaves
- one suction cup hook/participant
- scissors and hole punch
- autumn color photos
- sample of completed sun-catcher
- popsicle stick sticks
- Various acorns, Osage orange ball, nuts, huge leaves, rough leaves, smooth leaves, buckeyes etc. (for texture and identification)

HANDS-ON INSTRUCTION:

1. Show the various nuts and seeds, etc. and invite touching, identification guessing game and personal stories concerning these objects.
2. Spread the pressed leaves on the table, identify them, and match them with the nuts etc.
3. Show the sample sun catcher and distribute the sheets of pre-cut laminating paper.
4. Give them the choice of ribbon color to be used for the edging.
5. Peel off one piece of the paper to expose the sticky side. Probably help will be required in the positioning of the ribbon ¼" from the edge of the paper.
6. Give them a Popsicle stick to press the ribbon down onto the sticky surface. Warn that fingers, watches and arms will also stick to this surface!!

7. The choice of leaves is next. Once they know how they'd like to position the various leaves, have them stick them onto the paper and press in place with the Popsicle stick.
8. Unpeel the second sheet of laminating paper and place it over the first. I find it less frustrating for the participants if I do this placement.
9. Now, instruct them to press all of the leaves down tightly with their hands. This is also good exercise for some of the more frail participants.
10. Trim the edges evenly and punch a hole at the top.
11. Tie the remaining ribbon through the hole, making a loop to fit over the suction cup hook.

SPECIAL NOTES: These sun catchers are very lovely hung in the window, and on a bleak wintry day will be a pleasant reminder of the beauty of the season just past.

SESSION TITLE: The Nose Knows

PROGRAM DESCRIPTION: This session is extremely olfactory in nature and can be adapted for participants of any functioning level. It seems to always be enjoyed, and memories that are tucked away seem to come to the forefront, as the participants smell the various herbs provided in the little jars. Thus, the title - The Nose Knows!

The activity for this program is a sachet and since I've used it in October, I've incorporated Halloween colors into the project. Obviously you could use it for other months by varying the netting and ribbon colors. The most important ingredient for this session is the variety of dried and/or fresh herbs that are provided for rubbing and smelling.

Not only is the nose given a work-out, but the small motor skills are also utilized in stripping the leaves from the stems and blending them together. Conversation runs high and the socialization process is at work as well.

BACKGROUND INFORMATION: The definition of an herb is any plant that is used for fragrance, flavoring or medicinal purposes. Obviously the selection of herbs that you have in your jars will determine the information concerning usage and folklore. The internet is a great source for that kind of information.

Herb gardens are a delight to grow and to weed. The fragrances fill the air as you work amongst them and brush against their foliage. Herb gardens can be as elaborate or as simple as you want, depending on the number of herbs you enjoy using. The great herbal gardens around Abbeys, or in formal English gardens, can be daunting to say the least for someone wanting to begin growing herbs. I grow my herbs as borders to my flower gardens or in containers on my deck, or even in hanging baskets. Their only requirement is a nutrient rich soil in an area that receives at least six hours of sun each day. Our southernmost states can get by with less sunlight hours.

Most herbs prefer a slightly acidic soil with a ph between 6.0 to 8.0. The addition of peat moss or mulch will lower that number if it's too high in your garden. To raise the ph level, add lime to the soil.

One of my favorite fresh herbs is Lovage. It smells like and tastes like celery. Since I don't like to eat fresh celery because of the strings, I use Lovage leaves chopped in all of my salads. It's the best of both worlds; no strings, but still the fresh, clean taste of celery. A Lovage stem-straw is also a flavorful, novel way to sip a summer drink.

Borage has pretty blue flowers, but the leaves smell and taste like cucumbers! Once again, I like the cool flavor of that vegetable but I don't like eating it. Borage finds a place in my herb garden, right next to the Lovage!

Of all the lemon scented herbs, I find Lemon Verbena to have the most potent fragrance, and I use it all summer long in teas and when cooking fish. If you combine its leaves with those of lavender, mint and rosemary, the fishy odor on your hands is removed.

My herb garden wouldn't be complete without Lavender and Basil. Lavender cakes and cookies are a favorite summer treat. Three tablespoons of dried crushed leaves added to a yellow or white cake mix just before baking, is a favorite in our home anytime.

Did you know that in India, Basil is considered a sacred herb? In my garden, it is grown near my tomato plants because one enhances the growth of the other. This is called "companion planting" and it really does work! Most people know basil as the key ingredient in pesto sauce, but I use it fresh, snipped into any green salad and my taste buds rejoice. Sprinkle sliced tomatoes layered with slices of Mozzarella cheese with basil, oil and vinegar and it does become something heavenly.

As you can tell, not only do I enjoy working around herbs in my garden, but the harvest is delectable! I grow only those herbs which I enjoy using. I think I'll have to expand my herbal space this year!

Herbs should be harvested before they flower and after the morning dew has disappeared from their leaves, if you're after the strongest flavor. To dry them, just hang them in a dry, dark place. I personally prefer not to dry them in the microwave.

Fresh herbs are likely to have a greater medicinal value, and, generally speaking, one teaspoon of dried herbs is equivalent to three teaspoons (one tablespoon), of the fresh ones.

For teas, use one teaspoon of the dried herb / cup of boiling water.

MATERIALS REQUIRED:

- As many different varieties of dried herbs as you have available, removed from the stems and placed in baby food jars. I have about a dozen such jars placed in my "Nose Knows" basket, ready to be smelled and enjoyed.
- One piece of black netting pre-cut to 8" x 8" per participant

- One piece of thin orange ribbon pre-cut into 13" per participant
- Dried herbs for filling the sachet. I like to use any Mint and Scented Geranium variety and a little Sage. Other herbs can be used, as well. Use your nose to know which is a pleasant combination of aromas.

HANDS-ON INSTRUCTION:

1. The whole point of the Nose Knows basket is to demonstrate the many familiar herbal fragrances, so remove those lids and pass around the baby food jars, one at a time.
2. Invite them to bruise the herbs in order to release the fragrances. Take a good whiff and steer the conversation towards the experiences of the participants.
3. Make a guessing game out of identifying the contents of the jars.
4. Ask questions concerning their personal usage of the specific herbs. Did they grow them in their gardens? Did their Moms grow them too? What holiday comes to mind with the aroma of Sage? Do you drink Mint teas? Which is your favorite smell? Soon the group will be caught up in conversation and remembrances and the mind is being exercised.
5. Distribute the piece of netting, pre-cut ribbon, and the stems of dried herb varieties that you've chosen to use for these sachets.
6. Remind them to remove all leaves from any stems before placing the crushed leaves on to the center of the netting. You don't want stems poking through the netting.
7. Have the participants mix the dried leaves with their fingers to blend the fragrances. These leaves don't have to be pulverized or they will fall through the holes in the netting!

8. Pull the edges of the netting together to form a pouch and tie off with the ribbon.
9. Smell both the sachet and your fingers! Ahhh, the nose knows pleasure when working around herbs.

SPECIAL NOTES: If you are working with a very alert group, and if time (thyme) allows, you can go into a discussion of how to grow and dry herbs, as well as some of the herbal folklore and old remedies that were utilized before we had drugstores on every corner. This always stimulates the memories and is conducive to fun group conversation.

RESPONSES TO THIS SESSION:

"I always loved cooking with the herbs from my garden."

"We should have had the Chef who works here, come to this meeting."

"I remember smelling the mint in my Mother's garden, especially when my ball fell into it!"

"Mint tea? I'd much rather have a mint julep!"

After we had cleaned up our stems and scraps from the work area this comment was heard, "Even the garbage can smells pretty."

"I remember my Mom hanging bunches of Artemisia from our cabin's front door to smell pretty and keep out the flies. She also made a tea from fennel leaves to give to my baby sister when she had the stomach pains."

SESSION TITLE: The Wonderful World of Weeds and Seeds

PROGRAM DESCRIPTION: This is a session that points out the beauty of the various seedpods of plants that are considered desirable to have in the garden, and also of those that are listed as weeds. There is a lot of conversation going on as the participants touch and discuss the show and tell pods and seed heads of the common plants and weeds that I've brought with me.

I've included one project idea for an October session and one that follows a Christmas holiday theme, but I'm sure you'll be able to think of many other beautiful ways to use the graceful seed pods and dried weeds once you know and love them as I do.

BACKGROUND INFORMATION: Almost everyone thinks kindly of wildflowers growing in the woodlands, but "weeds" are more likely to be the object of scorn. "Oh, it's just a weed," we say. Many of the plants that are now called weeds were actually brought here from Europe by the early settlers for herbal usage. Those that were best able to survive with the least care, and readily multiplied where they weren't wanted, were referred to as weeds. Therefore, the word "weed," is applied to any uncultivated plant or a plant in the wrong place. Unfortunately, this condemns many beautiful native plants.

Weeds should not always be considered man's enemies. Common weeds can restore eroded land (the Fireweed of the Northwest is a perfect example of this), help hold water during dry spells, and add beauty to our landscape. A particular weed can be a nuisance to some people but a desirable plant to others. For example, clover is considered a weed in our lawns and gardens, but farmers intentionally plant certain kinds of clover as food for their animals and nourishment for the soil.

Dandelions in lawns are annoying, but in some areas they are planted as a garden vegetable. Young leaves are great in salads. Dandelion wine has been enjoyed by many for centuries. An entire field of blooming dandelions is worth a photo, and when thousands of their yellow flowers go to seed and produce their delicate white balls of fluff on a stem, that is worth two photos!

Plants of the Goldenrod, Milkweed and Sunflower families are also important soil builders, as well as playing an important part in the well-being of butterflies and birds.

Ragweed, unfortunately a nuisance to hay fever sufferers, is one of the best soil-improving weeds around. It detoxifies contaminated soil. It holds disturbed soil in place until other plants become established, and then, surprisingly disappears. However, it is quite difficult to convince a sneezing hay fever victim of those good qualities.

Not only do weeds improve the soil for us but they also supply food for birds and wild animals.

Aside from the ecological importance of weeds, they add beauty and diversity to our landscape. After they have released their seeds, the containers, (pods) remain in a variety of beautiful and interesting shapes to provide yet another gift of nature, the aesthetic beauty to feed man's soul. Walks along roadsides and fields become more interesting when you become aware of the beauty of weeds in their final display of the season.

The best time for gathering these treasures of the roadsides is after maturity, but before frost. By the time the pods are dry enough to pick, the wind has usually taken care of dispersing their seeds so they can once again become part of nature's cycle.

MATERIALS REQUIRED:

(These are the general necessities for any of the following projects)

- A variety of different seeds, pods and weeds for show and tell
- Pictures of flowers (weeds) in bloom that produced the various pods
- Plastic bags to cover the working surface
- Handy-wipes for clean-up

The Pumpkin Arrangement project:

- a small container (I've used a tiny wicker pumpkin found in a craft store) containing a piece of floral foam
- Variety of dried weeds and garden seedpods, as well as ones on stems for arranging. In the photo, I've used the following: Money Plant pods, Thistle, Yarrow, dried Ironweed, Grape Hyacinth pods and Silver King Artemisia. The

varieties are limitless and are dependent only on your roadside collecting and/or what you have in your garden.

- Pruning shears for trimming stems to desired height.
- Sample of finished project

The Milkweed project:

- Sample pods, some still filled with the silk threads containing the seed
- Two or three empty pods / participant that have a pipe cleaner loop already affixed to the top of the pod.
- A bag of purchased holiday fragrance potpourri.
- Glue and wooden craft stick
- Sample of completed ornament

HANDS-ON INSTRUCTIONS:

For the following projects, the most important part is the touching and observing of the various pods. Pass each sample around and encourage the participants to feel the different textures. Have fun peeling off the covering of the Money Plant pods. Beware of the prickly teasel (thistle)! Feel the papery, fairy-like bells of the Grape Hyacinth. Enjoy the strong fragrance of the Artemisia. Listen to the rattle of the seeds in the Lotus pod. This is sensory overload! If you have pictures of these seed pods when they were flowering, now is the time to show that comparison to the participants. Let the stories and reminiscences begin.

Pumpkin Arrangement:

1. distribute the pumpkins and bags to each participant
2. Display all the weeds and seeds (on stems) in the center of the table.
3. If you are working with a lower functioning group, begin distributing these stems, one variety at a time, and instruct them on pushing the stems into the floral foam. Their choice is the height of the finished arrangement
4. If you are working with a higher functioning group, distribute all of the available material to each participant and have them go at it! Don't forget the simple rule of thumb in arranging. Work with uneven numbers. For some reason the brain registers one, three or five stems of a particular variety as more pleasing to the eye than the even numbers of the same variety.
5. Everyone should be given the opportunity to show their finished arrangement to the group and to revel in the compliments that will follow. Self-esteem is high!

Milkweed Pod Ornament:

1. Distribute plastic bags for the work surface
2. Distribute glue and a craft stick to each participant
3. Allow each person to select their pods which will be different sizes and some may be more open than others. The choosing and decision making is not to be overlooked as part of the therapy.
4. Dump the bag of purchased potpourri in the

center of the table and enjoy the holiday fragrances filling the air.

5. Instruct them to put a thin layer of glue in the bottom and up the sides of the pod with their craft stick.
6. Press a single layer of potpourri into the glue. Add another thin layer of glue and another thin layer of potpourri. Repeat until the pod is almost overflowing with color and fragrance. The smaller pieces of potpourri are better for the bottom layers and the top layer should be embellished with a few larger pieces. When the top layer is dried, the ornament is ready to be hung on a tree or on a bulletin board.

SPECIAL NOTES: The following is a list of some beautiful roadside weeds that I've used in Show and Tell arrangements before they've gone to seed:

- Bishop's Cap
- Queen Anne's Lace
- Chicory
- Canadian Thistle
- Red Clover
- Mullein
- Wild Primrose
- Fleabane
- Smartweed
- Daisies
- Jewelweed
- Dandelions
- Wild Yarrow

- Ironweed
- Heal-All

There are web sites that can give you detailed folklore and interesting facts on these, and many roadside weeds. I can guarantee that your walks in the country will become more interesting with the knowledge and observation of these plants. No longer will you think of them as "just weeds!"

SESSION TITLE: Leaf Mosaic

PROGRAM DESCRIPTION: This foam leaf project is another activity that is a favorite used in conjunction with the Autumn Splendor module. It is a variation on the same beautiful autumn color theme that Mother Nature has provided for us. However, instead of using the gorgeous dried and pressed leaves in their entirety, we will crush them instead of laminating them, to create a mosaic effect. The completed project can be hung on a bulletin board or used as a fall décor in the participants' rooms. This is a project suitable for every functioning level, and conversation flows easily around fall activities, smells and sounds.

BACKGROUND INFORMATION: The same leaf information that is found in the Autumn Splendor session is applicable for this session also. Since the participants will be starting out with a green foam leaf form, it is noted that the leaves in summertime are green due to their chlorophyll production and once the cooler temperatures and shorter hours of sunlight take place, the beautiful colors are there for us all to marvel at and enjoy.

MATERIALS REQUIRED:

- One foam leaf shape with a hole punched into the top per participant. I like to cut a variety of different leaf shapes out of the foam paper in order to provide another dimension to this project…another choice for the participants to make
- glue
- one wooden craft stick for everyone
- plastic bags to work on
- handy wipes for cleaning sticky hands
- black marker for identifying leaf variety as well as their completed project
- Varieties of acorns, nuts, and seedpods.
- photos showing beautiful autumn color and scenery for show—and-tell
- completed sample for inspiration
- ribbon (16” lengths)

HANDS-ON INSTRUCTIONS:

1. Talk about the different acorns, nuts and pod shapes, passing each one around, asking if anyone recognizes them.
2. Give each participant their choice of the pre-cut foam leaf shape.
3. Spread the colorful dried leaves on the table in front of them and ask them to choose the colors that appeal to them.
4. Tell them to either tear their leaves into smaller pieces or to crunch them in their hands.

5. Either pass out the individual glue bottles or in low functioning groups, spread the glue on the foam leaf for them, using the wooden craft stick to spread the glue evenly over the entire foam leaf shape.
6. Using the torn leaf pieces, press them onto the glue-filled foam leaf creating a mosaic effect.
7. Be sure the leaves remain flat until the glue dries and then they can be displayed

On a bleak November day, it is nice to be reminded of the beauty that was once seen during the gorgeous "leaf-peeper season" and to anticipate Mother Nature's next gift to us.

RESPONSES TO THIS SESSION:

"We sounded like we were playing in the leaves."

"It sounded like I was taking a hike in the woods in the fall. We used to always do that."

SESSION TITLE: Autumn Tree Session

Here is another project geared towards the lower functioning groups that utilizes dried leaves. I call it the Autumn Tree Session.

Even though it is very simple, there are still choices to be made, directions to follow, glue to spread and leaves to press in place. These are all therapeutic actions. The result is something they can be proud to hang on their bulletin boards or doors.

The same background material as above can be used, gearing it to the group's alertness and interest.

MATERIALS REQUIRED:

- a variety of colors of 8" x 10" construction paper
- a black or brown marker
- a variety of colorful dried and pressed leaves, nuts and acorns.
- glue and wooden craft sticks
- handy wipes for cleaning sticky fingers
- pretty fall foliage photos (optional)
- small stickers of squirrels or birds (optional)

HANDS-ON INSTRUCTIONS:

1. Spread the leaves and nuts on the table in front of the group giving everyone the opportunity to touch and possibly identify them. At this point, many stories and reminiscences might be shared.
2. Talk about the different shaped leaves and see if anyone recognizes them.
3. Show the fall color photos, if you have them.
4. Give the participants their choice of colored paper and then tell them to pick out some of their favorite leaves from those on the table.
5. Using the marker, draw a tree trunk on each paper and tell them to arrange the leaves on their tree. Maybe they will even put some leaves on the ground!
6. Either give them the glue, if you feel comfortable with that option, or do the gluing of the leaves for them.
7. When they've finished their tree, offer them a sticker of their choice to place somewhere in or on their tree. This usually brings forth a lot of laughter, and we all know that laughter is the best medicine! As my Grandmother used to say, "It's good for what ails you."

If you want to do as the Victorian women did in the fall, you can treat branches of crimson and gold leaves with a glycerin solution and have them indefinitely as an autumn decoration in a beautiful vase.

Prepare a solution of one part glycerin (which can be purchased in drug stores), and two parts water. Bring it to a boil and simmer for ten minutes. Let it then cool completely.

Cut the branch of leaves at a sharp angle and lightly hammer the cut end. For best results cut your branches at night before any frost has touched them. This process will not work on leaves that have gone through a heavy frosting. Carefully observe the gradual change in the leaf color for proper timing for the harvest. Waiting too long will result in a dropping of the leaves from the branches.

Stand the branch in the glycerin solution and store in a cool, dark place until all of the mixture has been absorbed. This usually takes anywhere between one to three weeks to accomplish, depending on the leaf variety.

Wipe the leaves occasionally with a cloth dampened with the glycerin solution. This will help prevent the leaves from drying before the glycerin reaches the edge of the leaves.

Remove the branch from the glycerin water when you see tiny beads of the solution form and begin to drip off the tips of the leaves. Wipe down the leaves with a damp paper towel and then dry thoroughly.

Once again, Mother Nature has provided lasting beauty.

-- NOVEMBER --

* *

The thorns and briars, vermilion hue,
Now full of hips and haws are seen;
If village prophecies be true,
They prove that winter will be keen.

- By John Clare

* *

This is the month to tidy up the garden. By now the thistles (Cirsium), black-eyed Susan (Rudbeckia) and coneflower (Echinacea) seed heads have been picked clean by the finches, and the canoe shaped milkweed (Asclepias) pods have been harvested by crafters and horticultural therapists. Their silken threads weighted with small, dark seeds at the tip, blow on the wind, ensuring their longevity in the garden and fields. Surely, the fairies will come to gather those soft fibers and pods for their winter beds. The money plant's (Lunaria) drab, dirty-looking seedpod covering has been peeled off and its shimmering, silvery treasure beneath has been revealed. Stems of these "Silver Dollars" will make a striking arrangement for the bleak winter days that await us in the Ohio Valley. Sunflower seed heads have been harvested, and will be a treat for the winter birds at our feeders.

There are some flower seed heads that I don't remove from the garden during this clean-up period because I think they add interest and beauty and another dimension to my winter garden. I love seeing fluffy snow and crystalline beads of frost decorating them as my photo albums will prove. The tall decorative grasses bring a soft rustling sound to the garden as the cold winds blow through their beige plumage, releasing their seeds for the birds' enjoyment also.

This is the month of one of my favorite holidays, Thanksgiving. I always feel that it is rushed past and not given the attention it deserves on the way to the Christmas holiday festivities. It is for that very reason that I focus on it for the entire month of November. After all, it's Turkey Thyme and Pilgrim feasts that come to mind. I hope you will also enjoy using the following modules to incorporate this special time of the year into your horticultural therapy programs.

SESSION TITLE: Pressed Flower Projects

PROGRAM DESCRIPTION:

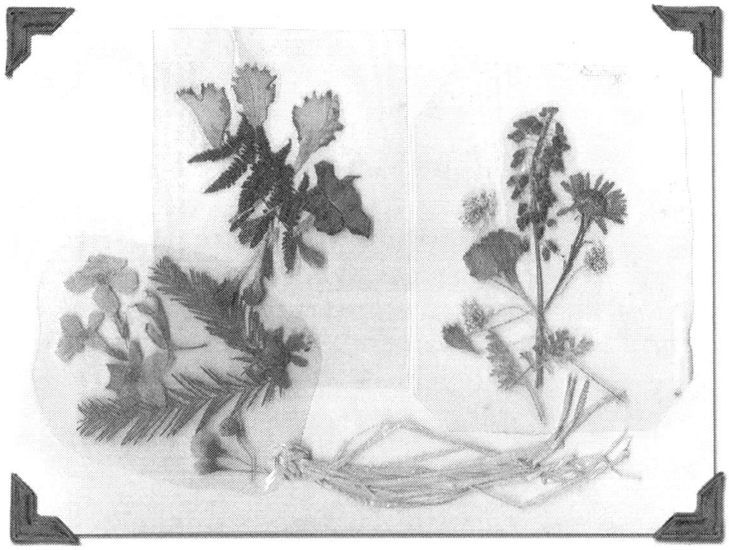

This group of sessions requires some manual dexterity and shouldn't be used as a hands-on project if you think frustration or impatience would prevail for the participants. It can be adapted to a "show and tell" type of session however. See the "Special Notes" section below.

In most cases, the hands-on participants are completely surprised and pleased with how simple and easy, a beautiful design is to make, even having "no artist ability".

Colorful, pre-pressed blossoms and/or petals are used to create bookmarks, frameable art or notepaper projects. Discussion will definitely commence when old time favorite flowers are used and past gardens are remembered. It is also an added bonus to have a bouquet of fresh flowers for use as a "before and after pressing" observation.

BACKGROUND INFORMATION: The art of pressing flowers and foliage is a centuries old process. Pressed flowers and plants seem to captivate nature lovers everywhere. Perhaps they bring back memories of family gardens enjoyed long ago, or historic gardens from places visited. Perhaps just the simple beauty of the miniature arrangement under glass is intriguing. Then again, maybe the amazement of seeing a woodland scene "painted" with pressed petal parts is captivating and stimulates not only the imagination, but causes admiration for the creativity of the artist and his completed work of art.

Often when you look at a pressed flower, you will notice subtle details that you would never have noticed when the plant was growing in the garden, along the highway or enjoyed in a beautiful floral arrangement. I am constantly amazed at what the undersides of some flowers can show us. Some have a perfect symmetry, others reveal subtle color changes, and some have strikingly beautiful veins that would never be noticed without the pressing process. Some single petals of a buttercup look like a heart when pressed, and butterflies can be created by the artistic placement of buttercup and bee balm petals. The imagination is at work and is a wonderful thing!

From the sixteenth through the nineteenth centuries, wealthy families, commercial nurseries and scientific institutions employed plant hunters who searched for new and exotic botanicals. That task was also part of the Lewis and Clark Expedition. They were the first to venture so far west into uncharted lands. President Thomas Jefferson was interested in the flora as well as the fauna that inhabited those remote areas. They documented one hundred and seventy-six new plants during their travels, and many of these are pressed and on display in the herbarium (a bound book of plants), at the Academy of Natural Sciences in Philadelphia.

Petal pressing became especially popular during the Victorian era, perhaps influenced by Britain's queen who was a legendary flower lover.

Extensive knowledge of flora was considered very ladylike and was actively encouraged. Collectors are always on the lookout for pressed plant art and herbariums that are signed by famous botanists. Twenty thousand dollars is not a far-fetched price for some of these herbariums.

Today there are many varieties of flower presses to be purchased, along with special papers and labels to be used if desired. Whether pressing flowers is being done for artistic purposes, or educational purposes, or just for the nostalgic feelings that the specific flowers elicit, this centuries old project is worthwhile. Everyone can become a painter. Just substitute flowers for the paintbrush and paint palette, and have a go at it! Not only is this a creative and therapeutic project, but it is very relaxing for many people. Participants love showing off their finished projects to the other members of the group and self-esteem is boosted by their compliments. This is also a good activity to aid in working the small hand muscles and encourages eye-hand co-ordination. Obviously, this is not a program suitable for anyone who is visually challenged.

MATERIALS REQUIRED: ***The Bookmark Project***

- two pieces of 2 ½" x 6" pre-cut, self laminating paper / participant
- scissors
- a hole punch
- raffia
- tooth picks and/or tweezers

- a selection of pre-pressed flower petals and delicate foliage (see below for pressing technique)
- a bouquet of fresh flowers (optional)
- show and tell samples of purchased pressed flower items such as candles, framed artwork or ceramic pieces
- finished project sample

MATERIALS REQUIRED: *The Notebook Project*

- folded, plain notepaper and envelopes for each participant (one of two sets for each person to make)
- tooth picks and/or tweezers
- clear drying craft glue
- scissors
- a selection of pre-pressed flower petals and delicate foliage
- wet paper towels to keep sticky fingers from causing frustration
- show and tell samples as above
- completed notepaper samples
- bouquet of fresh flowers (optional)

MATERIALS REQUIRED: *The Frame-able Picture Project*

- two pieces of 4 ½ " x 6 ½" self laminating paper / participant
- scissors
- tooth picks and/or tweezers
- a selection of pre-pressed flower petals and delicate foliage
- a bouquet of fresh flowers (optional)
- show and tell samples as above

Flower Pressing Information:

Do not limit yourself to pressing only garden flowers. A walk along a roadside or through a field can also provide interesting flowers and foliage to be immortalized. Do not pick wildflowers in National Parks. This is to protect our indigenous flora from being depleted.

Wait until after the dew has evaporated, and don't pick directly after a rain, or you'll be disappointed with the quality of the finished pressed result. You must work with thoroughly dry petals or they will end up looking brown. Try to pick flowers just before their peak, or shortly thereafter, when their colors will be strongest. Press the plant material as soon as possible after picking. Any plant that can fit into your flower press can be used, however, some flowers press better than others do. The pressing process may change the color of many flower petals. The colors may become more intense, muted or even disappear altogether. Sometimes even the latter can be useful in the midst of a variety of other colors in the design. A general rule of thumb is that the more succulent the flower or leaf, the greater the color loss. Conversely, the drier the petal or leaf, the better is the color retention. Usually the small flowers press better than the large ones, simply because they are less succulent. Have fun experimenting! It is important to remember that the brightness or intensity of the color of pressed flowers and leaves will be muted over time. This can be a matter of weeks or many years in the making.

In pressing plant material, you are removing moisture from it as you press it flat. This is not an overnight process. The old telephone book method of pressing is the most unsatisfactory method and often causes flowers to lose their color immediately or even become moldy. This is because of the type of paper and the lack of pressure applied. The best method is placing the flower in between sheets of blotting paper or paper towels that are then pressed in between books. Be sure to apply pressure, like bricks, to the top of your books, in order to remove all of the petal moisture. Also, be sure to check the dampness of the paper periodically. Dry paper is obviously more absorbent, thereby speeding the drying process, which results in better color retention. Remember that the way that you place the flowers on the paper is the same way that they will be permanently pressed. Once flattened, you cannot alter their shape. It is also a good idea to only use plant material of a similar thickness in any one layer of paper being pressed, to ensure that all material will press at the same rate of time.

For at least the first five days, be sure to check on the dryness of the paper. You may have to change it often, depending on your flower types being pressed. Your finished petals may take two to three weeks before being ready for use. Plan ahead!

I have been told that you can also dry petals in the microwave, as long as they're weighted down while drying. That procedure could save hours and days of time, but I'm unfamiliar with the timing process using that method. It might be worth looking into because I imagine that the color retention would be much stronger using that method of pressing.

HANDS-ON INSTRUCTIONS: *The Bookmark Project*

1. Talk about the flower pressing procedure and background information.
2. Display the pressed materials and compare them to the fresh flowers if you have brought along the optional bouquet
3. Show the finished project sample for inspiration. There is no right or wrong way to design these bookmarks!
4. Distribute the laminating sheets and a toothpick to each participant.
5. Encourage browsing through the garden of pressed petals and foliage and allow them to choose the material for their personal design
6. Tell the participants that a practice design should be made on the work surface first because once the petals and foliage have been placed on the sticky side of the laminating paper, they are very hard to retrieve and an unintended design may result. Some participants would rather make a random, impromptu design and this is fine, as long as they have been forewarned! Remember there is no right or wrong design! That should be the mantra for this session.
7. Do not place the design too close to the edges of the paper. You have to allow for trimming.

8. Peel off only one sheet of paper for each person.
9. When the design has been arranged on the paper to their satisfaction, have them press each petal down gently with the toothpick.
10. When they are completely satisfied with their design, and have decreed it finished, peel off the second piece of laminating paper and, beginning at the top of the paper, carefully press into place, squeezing out all of the air bubbles as you proceed to the bottom of the project. If you do this for them, a lot of frustration will be avoided, since there is a definite technique needed to insure success at this point. It would, after all, be disastrous to have their perfect design ruined by faulty laminating.
11. Trim the edges into the shape bookmark that they'd like, (square, oval, rectangle) leaving enough empty space at the top to be able to make a hole with the hole punch.
12. Cut the raffia into the desired length and loop it through the hole.
13. The raffia can be knotted or braided to complete the finished bookmark.
14. Now it is time for everyone to share their work of art with the others at the table.
15. Accept the compliments gracefully!

HANDS-ON INSTRUCTIONS: *The Frame-able Picture Project*

1. Follow the first ten instructions as above.
2. Trim the edges if necessary to eliminate mismatched laminating paper

3. Encourage them to put their finished project in a small frame when they return to their rooms or it can be taped to a mirror, or hung on a bulletin board.
4. Now it's time for everyone to share their work of art with the others

HANDS-ON INSTRUCTIONS: *The Notepaper Project*

1. Distribute the notepaper and envelope sets to each participant.
2. Encourage browsing through the array of pressed petals and allow them the time to choose the material for their notepaper design. This is all part of the therapy.
3. Encourage them to make a practice design on the notepaper before using any glue.
4. Using a small amount of glue in the design area, place the petals into the pre-arranged design. Advise against changing the petal placement once it is in the glue.
5. Gently rap the petal edges in place with a toothpick.
6. The back flap of the envelope can also be decorated, if desired, and if time allows.
7. Now it is time to stand back and be proud of their work! It's time for their Show and tell.

SPECIAL NOTES: If you need to make this session strictly a visual one due to participants' ability level, that can also be done successfully with this pressed flower program. It can be accomplished by using fresh flowers and showing samples of completed pressed flower projects. I have also shown purchased candles or ceramic artwork at this type of session with good results. The hands-on ability may not be there but the remembrances will become evident and that is an integral part of horticultural therapy also.

For a variation on the theme, I purchased a rubber ink stamp that had an impression of a Grecian urn. A terra cotta colored ink pad was used to stamp that impression on the notepaper. The pressed flowers were then arranged as if they were cascading from the urn. It was a very elegantly simple project and everyone had fun using the inkpad and rubber stamp!

RESPONSES TO THIS SESSION:

A botanist who was participating at my table was working happily, totally unassisted. When I commented on her ability, she said, "I have mounted many a plant in my day for class work."

I could tell that one other participant had been a schoolteacher. She wanted all of her flowers labeled with a black marker, "for educational purposes." I certainly complied with that wish!

"This is the first thing that I have ever done well."

"I will send my daughter a note on this paper. She'll be so proud of me."

SESSION TITLE: Turkey Thyme

PROGRAM DESCRIPTION: This seasonal project is fun, tactile and an olfactory stimulating one. Its superbly fragrant ingredient is the herb, Thyme. Dried golden rod is used for the turkey's feathers and is soft to the touch even in its dried form. The turkey wing is made of bits of pinecone and is again good for the sense of touch as well as the sense of humor. The turkey's gobbler is a dried mini-carnation, which again brings smiles and conversation. This is a project that everyone likes and is able to do, no matter what their functioning level is. Some may need help with the gluing but all can sprinkle the Thyme on the turkey shape and enjoy the fragrance and memories that herbs bring to mind.

BACKGROUND INFORMATION: Thyme is the oldest of known herbs. It is a perennial native to the Mediterranean and it was known and used by the ancient Greeks and Romans. It comes from a Greek derivative of a word meaning, "to fumigate," perhaps because they used it as an incense.

The Greek word, "thumus," signifies courage and the plant was held in ancient days to be a great source of invigoration, its qualities inspiring courage. Actually, the Romans added it to their bath water because they thought it gave them courage before battle. In the days of chivalry it was the custom for ladies to embroider a bee hovering over a sprig of Thyme on the scarves that they presented to their knights.

There are hundreds of Thyme varieties with scents and flavors ranging from lemon and orange to caraway and lavender. There are upright varieties that grow six to twelve inches tall, as well as the creeping varieties that grow well in between stepping-stones. There is nothing more delightful than walking along a pathway and having the wonderful aroma of Thyme released into the air as you tread upon its edges. It is very hardy and resilient and that variety can be used very effectively in that manner. Silver Thyme is the hardiest of all and has perhaps the best flavor. I also like its variegated leaves to add interest to the garden border.

All varieties bloom with delicate blue, pink or purple flowers and are a bee's delight! The excellent flavor of the honey near Athens, Greece is said to be due to the Wild Thyme, which grows there. The honey from this spot is of such special flavor and sweetness that in the minds and writings of the Ancients, "sweetness" and "Thyme" were synonymous.

The variety that was popular in ancient times was Thyme serpyllum, or "Wild Thyme." English Thyme was the variety known to Shakespeare and was grown in many Elizabethan gardens as a medicinal herb. They used it for the treatment of head and heart disorders as well as for "nervous complaints."

Lord Bacon, the first English essayist, devoted one of his essays to the arrangement of a garden. He thought that the plants, "which perfume are most delightfully not passed by as the rest, but being trod upon and crushed, are three-- burnet, wilde-thyme and mints. Therefore you are to set whole allies of them to have the pleasure when you walk or tread."

In the Middle Ages this herb was thought to be an antidote against fear. Seventeenth century English herbalist, Nicholas Culpeper, believed it to be a "certain remedy for that troublesome complaint, the nightmare."

Today Thyme is not only one of the most popular of all culinary herbs, but it is used commercially in everything from chewing gum to ice cream, and mouthwash to cough syrup. It is even used in making Benedictine Liqueur and some ancient books even recommend it as a hangover cure!

This herb has a fantastic aroma and imparts a great flavoring to all kinds of meats, stews and fish dishes. It is also used to make a wonderfully flavored vinegar and oil salad dressing.

It was, and still is, used for medicinal purposes because of its strong antiseptic qualities. Due to that particular quality, it is useful in making vinaigrettes since it prevents bacteria from spreading, thus preventing any spoilage.

Thyme, taken as a tea, has also been used to fight fevers, headaches and bronchial congestion. It not only acts as an expectorant and an antiseptic, but it also relieves bronchial spasms. The tea not only tastes pleasant if sweetened with honey, but it can also be used as a gargle for sore throats.

During WWII, dried Thyme was used as a substitute for pipe tobacco and you may encounter a few participants, as I did, who remember smoking it! It's amazing what you can learn from the participants in these sessions!

The American variety of Thyme is a creeping variety and is used externally to treat shingles. If used in bath water, it is also good for helping ease the aches and pains of rheumatism.

You can buy a tincture of Thyme in health food stores, and if used in steaming water as an inhalant, congestion will clear up quickly. In this tincture form, it goes directly into your lungs where it stimulates blood flow and helps to clear the congestion and coughing.

Even though bees love Thyme and provide us with a flavorful honey, insects do not like the plant. For a quick insect repellent, make a cup of Thyme tea, put it in a plant mister, and spray around doorways and windows in the summer time to repel insects. It really works!

In the language of flowers, Thyme means happiness, strength and courage.

I guess we just never have enough Thyme (Time) to do everything we'd like to do!

MATERIALS REQUIRED:

- Turkey cutouts from the shape of your hand (foam paper works very well). Have one per participant. Affix a loop at the top of the cutout ahead of time.
- A colored marker for placing an eye on the finished project
- Dried mini-carnations of various colors for gobbler of turkey (one / participant)
- Pine cone pieces for wings (prepared ahead of time)
- Dried, ground thyme for body trim
- Goldenrod pieces for feathers (can be fresh or dried)
- Glue, plastic bags to work on and handy wipes for sticky fingers
- Wooden craft sticks for spreading glue evenly (one / participant)

- Completed sample for show and tell
- Sprigs of various types of fresh thyme for smelling to demonstrate the difference in the fragrances.
- Pictures of thyme in bloom if available
- One whole pinecone for demonstrating how the wing pieces were obtained.

HANDS-ON INSTRUCTIONS:

1. Distribute one turkey cutout to each participant.
2. Distribute glue, plastic bags and a stick to everyone.
3. Talk a little about goldenrod.
4. Make a guessing game out of the wing material. Most people will not guess that it used to be the bracts of a pinecone.
5. Pass around the ground thyme so that everyone can enjoy the powerful fragrance and see if it brings back any memories of kitchens long ago.
6. Demonstrate how to glue one piece of goldenrod onto each "finger" of the turkey for its feathers.
7. Distribute the goldenrod.
8. The next step is construction of the wing. Give each person approximately a dozen pieces of pinecone pieces and have them, or you, put the glue on the turkey in the shape of a wing. The pinecone pieces glue easily if you just place the flat part into the glue. The glue will dry clear.
9. Next, we will spread glue all over the bottom body section and spread it thin with the stick. At this point handy wipes will probably become a necessity!

10. Distribute a couple of tablespoons of the ground thyme into each one's glue-free hand and demonstrate sprinkling it all over the turkey's glued body area.
11. Pat it into place gently and shake off the excess.
12. Smell your hands!
13. Allow each one to choose a colored mini carnation for the gobbler and glue it in place. Be prepared to hear gobbling sounds coming from some participants!
14. Last, but not least, use the marker to draw on an eye, giving the turkey its personality!

It will take a few minutes for the glue to dry, especially on the carnation, so advise everyone to keep their turkey flat for awhile before hanging it on their door or bulletin board.

Happy Thanksgiving with all of its wonderful
smells and reminiscences!

SPECIAL NOTES: For lower functioning groups, it might be better if you apply the glue to the appropriate areas and let the participants apply the materials.

RESPONSES TO THIS SESSION:

"My turkey has a cheerful personality!"

"This turkey stinks good!"

"My turkey smells like Thanksgiving dressing."

SESSION TITLE: Pilgrim Herbs

PROGRAM DESCRIPTION: This is a program that is more suitably geared to the independent living groups who would enjoy historic background information and who would enjoy tasting a session rather than creating a project for the Thanksgiving season.

BACKGROUND INFORMATION: Our first Thanksgiving feast probably included herbs and other seasonings native to New England, along with some that the immigrants had brought with them on the Mayflower

On September 6, 1620 one hundred and two hopeful passengers crossed the ocean bringing with them everything they thought they would need to start a new life in a new country. Every woman would have wanted to bring along her own store of favorite herbs, seeds or cuttings for planting in her new surroundings so that she would still have the familiar seasonings and known medicinal remedies that she would need for her family. Maybe she would also find space for a favorite rose or peony root to have at her new location to make it feel like her home once again. They possibly stuck those favorite plants into root vegetables bins, like potatoes, to keep them alive during the long sixty-six day voyage to Cape Cod.

Perhaps they tucked stick cinnamon, ginger root, black peppercorns and china tea into empty coat pockets and in any extra trunk space. There is no doubt that they brought Sage, Tansy, Mint starts, Pennyroyal, Bee Balm, Birch bark, Chamomile and Sassafras root in order to make their beloved herbal teas.

Rosemary, Sweet Marjoram, hardy Thymes and Horseradish are century old plants that are still found growing around old pilgrim home sites.

The earliest women settlers were too burdened and/or ill to make separate flower gardens but they planted Lilac bushes and Roses close to their houses and nurtured clumps of Hollyhocks, Peonies and Tiger Lilies. It was comforting to have familiar plants in a very unfamiliar new surrounding.

"Plimoth Plantation" is a living history museum in Plymouth Massachusetts, which reflects the English cuisine of the early and mid-seventeenth century. You can go there every November for a "First Thanksgiving Harvest Feast" re-enactment and enjoy the type of meal that the pilgrims prepared so many years ago.

It is recorded that they dined on wild duck, geese, turkey, swans and passenger pigeons that they shot. From the bay they feasted on cod, sea bass, lobster oysters and clams. Chief Massasoit's men contributed venison for that neighborly celebration.

The four surviving Pilgrim wives cooked simple dishes seasoned with their European herbs as well as the native ones that they had learned about since they arrived in their new land. Starchy roots, tubers, puddings, porridges and pones were served as fillers. Any spices or sugar that they had left from that difficult first year were added to dried fruits and Holland cheeses. Cranberries grew in nearby bogs and their Indian friends taught them about corn and native vegetables.

It was a delicious feast to celebrate all that they were thankful for in their lives.

The Pilgrims would have no doubt sat down to a hearty plateful of colorful, delicious food, just as we do centuries later. Many of those same herbs and spices and vegetables are served at our tables every Thanksgiving.

MATERIALS REQUIRED:

- Paper plates, cups and napkins
- Crackers and a knife and/or herbal breads
- Herbal butter (or margarine) made with Thyme **
- Sprigs of fresh Thyme varieties
- Water or fruit punch to drink. Perhaps you'd like to bring an herbal tea for the adventuresome participants.

HANDS-ON INSTRUCTIONS:

1. After sharing the background information with the group, pass around the fresh Thyme sprigs for bruising and smelling. I love when that fragrance permeates the air! Everyone's hands should also smell wonderful by now.
2. Distribute the paper products and offer everyone a cracker, spread with the tasty herbal butter varieties that you've prepared ahead of time. If you've made or bought herbal breads to sample, use plain butter on these so as to not hide the bread's herbal flavors.
3. This is a taste testing session. Enjoy! Be creative! Think like a Pilgrim!

SPECIAL NOTES: Be sure to check with the nursing staff or activity director before bringing in any kind of food.

* *

Herbal Butter

*** Any herbal butter is more full-flavored if made the day before it is to be served, thus allowing the flavors of the herbs to completely blend.*

As a general rule, combine:

- Tablespoon of finely chopped, dried herbs (my favorites to use together are Thyme, Parsley and Chives or Sage, Parsley and Chives)
- ½ pound of softened butter or margarine.
- 1 teaspoon lemon juice to enhance the herbal flavors (If dried herbs are used, soften the herbs first in the lemon juice before adding them to the softened butter).

Refrigerate in a tightly closed container before serving. Remember that dried herbs are more potent than fresh ones. One teaspoon of any dried herb equals approximately one tablespoon of the fresh herb's flavor.

Herb blends should be subtle. Use one strong flavored herb as a basic flavor and add other herbs to compliment it. Basil, Rosemary, Oregano, Thyme, Sage and Tarragon are dominating herbs. As a rule, do not mix these herbs with one another.

You can freeze and store herb butters for several weeks. After mixing the herbs of choice with softened butter or margarine, freeze them in ice cube trays. When they are frozen solid, pop them out and continue freezing in bags until you're ready to use them in vegetable or meat dishes.

Basil-Parsley butter is delicious when used with zucchini, green beans and stewed tomatoes.

There is nothing tastier to me than using an herbal butter on fresh corn-on-the-cob!

We should be grateful to those brave Pilgrims for stuffing those herb cuttings into their pockets!

~~ DECEMBER ~~

* *

Silly gardener! Summer goes
And winter comes with pinching toes,
When in the garden bare and brown
You must lay your barrow down!

by R. L. Stevenson

* *

Our year of horticultural therapy is winding down even as the days of the month grow shorter. The winter solstice marks the shortest day of the year but is also the turning point of the year. From this point onward, we have more daylight hours and that is something to be happy about.

Throughout the ages there have always been festivals of light associated with this time of year, and they were all linked to the fertility of the soil and the longed for return of the sun. There are certain plants and trees and foods that are linked to these solstice celebrations, and they themselves are the food for an interesting December program.

The Holly bush, the Poinsettia and the Mistletoe berries, along with the powerful aroma of pine needles, are just a few of the plants that can be worked into horticultural therapy programs this month. And don't forget the wonderful milkweed pod that we harvested last month. Read on to see how they can be used for the holidays.

Somewhere in my garden literature many years ago, I came across the following words that I've had taped to my refrigerator amidst the photos of grandchildren and other important things! I don't know who the author was but he/she certainly knew the mind of the avid gardener. I now think that these words apply to the horticultural therapist as well.

> *"The best gardeners are those for whom the garden is a year long process, not a goal. Spring brings an irresistible urge to stick their hands in wet, black dirt. Summer means weeding, the best form of meditation, a time for sorting things out. Fall celebrates those hardy crops that, like us, get a burst of new energy from frosty air. Winter means time to read about gardens, fantasize about them, and plan them. A gardener's pleasure is never done."*

SESSION TITLE: Happy Holidays, Naturally

PROGRAM DESCRIPTION: These programs that follow fill the air with fragrance and are enjoyed by all levels of functioning participants. The projects work with either purchased bags of potpourri or dried flower petals that are used in the making of potpourri, which is a separate session described elsewhere in this book. You can choose to work with dried milkweed pods, wide strips of red velvet ribbon, pinecones, sachet bags or Styrofoam balls and cinnamon sticks. Perhaps you will even come up with additional ways to be creative for the holidays using the natural ingredients you may have on hand. Let your imagination take wing! Have fun and enjoy the uplifting fragrances of the season.

BACKGROUND INFORMATION: Holiday memories often begin with the wonderful fragrances of cookies baking, or that of pine boughs, or herbs and spices being used for craft projects, like the clove studded oranges and lemons. The home is full of different aromas at this time of year, all of which are stored in our memory banks just waiting for a stimulus to trigger that memory. The sense of smell is a sure way to take you back in time to a remembered place or a favorite activity. The Christmas scents used in these projects may be just that trigger which sets the memories in motion and brings smiles to the faces of the participants.

MATERIALS REQUIRED: *The Red Banner Project*

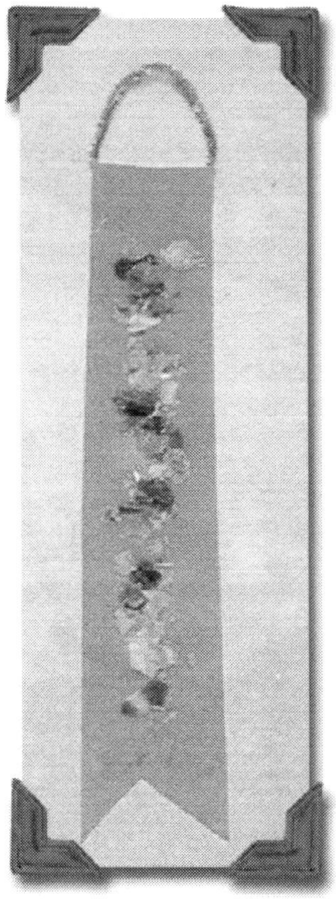

- One piece of pre-cut, red velvet craft ribbon (approximately 18" x ¾") per participant. Have a pipe cleaner hanger already in place at the top of the banner before the session begins. I find it easier to fold down the top of the banner over the pipe cleaner edge and hot glue it in place.
- A purchased bag of potpourri, or if you've made your own from an earlier session, you can use that instead.
- Clear drying glue and wooden craft sticks
- Plastic bags to cover the working area
- Wet-ones for sticky fingers
- A black marker
- The completed sample for show and tell

MATERIALS REQUIRED: *The Scented Topiary Project*

- same as above without the red ribbon plus:
- one 4" Styrofoam ball / person
- one 8" cinnamon stick for the stem / person
- one 4" flower pot / person
- floral foam
- completed sample project

MATERIALS REQUIRED: *The Potpourri Ornament or Sachet Bag*

- one 4-5" new square / person
- purchased or made holiday potpourri mix
- one red or green 6" piece of thin ribbon / person
- one small cinnamon stick / person
- completed project sample

MATERIALS REQUIRED: *The Pine Cone Ornament*

- one pine cone / person
- dried flower petals
- a glittery pipe cleaner for hanger
- clear glue and wooden craft sticks
- wet ones for sticky fingers. That happens a lot with these projects! There is nothing more frustrating than trying to pick up dried flower petals with sticky fingers.
- Plastic bags to cover the working area
- Completed sample

HANDS-ON INSTRUCTIONS: **For the Banner Project**

1. Have the ribbon pre-cut, with the pipe cleaner loop already in place.
2. Ask each participant if they'd prefer "Happy Holidays" or "Merry Christmas" written, with the black marker, at the top and bottom of the banner.
3. Spread out the potpourri on the table in front of them. Ahhh, great fragrance!

4. Distribute one ribbon banner per participant.
5. Show the completed project sample and let them smell the wonderful aroma of the holiday season.
6. Distribute the glue, sticks and bags and show them how to make a design with the glue, on the banner. Perhaps they will want to cover the entire banner with glue. Great idea! The more surface covered with the smaller pieces of the potpourri, the more fragrance will be there to enjoy.
7. Instruct them on covering the glue with the smaller, finer parts of the potpourri, patting it gently into place. They can then add the larger, more decorative parts of the potpourri as a second layer. More glue may be necessary to affix these larger pieces into place randomly. The creativity and color themes come into play at this point with some of the participants.
8. Remind them to keep their banner flat until the glue dries before using it as a door or wall decoration.

Using the marker put their initials on their work of art. All artists sign their work! Invite them to smell their hands also when they've completed the project.

HANDS ON INSTRUCTIONS: *For the Scented Topiary Project:*

1. Distribute the glue, sticks, bags and potpourri as above
2. Give each person a Styrofoam ball, flowerpot and cinnamon stick
3. Direct them to put the cinnamon stick into the bottom of the ball, as a stem, and then to put it into the floral foam in the flowerpot. Already their hands should smell sweet.

4. Using thick glue, instruct them on covering the ball initially with the small powdery pieces of the potpourri .They can then use the larger, more decorative pieces for embellishment The base of the flowerpot can also be sprinkled with potpourri to complete this pretty, fragrant project.

HANDS-ON INSTRUCTIONS: *Potpourri Ornament or Sachet Project:*

1. Pass around the completed project so that everyone can enjoy the fragrance and know what they are about to make for their own enjoyment.
2. Distribute one net piece / person
3. Invite them to take a handful of the purchased potpourri mix to place in the center of the square.
4. Can they identify the types of flowers and/or botanicals that comprise the potpourri?
5. It's time for them to smell their hands!
6. Give them a choice of ribbon color for the hanger
7. Gather the edges of the netting together and secure with the ribbon piece. Put a cinnamon stick in the first knot. Then make a loop and tie it off with a bow, creating a loop for hanging purposes, the fragrance is theirs to enjoy whether it be on their tree or bulletin boards.

HANDS-ON INSTRUCTIONS: *For the Petal Pine Cone Project*

1. Give each person a pinecone that already has a loop hanger affixed to the top.
2. Distribute the gluing materials and bags as above.
3. Show the completed sample as well as the big container of dried flower petals.
4. Give them a chance to smell the full container of petals. Are there any recognizable individual flower fragrances?

5. Invite them to take a handful to work with, feeling how soft yet dry they have become. Can they recognize which types of flowers the petals were part of?
6. Give instructions on putting glue and flowers on each of the pinecone bracts. Continue until the entire cone is filled with flowers.
7. Be sure to offer the wet ones for sticky fingers often throughout this project, otherwise the frustration level will definitely peak and the therapeutic value will diminish proportionally!

SESSION NOTES: You can choose from the projects listed above depending on the functioning level of your group. The important thing is the aroma induced memories and the conversation that naturally follows as thoughts and memories of long ago are shared with others in the group. Eye-hand coordination, cognitive skills and small motor skills are all employed in these very simple but enjoyable holiday projects....and that is horticultural therapy!

The topiary tree project will be the most time consuming, and possibly the most difficult to do, and so I recommend that one for an independent living, or very high functioning group of participants. The background material for these projects can be pulled from the Potpourri session or the session on conifers if you want more in depth programs.

RESPONSES:

"I just love doing Christmas projects. I always did that with my Mom when I was a little girl. That was such a long time ago!"

SESSION TITLE: Osage Ornaments, Flowers and Wreaths

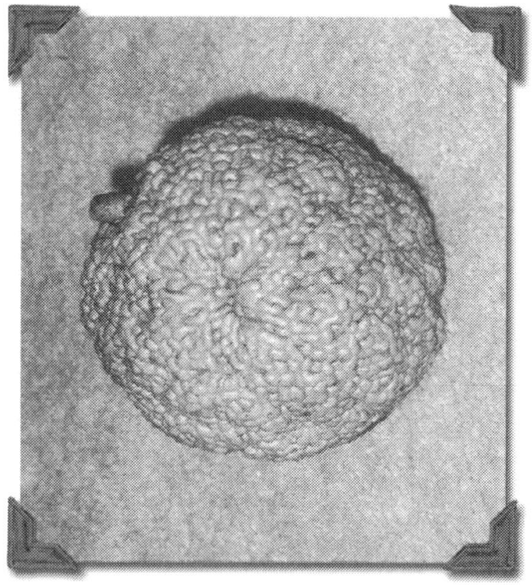

PROGRAM DESCRIPTION: This is a hands-on project using the fruit from the Osage Orange tree as a Christmas ornament. The fruit has to be sliced and baked in a 300 degree oven until it is no longer fleshy. Your kitchen may have a strange "fragrance" for a short time after baking!

BACKGROUND INFORMATION: This funny, bumpy fruit is also called a Monkey Ball, a Hedge Apple, a Horse Apple, and a Mock Orange ball. The tree is part of the Mulberry family and was probable given the name Osage Orange due to the fact that it was growing in Osage Indian territory. In 1804, Lewis and Clark recorded the presence of Osage Orange apples. They hang from the tree's branches like giant ornaments and when they fall to the ground or on a car roof, (mine!) they make quite a thump. I often wonder how many squirrels have been knocked silly by a falling Osage Orange ball.

The tree is found throughout Ohio but doesn't, as a rule, occur as a forest tree. It grows chiefly in open fields, along fence rows. It can reach a height of sixty feet, but it usually grows to between twenty and forty feet. The trunk is four to twelve inches in diameter. The bark is thin, grey, sometimes tinged with yellow, and on old trees, it is in strips or flakes. The bark contains tannin, which is used for tanning leather. The most common usage, however, is for living fence posts. The oblong leaves turn bright yellow in the fall and are shiny green in the summer. Beware! There are vicious, long thorns along the trunk. The wood is heavy, exceedingly hard and very strong. Therefore, its use for posts, wheels, lumber and fuel is a given. The Indians prized the wood for bows and war clubs.

MATERIALS REQUIRED:

- Sample of real Osage Orange ball, or photo of one.
- Gold spray-painted slice of orange (2/person) with a wire loop affixed to the top
- Dried flowers and weeds that have been spray painted red, green, white or silver.
- Samples of weeds and flowers before they were painted for show and tell purposes
- Elmer's no-run glue, one wooden craft stick/person and handy wipes for clean-up.
- 14" piece of red or green narrow ribbon/ornament.
- A plastic bag for each person to work on.
- The finished sample.

HANDS–ON INSTRUCTIONS:

1. Pass out the bags, wooden sticks and glue to each person
2. Give the participants their choice of Osage Orange slices to be decorated

3. Show the finished sample
4. Allow them to choose the dried material that they like for decorating the slice
5. Let the creativity begin as they design their ornaments and glue the dried flowers in place.
6. When the ornament has been decorated with the floral material and completed, give the participants the choice of ribbon color, and tie it around the wire hanger at the top of slice
7. Allow the ornament to lie flat for a little while to give the glue a chance to harden before having a show and tell period.

SPECIAL NOTES: While the glue is drying, it is a good time to let them talk about their own personal experiences with these fruits. Some of the stories can be humorous! Any small, dried flower can be used. I've used Golden rod, Ageratum and Ironweed very successfully. Ironweed takes spray paint very readily once it's dried.

To prepare the Osage Orange balls for use after collecting them in late September, first slice the balls into one inch thick slices. Put them in single layers on a cookie sheet and bake at 300 degrees for approximately 25 minutes, or until lightly golden in color. Cool on wax paper and store in airtight container until ready to use. Affix a small floral wire loop at the top of the slice, with a drop of glue from a hot glue gun. Spray paint when ready to use.

SESSION TITLE: Osage Orange Flowers

PROGRAM DESCRIPTION: A hands-on project for lower functioning patients, in which a flower arrangement can be accomplished with a minimal amount of dexterity needed.

BACKGROUND INFORMATION:
The same Osage Orange information as above.

MATERIALS REQUIRED:

- One 4-inch clay or plastic flowerpot (Have a block of floral foam already fit into it.)
- Sprigs of Statice or Baby's Breath to be used as filler flowers
- Three baked and brightly painted Osage Orange slices/participant (red, orange, yellow and pink work nicely.)
- Silk leaves attached to a wooden craft stick with green floral tape (done ahead of time)
- Black-eyed Susan's (Rudbeckia) dark centers

- No-Run Elmer's glue
- Plastic bags on which to work
- Spanish moss

HANDS-ON INSTRUCTIONS:

1. Pass out the plastic bags.
2. Have the floral wrapped craft stick already stuck on to the Osage Orange slice with a hot glue gun.
3. Give the group their choice of colored Osage Orange slices, which will become their three flowers.
4. Pass out the glue and three Rudbeckia centers to each participant.
5. Have them glue that center on to the middle of the slice.
6. Talk to them about the Osage Orange background while their flowers are lying flat and the glue is drying.
7. When absolutely dry, have them arrange these colorful flowers in the provided flowerpot using the Statice and/or Baby's Breath as the filler material.
8. Arrange a small piece of Spanish moss around the base of flowers to give it a finished appearance.

SPECIAL NOTES: When you collect the Osage Orange balls in late September for the Christmas ornaments you can also slice, dry and store extras for this summertime project.

I have also made wreaths from these colored slices by gluing them onto a stiff cardboard or foam board circular shape. I glue moss onto the form prior to the session so that the participants only have to arrange and glue the pre-painted slices on the wreath shape. Add a Christmas ribbon and presto, a unique wreath to decorate an inside door or bulletin board.

RESPONSES TO OSAGE ORANGE SESSIONS:

"It's always interesting seeing outdoor things we'd never be able to see anymore."

"I remember we had a fence made out of those trees and my brother used to throw those balls at me. I learned to be a fast runner."

"Did you know that if you put one of these monkey balls in your basement, it will keep the bugs away?" It is amazing at how much I always learn from these sessions.

SESSION TITLE: Celebrating the Winter Solstice

PROGRAM DESCRIPTION: This session is geared more to the independent living participant, rather than to a resident of a health care unit. There is detailed and symbolic information given, and the hands-on-activity of making a solstice ball would be tedious for most health care unit participants.

BACKGROUND INFORMATION: Our ancestors lived at the mercy of the elements and were therefore, very aware of the winter solstice. This is the point in the year when the days begin to lengthen again, heralding the coming of spring and the growing season. The cold and darkness of winter is past and Mother Earth, with her life-giving elements, is about to awaken. Many cultures around the world celebrate this occasion and it continues to be an important holiday for the Hopi and Tewa people of the American Southwest. Most of the celebrations revolve around the creation and rebirth of the earth and a welcoming for the return of the sun. Included are rituals of purification and offerings of corn and tobacco and usually ends with a feast and a blessing.

Most of us today don't have these rituals surrounding that day in December, because we are no longer totally dependent on nature for our survival. The ancient Babylonians and Persians marked the day "when the sun gains victory over the darkness" with festivals and feasts. I personally, feel a surge of energy on that day, which stems from the fact that the days will now be getting longer and soon it will be warm enough for me to work in my yard once again!

Carl Jung has said, "By honoring and remembering the sun's rebirth, we also think of our own rebirth, connecting to the creative power of our own soul."

There are a number of specific plants that are considered the "sacred plants of the Winter Solstice." Wheat symbolizes abundance, fertility, sustenance and good luck. It can be used in the forms of grain, straw figures, cookies, cakes and breads. Ivy symbolizes fidelity, everlasting life, protection and healing. It can be in the form of crowns, wreaths and garlands. Evergreens symbolize the continuity of life and can be found in pine, fir, cedar, and juniper boughs. Holly symbolizes the Old Solar Year, and takes the form of boughs over doorways. Oak symbolizes the New Solar year and can be in the form of acorns and Yule logs. Mistletoe is the most commonly thought of and it represents peace, prosperity, wellness and fertility. It can be used in the form of boughs, kissing balls or sprigs above doorways. Frankincense and myrrh symbolize purification, spiritual illumination and inner peace. They are most usually represented as incense or oils.

MATERIALS REQUIRED:

- purchased vine balls (silver and gold)
- fresh ivy sprigs (house and ground ivy works well)
- metallic ribbon (silver and gold) for loops at top
- red berries and/or red and white dried globe amaranth
- thick white glue and wooden craft sticks
- pruning shears and scissors
- handi-wipes
- gold and silver painted wheat sprigs

- a paper cup to set the ball on top of while working on it

HANDS-ON INSTRUCTIONS:

1. Distribute the vine ball of choice to the participants along with the matching metallic ribbon.
2. Tie the ribbon into a loop for hanging when completed.
3. Pass out sprigs of ivy and/or single ivy leaves used to trim the vine ball. Some ivy stems may be inserted in between the vines and other single leaves can be glued on top of vines, with patience.
4. Glue the globe Amaranth blossoms on top of the ivy or fill in the empty spaces with them.
5. Attach the gold or silver wheat sprig to the bottom of the ball with glue.
6. When completed, explain again to everyone, how some of the solstice plants were used in making this ornament and reminding them of their significance and meaning.

SPECIAL NOTES: you can also have a solstice tea party by trimming the tabletop with long ivy vines and acorns. Serve corn chips (the Indian ritual of offering corn), cakes, cookies and breads. Include a fragrant wassail as the beverage. This can be an unusual way to end the year of sessions, while looking forward to the rebirth of the horticultural therapy program in January!

SESSION TITLE: The Fragrance of Conifers

PROGRAM DESCRIPTION: The following sessions stimulate the sense of smell with all of the magic that is conjured up with a walk in the woods or a sparkling Christmas tree. There are many varieties of sessions that can be worked around the use of fresh evergreen branches or dried evergreen needles, which have been finely ground in a blender. Fill any holiday container from baskets to stockings with a variety of evergreen boughs, dried carnations and baby's breath to create a seasonal arrangement or door hanging. The important thing to build on is the wonderful fragrance of the pine and other conifers. This session can be adapted to every functioning level.

BACKGROUND INFORMATION: The word "Conifer" means cone-bearing, and any tree that produces cones as their seedpod, is considered a conifer. The cone is to the conifer as the acorn is to the mighty oak.

There are nearly five hundred species in five different tree families that are considered conifers: *1.* Spruce *2.* Pine *3.* Fir *4.* Hemlock and *5.* Juniper varieties.

The Pine is the best known, as well as the first seed-bearing tree to have been on our earth! Pines have existed even before the dinosaurs roamed the land. This is due to their flexibility in adaptation, which has allowed them to survive the changing climates and natural catastrophes that have occurred over the eons.

Their needle shaped leaves minimize their surface area, thereby enabling them to shed the weight of snowfalls and not suffer the damage of broken branches. The waxy coating on their needles cuts down on evaporation and the subsequent drying out of their branches during windy and dry times.

Many of the species have a fire adaptation as well. The White and Red Pines have a thick outer bark which insulates the sensitive growth cells from the scorching and deadly heat of a forest fire. Interestingly, cones of the Lodgepole Pines and the Jack Pines, need the extreme heat of a forest fire to open their cones, (seeds) thereby preserving their species by reforestation after the fire has subsided.

There are many varieties of each of the five different families mentioned above. Some of them are as follows: The Virginia Pine is also known as the scrub pine. The Pinyon Pine provides us with the delicious tasting pine nuts that we can buy at the supermarkets. The Longleaf Pine is cut for Christmas greens and the Scotch Pine is a popular cut Christmas tree. Arrangement of needles is also an identifying characteristic. The Scotch Pine is identified by having two needles per bundle, the Ponderosa Pine has three needles per bundle and provides great lumber for furniture, while the White Pine has five very soft needles per bundle.

The Pitch Pines are used for torches and campfires, and their trees become very gnarled as they get older. This is one of their identifying characteristics. The Australian Pine has a very tiny cone and this is very identifying for this species. The Giant Redwoods are part of the Pine family also, and are the largest living things that have ever existed on the face of this earth. The giant Sequoia is a cousin to the Redwood tree. Anyone who has stood at the base of one of these beauties has no doubt that it is the largest living thing on the planet.

The Balsam Fir is extremely fragrant and springy and because of these two facts, campers in the north woods always like to make a bed of those needles upon which to rest their weary heads at the end of a long hiking day. The needles of the Fir have a white stripe on the underside, which is also a good identifying tool.

Another member of the Fir family is Douglas, a fir tree that is second in height only to the Giant Sequoia.

The Hemlocks have a moist inner bark that was used for healing poultices long ago and is still used today in a variety of liniments.

The Colorado and the Blue Spruces have very short, sharp needles and the Norway Spruce has a very swooping growth pattern, which is its main identifying feature. As many different types of conifers that there are, that's how many different shapes and sizes of cones we can find.

When the first pioneers came to this country, the White Pine was the monarch of the eastern forests. Its trunk was six feet in diameter and soared two hundred and fifty feet heavenward. In the days of majestic sailing ships, the long straight trunks of these trees were preferred for masts.

Still today, the Pine is one of Ohio's best trees for reforestation and is a leader in the lumber industry. The Indians used the resin, as well as the inner bark of these trees, as an emergency food source. They also used the resin to seal the seams in their canoes. They would mix the resin with beeswax to make the seams watertight.

The Pines are second only to the Oaks in providing food for wildlife, and for that reason, every yard should have one. Rabbits and deer eat the young bark, and squirrels and the Pine Siskin, a small bird, eat the seeds that can be found inside the cone.

MATERIALS REQUIRED FOR CONTAINER ARRANGEMENT:

- Insert a block of oasis in the containers prior to the session, to make arranging easier. Use one container / participant
- Take clippers for trimming and shortening the branches
- Take a variety of evergreen branches. Oftentimes scraps from Christmas tree dealers provide a good source of a conifer variety.
- Have a variety of cones for show and tell purposes.
- Have enough dried Baby's Breath, Carnations and Eucalyptus to give to each participant for filler material.
- Take a variety of bells, berries or other holiday picks

- Have your finished sample to display

HANDS-ON INSTRUCTIONS:

1. Present the background information and allow time for a lot of smelling and touching of the pine branches.
2. Distribute the containers to be filled to each participant
3. Distribute a variety of different evergreen boughs and emphasize again the fragrance and feel of the different branches. Some are stiff, some are soft, some have long needles and some have short ones. How many needles per packet are there in the different samples? What images do the fragrances bring to mind…holidays, walks in the woods? You may be surprised at the memories that are evoked and shared.
4. Once the greens are placed in their container, distribute the dried flower material for arranging.
5. Last, but not least, add the glittery box, berry or bobble to the arrangement and sit back and admire your holiday creation!

MATERIALS REQUIRED FOR THE FOAM TREE PROJECT:

- One green foam Christmas tree cutout / participant. Affix a tinsel loop to the top of the tree beforehand
- plastic bags on which to work
- glue and wooden craft sticks
- a black marker for identifying each participants project when completed
- a supple of dried pine needles, finely chopped
- a variety of branches and cones for show and tell and smell
- tinsel and other tree trimmings such as dried carnations and/or everlastings
- pieces of pine cone to be used for tree trunk
- handy-wipes for sticky fingers
- a star sticker for the top of each tree
- a finished sample for show and tell

HANDS-ON INSTRUCTIONS:

1. Distribute the bags, tree forms, glue and wooden sticks to each person.
2. Demonstrate how to spread the glue all over the surface of the tree, using the wooden stick. A thin covering will do.
3. Give each participant a pre-cut piece of tinsel and have them lay it in the glue in any draping pattern that they'd like.
4. Have each person take a handful of the dried, ground pine needles, inhale deeply and enjoy the fragrance.

5. Sprinkle the pine on the rest of the glue. Gently pat the needles in place. Now you have a foam tree that smell like the real thing!
6. Glue the individual pine cone pieces onto the trunk of the foam form
7. Give each person a choice of tree trimmings to glue on to the tips of the branches and in the body of the tree shape. Here originality reins!
8. The final touch to their tree is the star sticker for the tip-top
9. Give instructions on keeping the tree flat for a few hours, until all of the glue has dried sufficiently. There is nothing worse than having your tree become un-trimmed before your eyes.

MATERIALS REQUIRED FOR A SACHET SESSION:

- one coffee filter / participant
- cedar shavings (can be purchased in a pet department)
- pulverized, dried pine needles
- staple gun plus extra staples. You know you will run out before the session is completed!
- either scotch tape or green vinyl tape to cover over the staples to prevent being poked by their edges.
- a green marker
- a variety of fresh pine boughs and cones for show and tell
- a pair of scissors for any necessary trimming of tape

HANDS-ON INSTRUCTIONS:

1. Show the sample and encourage everyone to smell it
2. Distribute one coffee filter per participant
3. Present the option to draw evergreens and/or their names on half of the coffee filter, using the green marker. (Optional, depending on the capability level of those participating)
4. Have each person take a handful of the ground pine, and place it in the center of their opened coffee filter.
5. Time to smell your hands.
6. Have each one put a pinch of cedar chips on top of the pine on their coffee filter. The cedar fragrance is much stronger and overpowers the pine fragrance if used in equal quantities. You don't want that to happen. Just a pinch will be sufficient.
7. Using hands, mix the two ingredients together
8. Time to smell your hands once again.
9. Fold over the open edges of the coffee filter with a narrow double fold, and staple the edges closed.
10. Cover over the bottom edges of the staples with the tape to prevent scratching by the staple's edges.
11. Time to smell the finished product.
12. It can now be used as a sachet in their closets or drawers.

NOTES: As in any project that you do, if working with an Alzheimer Group, be sure the participants aren't going to put any of the materials into their mouths.

RESPONSES HEARD IN VARIOUS SESSIONS:

One of the participants had a son living in Helena, Montana and she told us that she recognized, and knew "those great pine smells" from visiting him there. "Those were nice times," she said.

A woman from West Virginia told the group that she had lived on a farm where they'd just go to their hill and cut down their own tree for the holidays. Others present also remembered cutting down their Christmas trees. That is the interaction that is therapeutic.

A lady remembered, "a big old pine tree in our front yard at the farm and Mom would ask me to collect all of the fallen needles for my Dad's pillow. I was little and didn't know then why he wanted to sleep on them." She said that later she found out that the doctor had made that recommendation since her Dad had asthma and that fragrance helped his breathing. (See the session on making sleep pillows, entitled "Sweet Dreams")

Another woman remembered her old cedar chest (her hope chest), with fond memories.

A male participant told us that pine was a soft wood and easy for carpenters and woodworkers to use. His Dad used to whittle it.

"The smell of pine is always stronger after a rain or on a foggy morning," was another comment shared.

~~ ADDITIONAL PROJECTS ~~

SESSION TITLE: Sweet Dreams

PROGRAM DESCRIPTION: A hands-on as well as "a nose-on" type of session. In this session, the discussion centers on the "sleep pillows" of yesteryear and culminates in the actual making of these fragrant pillows with a purpose.

BACKGROUND INFORMATION: Dream pillows, or sleep pillows, are one of the oldest remedies for encouraging restful sleep. The Romans used rose petals, and King George Ill and Abraham Lincoln preferred a filling of wild hop blossoms. At naptime, Victorian women rested on lacy pillows of lavender and rose petals. Christian legend tells us that the baby Jesus lay on a bed of fragrant, sleepy-time bracken, a wild herb later called Lady's bedstraw. (Galium verum)

Unlike flower scents, leaf odors are more permanent. Fresh or dried herb cuttings have filled cushions, bedding and little sweet bags for centuries. Lady's bedstraw and sweet woodruff (Galium odoratum) were mixed with rushes and straw for filling mattresses. They were also valued for their dried-leaf perfume of new-mown hay, and for repelling insects. In some parts of the world, dried grass, hay or straw is still used as mattress fillers.

Sleep pillows can be of any size. Traditionally, they are small and relatively flat so they lie smoothly and unobtrusively inside a pillowcase or under a pillow. Use fabric remnants with pretty patterns and colors, and if desired, trimmed with lace and ribbons to make sleep pillow coverings. Ideally, each pillow is formed into an envelope designed to hold a separate herb bag made of muslin or another thin fabric. The pillow covering should be washable and the herb bag replaced or refreshed when the fragrance fades--every four-to-six months.

NOTE: For this session, I use a single bag instead of using one inside the other. It is much less confusing to the participants.

The sedative effect of a sleep pillow comes from its essential oils. Their effectiveness in the minute quantities in a pillow is up for interpretation; still, the scents are comforting and pleasant to wake up to.

Be sparing when filling the herb bag, to keep the finished pillow fairly flat and comfortable. Gently crush the mixture so that no sharp parts remain. The flower, leaf and herb ingredients in the recipes used should all be thoroughly dry before using.

Pillows are used to aid in sleep as well as relieve headaches. Some pillows are placed over the eyes to relieve stress or eye strain.

Five hundred years ago, Native Americans discovered the benefits of balsam fir pillows in clearing congestion and treating head colds. Today some doctors are prescribing balsam pillows for their asthma patients. Some pillows just have a pleasing fragrance to send you off to dreamland.

RECIPES FOR PILLOWS:

A Headache Pillow—

Two parts Lavender and one part each Lemon Thyme,Lemon Verbena and Sweet Woodruff, and a pinch of Rosemary.

A Sinus Pillow—

Two parts crushed pine needles to one part of each Rosemary. Lemon Verbena and Spearmint. Eucalyptus can be substituted for the Spearmint.

A Pleasant Dream Pillow—

Use equal amounts of Rose petals, Mugwort, Chamomile flowers, Lavender flowers, Catnip and Peppermint.

MATERIALS REQUIRED:

- Pre-sewn pillowcases. (five inches-by-five inches)
- Ingredients for chosen pillow
- Staple gun and extra staples
- Scissors
- 5 Colored vinyl tape
- Paper towels to mix ingredients on
- Samples for show-and-tell-and-smell.

HANDS-ON INSTRUCTIONS:

1. Show the samples and pass around for each participant to smell.
2. Distribute paper towels and pillow cases.
3. Smell the individual ingredients that are to be used for the pillows.
4. Distribute the ingredients and have participants mix together with their hands.
5. Stuff bags.
6. Staple unfinished edge.
7. Cover the staples with the vinyl tape.
8. Enjoy the finished product.

SPECIAL NOTES: This is an especially good session for those with physical challenges. The nearly blind can feel accomplished at the completion of this project.

Even most arthritic hands can stuff the bags with the lightweight herbs and flowers and this activity provides good, gentle exercise for them, as they enjoy the fragrances filling their area.

SESSION TITLE: Bath Thyme

PROGRAM DESCRIPTION: A simple, hands-on session that involves making an herbal bath bag. The fragrances used are stimulating, the textures of the ingredients are interesting and the end product is useful as well as pretty to look at.

BACKGROUND INFORMATION: Almost everyone takes a bath sometime, whether its purpose is to cleanse the skin or just to enjoy a nice, long, relaxing soak in the tub. Maybe a bath is taken to relieve aches and pains, or maybe it is taken for pure relaxation. Whatever the reason, an aromatic herbal bath is one of the best and most pleasurable ways of doing these things. The addition of herbs to the bath water can either invigorate and stimulate circulation or relax and sooth muscles. It is a perfect way to unwind the body for a peaceful night's rest. You can choose herbs for a healing treatment or simply because of a favorite aroma.

The temperature of the bath water is an important part of the procedure. It should be just a little warmer than body temperature. If the water is hot enough to cause perspiration then the therapeutic effect of the absorption of the herbs is lost.

The easiest way of adding herbs to a bath is to hang three-to-four herbal tea bags from the tap or to place a small, herb-filled tea ball directly into the water. You can also hang an herb-filled muslin pouch, with a long loop, over the hot water faucet, so that the water runs through the bag. You can use a single herb or mix up to four different ones per bath. For a body scrub, add a little fine oatmeal or bran to the herb bag. Rub this over the skin near the end of the bath time. These two ingredients also help soften the water.

Another method for an herbal bath is the infusion method. Instead of adding the herb directly to the water, you can extract its therapeutic properties by steeping a handful of fresh herbs in two-and-a-half cups of boiled water for ten minutes. Strain and pour the "tea" into the tub water.

A skin-softening herbal bath can be made by adding three tablespoons of powdered milk to two ounces of dried or four ounces of fresh herbs.

Herb-scented waters are also a pleasant addition to the bath water or used as a body splash. Use any herb you like and steep in boiling water. Cool, add two tablespoons of rubbing alcohol, strain and bottle for future use.

Therapeutic Bath Herbs:

Relaxing - Chamomile, Jasmine, Marjoram, Linden flowers.

Healing - Calendula, Comfrey, Lovage, Lady's Mantle, Spearmint, Yarrow.

Stimulating - Basil, Eucalyptus, Fennel, Lavender, Lemon Balm, Lemon Verbena, Mint, Rosemary, Sage, Thyme.

To relieve stress or fatigue - Lavender, Pine, Sage

MATERIALS REQUIRED:

- Pre-sewn muslin pouch
- Green stamp and stamp pad
- Twenty-two-inch length of ribbon
- Paper cups and plastic spoon
- Herbs of choice
- Powdered milk (softener)
- Oatmeal bran (scrub)

HANDS-ON INSTRUCTIONS:

1. Distribute the muslin bags and give the participants the option of decorating and personalizing their bags with the stamp.
2. Distribute the paper cups, spoons and herbs.
3. Use the cup for mixing the herbs and/or milk and bran.
4. After spooning the mixture into the bags, tie with ribbon and form a long loop.
5. Give usage instructions. ENJOY!

SPECIAL NOTES: The simple task of spooning the ingredients into the muslin bag can be a rewarding accomplishment for physically challenged participants and the herbal fragrances can be a source of enjoyment for everyone.

SESSION TITLE: Terrific Topiaries

PROGRAM DESCRIPTION: This is a hands-on session that begins with the discussion of topiary as a living art form and progresses to the actual planting of an ivy topiary.

BACKGROUND INFORMATION:

Topiary is the art of forming living plants into ornamental shapes. This art has been practiced for centuries, dating back to the Hanging Gardens of Babylon. Topiaries have always been very popular in English gardens. Many shapes in the English gardens were formal, such as globes or pyramids. Today you can see a variety of shapes from formal to playful and whimsical. Walt Disney has taken the art of topiary to a new dimension. Two types of topiaries exist; the slow-growing shrub variety and the quicker growing sphagnum topiary. The shrub varieties can take anywhere from three to ten years to complete. Once mature, regular shearing is needed to keep the original shape. The second type of topiary is the sphagnum topiary. With this method, a complete topiary is produced in less than three months. With this method, chicken wire or metal framing is used to produce the desired shape. These also require regular pruning to maintain their shape and to promote multiple branching. Fertilizing regularly is also necessary to encourage abundant growth. A wide variety of English ivies or creeping fig are very simple to work with and are quick growing. Floral topiaries have become popular as well as the very practical herbal designs. The best part about creating an herbal topiary is that you can eat the material that you have pruned!

MATERIALS REQUIRED:

- One clay flowerpot and one ivy rooting per participant
- One topiary frame, made from a coat hanger, per participant
- Plastic bags to work on
- Potting soil and "spoon shovels"
- Small sized gravel (optional)
- Green waterproof markers or stamps and stamp pads to decorate clay flowerpot (optional)
- Watering can
- Show and tell examples of indoor topiaries and/or photographs of various types of topiaries
- Hand wipes and paper towels for clean up

HANDS-ON INSTRUCTIONS:

1. Distribute the bags to cover the working surface.
2. Distribute the pots and markers for decoration if the dexterity of the participants allow for this optional step. Assist in the pot decoration, if necessary. If the pot has a drainage hole, allow each participant to scoop out the potting soil into the decorated pot. If there is no drainage hole, each person will need to place approximately one inch of gravel in the bottom of the pot before adding the soil.
3. Distribute the ivy cuttings and assist in the planting if necessary. Be sure that the ivy is planted in the center of the pot.
4. Give each person a wire frame and give instructions for inserting it behind the ivy plant.
5. After clean up is completed, let them water their new plant and give them further watering instructions and light requirements.

SPECIAL NOTES: This session is great for all levels of participants except for the Alzheimer patient who may be inclined to eat the gravel and/or the soil. Future discussion of the plants' progress just enhances the therapeutic effect of this project for weeks to come. Be sure to show photographs of various types of topiaries. The pictures start good conversation.

SESSION TITLE: Herbal Salt

PROGRAM DESCRIPTION: This session utilizes a variety of dried herbs and is combined with a taste-testing segment. If your participants have dietary restrictions this may not be a suitable program for them. It is always advisable to check with the nursing staff before presenting this program to a group. A discussion of the benefits of cutting back on salt consumption and using herbs instead, to enhance flavor, is the main focus for the program. Each participant will have a small shaker top container to take home with him or her and will have tasted the finished product on crackers during the session. The program awakens the senses of smell and of taste and any level of participant seems to enjoy it.

BACKGROUND INFORMATION: There is an increasing awareness of the dangers of too much salt in your diet. From fluid retention, toxemia, and high blood pressure to kidney and heart problems, too much salt can be detrimental to your health. Salt enhances the flavors of foods, but there is an alternative way to accomplish the same thing and that is by the use of herbs. Not only do herbs enhance the flavor of the foods that you eat, you know that you are doing something good and healthy for yourself at the same time. There is so much sodium in processed foods that is advantageous to cut back on as much added salt as you can from your meals. You can make a completely salt free substitute or you can make a minimal salt substitute. Either way you may be surprised at how full flavored foods can be without much, if any, salt added. Be good to yourself and give this a try!

MATERIALS REQUIRED:

- Your choice of dried herbs–my favorite recipe follows in the Notes section below.
- Salt (optional)
- One container with a shaker top per participant
- Measuring spoons
- One paper cup and teaspoon, for mixing purposes per participant
- Mortar and pestle (optional)
- Finished sample
- Labels and colored markers or a pen
- Napkins, margarine, knife and crackers for sampling
- Punch or water.

HANDS-ON INSTRUCTIONS:

1. After talking about and discussing the benefits of less salt in your diet, proceed with the taste test.

2. Spread margarine (small amount) on crackers, sprinkle generously with the sample blend and distribute to each participant to enjoy. They may also enjoy a drink at this point and come back for seconds! A lot of interesting discussion and sharing of thoughts ensues at this time.
3. Distribute the cups, teaspoons and containers to each participant.
4. Distribute each dried herb separately and strip from the stem. Crush with the back of the teaspoon or in the mortar and pestle. Continue this process until all of the desired herbs are measured into the cups.
5. Mix all together thoroughly
6. Carefully spoon into the containers and close with lids.
7. Distribute labels and markers so that each participant can creatively, or otherwise, identify their containers.

Recipe for Herbal Salt *(Be sure to use dried* herbs)*

Two tablespoons Parsley

One tablespoon Basil

Two teaspoons Thyme

Two teaspoons Oregano

One teaspoon Rosemary

One teaspoon Sage

Two teaspoons salt (optional**).

Before using, be sure to invert the container in order to get a true blend of the herbs.

* *They must be dried to prevent moisture from being trapped inside the closed containers, causing mold to form. If you do not have a source of fresh herbs to dry, use purchased herbs from the supermarket. That is a more costly way to do it, but the result tastes the same. Part of the therapeutic value, however, comes from the actual stripping and crushing of the herbs from the stems which will be lost if purchased dried herbs are used.*

** *If skipping the salt, add one-eighth teaspoon pepper, one teaspoon Marjoram and one-half teaspoon onion powder.*

<u>SESSION TITLE: The Antiquity of the Carnation</u>

PROGRAM DESCRIPTION: This is a hands-on session, which can utilize a wide variety of craft ideas. The strong fragrance produced by fresh carnations and the vivid color retained in the dried carnation make this a good session for those who are able to participate as well as for those who can just enjoy the perfume.

BACKGROUND INFORMATION: The carnation is known by a variety of names. Clove Pinks, Dianthus, and Gillyflower are the most common. The Carnation has been grown for over 2000 years. It arrived in England with the Normans and was a favorite plant in Tudor knot gardens. Some of the old varieties are still available.

The ancient Greeks were equally enthusiastic about this flower. They called it Dianthus. "Did" is Greek for "of Zeus" and the suffix "Anthon" means flower. Literally translated it means "the flowers of Zeus" or "divine flowers". They really are divine in their colors, shapes and fragrance! The Greeks and Romans used the carnation in garlands and coronets and the actual word "carnation," comes from the Latin "corona," meaning a garland with which to crown notable men.

The Carnation has an unparalleled perfume. It can be either sweet or spicy. Its petals can be fringed, stripped, or solid colors. It is long lasting and, all in all, the perfect flower! The Carnation is second in popularity only to the rose. The scarlet Carnation is the state flower of Ohio.

There are different species of Carnation: a) Clove Pink - a clove-like fragrance; b) Maiden Pink - the color of a maiden's blush; c) Grass Pinks - so named because of the type of foliage it has; d) Border Pinks - good for borders because of short growth habits.

The Sweet William is from the same family and was named for William the Conqueror. The clove-scented flowers were used to spice wedding wines because it was thought to be an aphrodisiac. To this day, in Italy the Carnation is a symbol of ardent love as is the red Rose in this country.

Fresh Carnations were used to test for gas leaks in rooms. Fresh Carnations will last for a week or longer. If gas is present, the fresh flowers will close up their petals within just a few hours.

There is no medicinal use for this flower. It is grown for its sheer beauty, fragrance and lasting qualities. It gives joy just by being.

MATERIALS REQUIRED:

- A variety of dried Carnations.
- Elmer's glue.
- Plastic bags to use for a working surface.
- Wreaths, forms, mini-Christmas trees or gift bags, depending on the craft used.
- Finished sample.

- Fresh carnations to demonstrate the fragrance and/or pictures of wide variety of species.
- Ribbon, netting or baby's breath, depending on the chosen craft.

HANDS-ON INSTRUCTIONS:

1. Show the finished sample and distribute the plastic bags for the working surface.
2. Show all of the colors of the dried Carnations and let each participant choose the flowers for the chosen craft.
3. Distribute glue to each capable participant, and instruct in the placement of the dried flowers, again depending on the craft chosen.
4. Be sure to allow time for glue to harden before hanging any of the items.

SPECIAL NOTES: You can either enhance or simplify this session depending on the level of capability of the participants. It is also an effective session for the Alzheimer patient because of the fragrance and colors involved. At the end of the session, the fresh Carnations can be given to the participants.

A RESPONSE TO THIS SESSION:

We used a starched doily form in this project. An Alzheimer participant commented on those doilies, "They are a nice thing to think about…how it was then. My Grandmother had doilies everywhere." And the reminiscences followed and were shared with the group. Of course, others then had their own stories to add….and that is part of horticultural therapy.

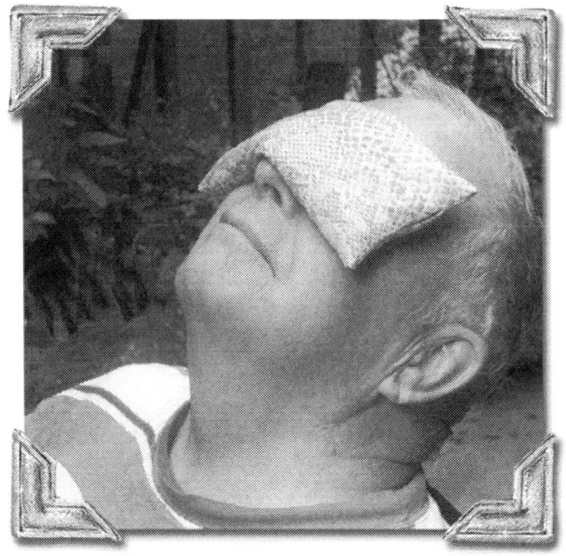

PROGRAM DESCRIPTION: This is a very sensory stimulating session. The fragrance of Lavender abounds and the smooth, silky texture of the flax seed is interesting to touch. The finished product is a comfortable weight to lie across the eyes and the participants enjoy its fluid movement on their foreheads. You can use this session for low functioning groups as well as for independent living participants. The interest of the individuals determines the amount of background material that you'll want to give. At the end of this session, each participant will have his or her own eye pillow to enjoy.

BACKGROUND INFORMATION: Look under the January program for Lavender Bath Powder for the background material for the herb, Lavender. You can talk a little or a lot about the Lavender ingredient in these eye pillows, or you can focus on the interesting Flax plant, which is another important ingredient for this project.

Herbalists know that Lavender is unsurpassed for calming frayed nerves, relieving insomnia and depression, and aiding in healing. More than a pleasant scent, natural Lavender has the power to relax tense muscles, relieve burning, irritated eyes, and soothe away that tension headache. Your entire body will feel the benefit. The pillow that you will make in this session eases eyestrain with soothing darkness and the refreshing, relaxing scent of the

Lavender flowers. Flaxseeds give the pillow a long shelf life and provide the soft, fluid feel and slight weight.

Flax (Lignum usitatissimum) is of the family Linaceae and the common synonym is Linseed. It is one of the English-grown medicinal herbs, the products of which are included in the British Pharmacopoeia. The seed is widely used in medicine.

Its cultivation reaches back to the remotest periods of history. The Flax seeds, as well as the woven cloth, have been found in Egyptian tombs. It has been cultivated in all temperate and tropical regions for so many centuries that its geographical origin cannot be identified since it seeds itself wildly.

The "fine linen" mentioned in the Bible has been satisfactorily proven to have been spun from flax; it was the plant to which the plague of hail proved so disastrous in the Book of Exodus, and it also furnished the garments of the Jewish High Priests. In the New Testament times, it formed the clothing of the Savior in the tomb where Joseph of Arimathaea laid Him.

It was used for cord and sailcloth ("white sails" are mentioned by Homer in the "Odyssey") and it was used for lamp-wicks, as mentioned in the book of Isaiah.

Bartholomew, the medieval herbalist refers to the making of linen from the soaking of Flax in water until it is dried and turned in the sun and bound in bundles for further beating and bleaching.

Flax is an ancient crop grown for its seed and fiber production. In 3000 B.C., it was cultivated in Babylon. In 650 B.C., Hippocrates wrote about it as a relief for abdominal pain. In the eighth century A.D., Charlemagne thought its consumption so important that he passed laws requiring his subjects to eat it. In 1617 A.D., a Canadian farmer brought it from France to North America. World wars increased the demand of it as a source of oil in factory products; in the first half of the twentieth century, linoleum became popular. In the 1960s and '70's it became part of a healthy diet, and now it has been shown to contain the fatty acids (omega 3), which have been proven to be nutritionally important. Flax seed prevents hypertension, helps to retain Calcium, Magnesium and Phosphates in the body and may prevent immune disorders and possibly, cancer. Therefore, you can see this tiny flower has been around for centuries and it has many important uses.

The Flax is a graceful little plant with blue blossoms, that stands about one to two feet high. It blows gracefully in the breeze and looks very fragile. You would never guess at its importance in the scheme of historical, medicinal and practical uses. All parts of the plant are useful, from the root, to the seed. A yellow-gold dye is produced from its roots, its fibers are used in weaving, its flowers are beautiful and produce a seed that has a multiple of uses.

The tiny Flax seed is thirty to forty percent oil, and this oil also has a variety of uses. Mixed with an equal amount of limewater, it is then known as Carron Oil, and is used in treating burns and scalds. Mixed with honey, linseed oil is used as a cosmetic for removing spots from the face. Linseed oil also has a place in veterinary pharmaceuticals.

Farmers use the oil to coat shovels and other farm implements to prevent rust from forming.

This oil is also a major ingredient in many fine oil paints, varnishes and stains. It preserves and beautifies wood surfaces and is used in furniture polishes as well.

In 1863 it was discovered that by oxidizing linseed oil, a thick mixture called linoleum cement was produced. By adding a backing, and drying with pine resin and wood flour, tough, strong sheets formed and the flooring that we know was invented. Because Linoleum is flooring made of all natural ingredients, it helps reduce pollution because it decomposes completely, unlike vinyl flooring, in landfills.

So, we can now understand that the tiny flax plant suits the world of yesterday, today and the future as well.

MATERIALS REQUIRED:

- Two pieces of a soft fabric, five-by-nine inches each, sewn together into a bag, with a one-inch opening on one side for each participant
- One cup of flaxseed per participant (can be purchased in health food stores)
- One tablespoon of dried lavender flowers per participant.
- One paper cup per participant, for mixing purposes
- One teaspoon per person
- A fabric glue stick
- A funnel
- The finished sample
- Sprigs of fresh lavender or a potted plant for show and tell.
- A picture of the blue flower of the flax plant.

HANDS-ON INSTRUCTIONS:

1. Pass out the sewn bags to each person
2. Show them, and let them smell, the finished sample
3. Distribute one cup of flaxseed to each person and let him or her feel it as they pour it into the paper cup.
4. Pass out sprigs of dried lavender and instruct on how to strip the flowers from the stem and crush them between their fingers to release the fragrance. Do enough sprigs so that there is approximately one tablespoon of dried flowers to put into each cup. The fragrance in the room should be beautiful by now!
5. Mix the seeds and the lavender together with the teaspoon
6. Using the funnel, slowly pour the mixture from the cup into the bag.

7. Close the opening in the bag with the glue stick
8. Have them place the finished bag over their eyes. They can feel the softness and smell the fragrance.

NOTES: Tell everyone about the great relaxing and soothing benefits produced by frequent use of this eye pillow. It is a great companion for their afternoon naptime as well as for going to sleep at night. If it falls off during sleep, it will make their pillowcases smell wonderful!

If you can't find flaxseeds at the health food store, substitute short grain rice instead. Old silk scarves or ties make an excellent fabric for the bags.

The mixing, stripping and smashing of the Lavender, the pouring from cup into funnel as well as using the glue stick are all helpful small muscle activities.

The conversation that results from the many uses of the Flax is very interesting. Many participants remember their mother using it for many varied purposes.

SESSION TITLE: The Enjoyment of Potpourri

PROGRAM DESCRIPTION: A treat for the nose is the best way to describe this uplifting session. Anyone can enjoy making this mixture of petals, herbs and spices, and the more cognitive participants will enjoy the history as well as the finished product. This session is not appropriate for participants who are prone to taking everything from the table to the mouth. This is a good session for eye-hand coordination, following simple instructions and the use of hands and arms. The latter is worked by the shaking motion required after each step in the procedure. Obviously, it also stimulates the senses of smell and touch, since the participants are using handfuls of dried flower petals and herbal leaves. Since there is "homework" to do with this session, the effects of horticultural therapy last longer than the one hour that we are together. It takes three to four weeks before the product is considered finished and ready for their complete enjoyment. They have to think about it and shake it every day for those three to four weeks and so it becomes a topic of conversation as well as a looked forward to activity to be performed. They remind each other to "do our homework."

BACKGROUND INFORMATION: "Potpourri" is a French word that when translated literally into English, means, "a rotten pot!" That is certainly not a pretty meaning for something that turns out to be so lovely to both the eyes and the nose. The term was originally used as a culinary term meaning a stockpot of vegetables and meat. Now it is strictly used in reference to a pot of fragrant plant material (botanicals).

Humans have always enjoyed perfumes. The perfuming of areas is an ancient practice. The cave men burned scented woods near or in their caves and their environments were "perfumed" by the different smoke scents. The term "perfume" comes from "per fumin" translating into "by means of smoke".

The early Egyptians used sweet smelling oils to appease the gods and to anoint the body. Perfumes were also an important part of the lives of the ancient Greeks and Romans. They used fragrances for religious celebrations.

The Arabs, however, perfected the art of distillation, which is the process used to separate the essential oils from the fragrant part of the flower. That process caused the art of making perfumes reach a new height.

Essential oils are the life-blood, the soul of each and every flower. The essential oil is what makes a rose a rose and not a carnation.

Four hundred years ago, the Victorian homes were perfumed by mixes of scented flowers, and set out in beautiful containers in their parlors. This was the beginning of the "Rose Bowl" and I'm not referring to the football game! Two hundred years after that, the term "potpourri" came into common usage in the English language, in reference to a beautiful fragrance.

There were many ways of displaying potpourri other than the rose bowl. These mixtures were put into baskets and jars, sachets and pillows, and coat hangers were lined with fragrant coverings. The versatility of potpourris caused them to be found in every room of the house. There is nowhere in the home that cannot benefit from the delightful, natural perfumes of potpourri. It can also be a keepsake of special occasions. For example, flowers from a wedding bouquet or those roses received on an anniversary or other special occasion, can be the foundation for a memorable potpourri that not only delights the sense of smell, but also delights with the memories brought to mind.

The pioneer women also had uses for fragrant herbs. Other than using them as deodorizers for their cabins, they also knew that specific fragrances deterred bugs from their straw mattresses (e.g. lavender and tansy). They referred to the herbs used to keep their dirt floors fresh, as "strewing herbs," because they were handled in just that way.

Today potpourri can be color coordinated with its location in the house. It can please the eye as well as the nose. We aren't necessarily using it to repel bugs, or deodorize rooms, as our forefathers did, and so we can choose flowers for their colors instead of strong fragrances.

The Victorian women all had a "still room" off their kitchen area. It was a room specifically used for drying and preparing herbs for their household needs, whether it was for cooking, housecleaning, or for medicinal purposes. There was always a fire burning in the fireplace in this room with a large pot suspended over its flames. The Victorian woman would mix spent flower petals and herbs in this pot and add a little salt and brandy and/or brown sugar to the mixture for curing. It would simmer for weeks and she would continue to add left over flowers and herbs from her kitchen garden, to this mixture. It took about two to three months of simmering and adding to this mixture before a fragrant "stock pot" was created. It didn't look very pretty in its brown mushy form; in fact it looked like a "rotten pot." The fragrance, however, was unsurpassable! It would then be scooped out and placed into a pretty container with perhaps a lace doily covering, so that just the fragrance could be detected. This wonderful concoction had to be given a name and "rotten pot mix" wasn't too appealing. The Victorians translated that phrase into the French and decided that "potpourri" had a much nicer ring to it!

The Victorian method of making potpourri was known as the "moist method" and did require more time and patience than the "dry method" of making potpourri that is used today. The modern way of making it takes only three to six weeks to achieve the beautiful, long lasting fragrance instead of two to three months.

No matter how you make a potpourri there have to be the five following ingredients contained in the mixture:

1. dried scented flowers and petals – the faster the materials are dried, the more color they will retain. Hanging herbs and flowers are a beautiful display in themselves. They shouldn't be hung in strong sunlight.
2. herbs with desirable fragrances (rosemary, lavender, thyme, mints, scented geranium leaves etc.)
3. spices (nutmeg, vanilla beans, cloves, cinnamon etc)

4. a fixative which will absorb and retain the fragrances. It this ingredient isn't used, the fragrance is quickly lost. (cat litter or vermiculite is the most common since they both have the capability of absorption)
5. essential oils of your choosing. (rose, lavender, citrus, gardenia etc.) We rely on these much more than did our ancestors and they are the reason why this method takes much less time to produce a finished product.

To have the fragrance of a bowl of potpourri in your house is like bringing a flower garden indoors. It is so uplifting on a dreary day, to be able to smell mints and roses and pine needles and lavender! It is like summertime all year round!

MATERIALS REQUIRED:

- a variety of dried flower petals
- dried herbs
- pre-mixed blend of cinnamon, cloves and/or nutmeg. In a baggie with a small scoop
- vermiculite and measuring cup
- a variety of essential oils and an eye dropper (use approximately 12 drops / participant)
- quart size Ziploc-type bag
- dried orange peels

- aromatic foliage, wood chips, pine needles, pine cones or seeds pods (optional depending on the season)
- samples of potpourri in a variety of containers for show and smell!
- a bouquet of fresh flowers to show the before and after of the dried petals. (optional)

HANDS-ON INSTRUCTIONS:

1. Distribute the plastic bags to each participant.
2. Instruct them to open the bags as you put a small amount of vermiculite into each bag (1-2 tbsp.)
3. Now give them a choice of the essential oil Let them smell each one and pick out their favorite.
4. You add about 12 drops of the chosen one, into the vermiculite.
5. Have them seal the bag and thoroughly mix all of the oil into the vermiculite, even that which may be clinging to the sides of the bag.
6. It's time to open the bag and add a big handful of dried flower petals. They find it enjoyable to reach into the container and feel all of the petals and smell the aroma that the great variety of petals mixed together will bring.
7. Once they've added the petals to the vermiculite/oil mix, they have to close the bag tightly and mix completely.
8. Go through that same mixing procedure with each newly added ingredient. You can add up to three herbs as well as any of the optional ingredients at this point.
9. After the last shaking-mixing time, add the blended spices. Don't use more than one tablespoon.

10. Give them the opportunity to smell the bag after each new addition and explain that once everything is blended together, it will take on an entirely different fragrance. If the citrus fragrance of the orange peels is used, have them try to tear the larger orange pieces into many smaller ones. It not only provides more surface area of fragrance but that step also gives fingers a chance to be exercised.
11. After the final ingredient is added and mixed, let them smell the blended product. Then tell them to seal it up and not to sneak a smell for the next three to four weeks! The ingredients need to be in their closed container (their plastic bag), for that period of time so that the fragrances have a chance to blend together and become stronger. However, they must gently mix their bag every day, while keeping it closed, allowing the vermiculite to sift down through the petals and herbs and spices. This is an important step in both the making of the potpourri, as well as the therapeutic exercise and interest it creates.
12. At the end of the three to four week period of time, they can then open up their bag and put their potpourri in a pretty cup or spread it out on a saucer so that they can enjoy the smells of a flower garden all year round!

SPECIAL INSTRUCTIONS: This potpourri project can become seasonal depending on the types of flower petals or foliage and essential oils that you use. A springtime potpourri can be made using a larger number of dried daffodils and hyacinth petals. A fall potpourri can be attractive with the addition of rose hips, seeds or cones. Use an appropriate autumn scented essential oil instead of a floral scent. A holiday potpourri should be heavy on the pine fragrances and cinnamon oils. More cloves also add to the festive fragrance blend.

SESSION TITLE: Ivy League and Otherwise

PROGRAM DESCRIPTION: This program delves into the many varieties of ivy and the creative uses for it, ranging from note paper to topiaries. The participants only need the ability to glue ivy onto a pre-cut piece of notepaper to enjoy this session. If a "play-in-the-dirt" type of activity is desired, ivy comes to the rescue. It's a perfect plant to use for planting a topiary shape.

BACKGROUND INFORMATION: True ivy belongs to the botanical genus Hedera and it can take many forms. There are more than three hundred and fifty cultivars of the most familiar species, Hedea helix, or as we know it, English Ivy. An ivy can be solid dark green or silvery in appearance. It can be variegated, with gold or white throughout its leaves. There are ivies with leaves that resemble lettuce, maple leaves, stars and even dragon's claws. These natives of northern Europe, are not often attacked by pests or diseases. They can tolerate all kinds of weather and grow in just ordinary soil. They grow best in a northern or western exposure and easily propagate by the aerial roots that form on their stems.

There are two stages to the ivy plant - the juvenile and the tree ivy stages. While they are still in the juvenile state they climb and/or trail. There are no flowers during this stage but the aerial roots are present at this time. When they reach the top of their tall support, the stage changes. The climbing habit gives way to a bushy form and the aerial roots cease to appear. The leaf shape also changes and it is now in the tree state. Flowers during the autumn season are yellow/green and in clusters, and fruits develop during the winter months. True ivies shouldn't be confused with the many other plants that are also called ivy, including Boston, Swedish and Poison ivy. These plants belong to an entirely separate genus. Boston ivy, actually a native of Japan, belongs to the same family as the Virginia Creeper.

In general, large leaved varieties grow faster and more vigorously than the smaller ones and make a greater impact from a distance. Small types can be tucked into planters. H. helix "Spetchley," is one of the smallest of the miniature ivies, having leaves only a half-inch wide. H. helix "Harrison," has dark green lobed leaves and is the classic ivy look.

Ivies are highly adaptable and as houseplants have very minimal care requirements. Plant them in ordinary soil-less potting mix and add extra Perlite to ensure good drainage. Water the plants only when the mix is dry to the touch and mist the leaves frequently with water to avoid spider mites, which are one of the few pests that plague ivy. Feed ivy sparingly. If its leaf color is pale, or if its leaves lose their crispness and its growth begins to weaken, then listen to what it's telling you. It is pleading with you to feed it!

Periodic light pruning will increase its branching and give a shape to one in training as a topiary form.

Potted ivy was so popular during the late nineteenth century that it could be found in almost every parlor, either winding around windows or draping from picture frames or fire screens. The Victorians loved it because it would thrive in low light situations. They revered it for its symbolic connection with marriage and fidelity. In the language of flowers, it means friendship and fidelity. It is also the symbol for everlasting life because it remains green throughout the year.

Ivy has never lost its popularity over the centuries, perhaps because of its versatility. It looks great in gardens as a ground cover and it is interesting on its own because of the varied leaf shapes and colors.

They are also climbing vines that cling to upright surfaces by roots that sprout from their stems and work their way into any available crevice. Given the support of a thin stake, a single stem can be trained to grow upward and then branch out to make a little ivy tree. Of course, the trailing stems that are allowed to cascade over the sides of pots or hanging containers are also very gracefully beautiful.

Did you know that the Ivy League Universities were first given that designation because of their football teams? Harvard, Yale and Princeton were old institutions with thick vines of ivy covering their walls. A sportswriter first coined the term in the

1930's by saying of their losing football teams, "They're just Ivy League, what do you expect?" It was said in a humorous, yet sarcastic manner, but the term stuck.

And you thought you would only be learning about the Hedera species in this session!

MATERIALS REQUIRED:

- dried and pressed ivy leaves, approximately four leaves/ notepaper
- two – three pieces of notepaper with envelope / participant
- colored markers, especially a green one
- glue
- clear acrylic spray
- a shoe box in which to spray finished projects with the acrylic paint
- samples of completed designs
- scalloping scissors (optional)
- wet wipes to clean sticky fingers
- various samples of houseplant ivies
- plastic bags to cover the working surface.

HANDS-ON INSTRUCTIONS:

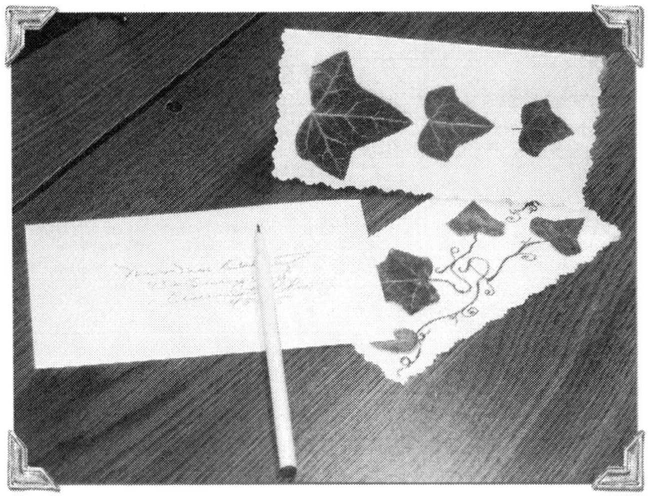

1. Discuss and pass around the houseplant variety of potted plants that you've provided for show and tell.
2. Distribute the plastic bags.
3. After spreading out your supply of dried and flattened ivy leaves of various sizes and shapes, give them their choice of three or four. You will be surprised at the lengthy decision making process at this stage of the project. I had one lady who had decided to do her initials in overlapping leaves. Obviously, she wanted the same sized leaves for her very creative idea.
4. Give instructions about having their leaves in place BEFORE gluing them on the notepaper. That way, they can play with the design a few times before making the final placement decision....and they will!
5. After they have glued their leaves onto the notepaper, spray the project (inside the shoebox for protection), with the clear acrylic spray to make their project permanent, and to give a nice sheen to the leaves and paper, as well.
6. Wait a few minutes for the spray to dry and then using the markers, let them personalize their notes if desired, with their initials or a design. It is important to apply the spray before the personalizing is done, because it could cause the marker color to bleed into the paper and ruin the project.

7. Distribute the envelopes and suggest that they even glue a small leaf on the back flap to complete the artistic, designer look.

SPECIAL NOTES: If you would like to have this be a planting session with ivy cuttings, follow the planting instructions and materials required found in the "Terrific Topiaries" chapter of this book.

RESPONSES TO THIS SESSION:

A female participant remembered that on her wedding day she had carried ivy cascading from her Bible. Others commented on that as something they had also done.

After talking about ivy-covered buildings, one woman, who hadn't participated in any of the preceding conversation, said, "I used to live in an ivy covered house when I was little."

I'm guessing that she took that thought and many related ones with her long after our one hour together was completed. It is interesting to see just what triggers wonderful memories…and that shows how horticultural therapy can be more than just playing in the dirt.

SESSION TITLE: Sycamore Bark Painting

PROGRAM DESCRIPTION: This is a very tactile session which is better suited for the higher functioning groups although it can be adapted as strictly a show and tell session if need be. There is a great variety of show and tell objects connected to the majestic Sycamore tree. The grey-white bark itself is unique in its peeling, puzzle-like pattern. The fruiting bodies are interesting to feel and to take apart, to show the seeds that comprise this long stemmed sphere. Its gigantic leaves are always a conversation piece and once the photos have been shown of the very distinctive appearance of this tree along the roadside or near creeks and streams; everyone will recognize it and have a story to tell.

BACKGROUND INFORMATION:

The Sycamore tree (Platanus occidentalisi) stands out along streams and the edges of moist floodplains in the brown winter landscape. The pale gray to yellow-brown, to bright white bark of the upper trunk and spreading limbs is eye catching and an easy source of identification, even for the most untrained eye. The beauty of its peeling, multi-colored bark resembles a camouflage uniform of a soldier on duty, standing straight and tall and guarding his territory. The outer bark, unable to grow along with the limbs and trunk as they expand, peels off in sizable, irregularly shaped chunks to reveal the inner bark, thus giving us the beauty of the Sycamore in camouflage gear. It is hardly camouflaged however, since it makes such a striking statement on the landscape.

These large widespread trees are an important source of timber. It is one of the biggest, sturdiest and most durable of the North American hardwoods. It flourishes in wet situations and some of its proudest specimens grow along the winding riverbanks of the Midwest.

In Colonial times, the cores of the round fruits, along with the very tough fruit stalk and a short piece of the twig, were used for buttons. That is definitely a case of "necessity being the mother of invention." Perhaps that is why it is also called the Buttonwood tree. These single, round fruits are composed of many small, hard seeds, each with a plume of brown hairs that set it adrift on the breeze.

The California Sycamore (Platanus racemosa) has seed balls in necklace-like strings of 3-7, while the Arizona Sycamore (Platanus wrightii) has seed balls in groups of two to four. These "buttonballs" dangle on wiry stems, turn brown, and remain on the tree all winter long. They resemble ornaments on the winter trees until they split open in the spring to release their tiny elongated seeds with the attached fluff-sail. Then their search for favorable growing conditions begins. Yes, Mother Nature is wonderful!

Its leaf is often times mistaken for that of the Maple (Acer) leaf, but the Sycamore produces a much larger leaf and its bud and leaf arrangement is alternate, while the Maple's is opposite on the stem.

When we can identify a tree and call it by its own name, we become more closely linked to our forefathers, who would have no more confused a Maple with a Sycamore, than we would mistake a hose for a shovel! They knew the value and uses of the trees that grew around them. They respected the trees and understood the glory of how they functioned.

MATERIALS RERQUIRED:

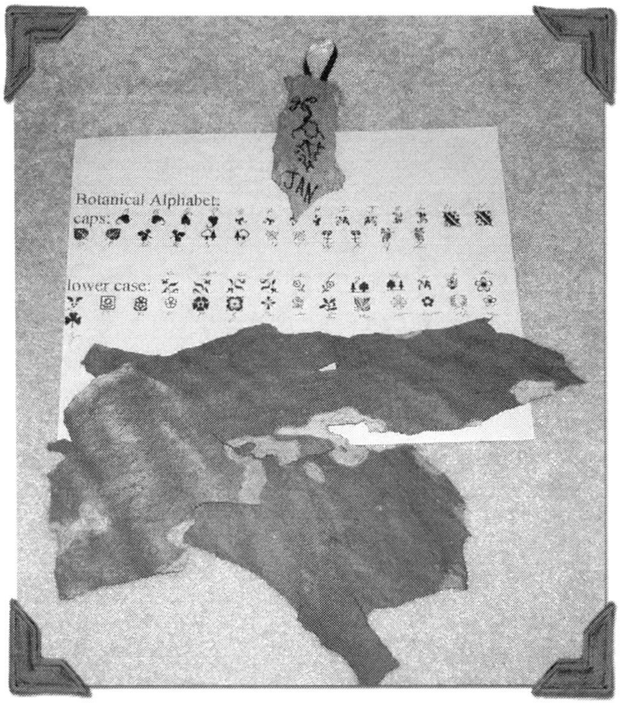

- pieces of peeled off Sycamore bark
- show and tell items such as a leaf, seed ball and photos of the distinctive trees in the landscape
- a botanical alphabet sheet for each participant, (optional) this can be found on the internet
- colored markers, pencils or crayons
- your finished sample showing both a hanging and a framed version

HANDS-ON INSTRUCTIONS:

1. After presenting the background information and having a group discussion about this distinctive looking tree, pass out the samples so they can touch and feel the rough bark and prickly seed ball.
2. Give each participant their choice of collected bark pieces. Have a ribbon loop already affixed to some of the smaller pieces. Once again the decision making process is an important therapeutic tool. "Do I want to make something to hang or to frame?"
3. Describe the Botanical alphabet and distribute one sheet to each person, (optional) in case they'd like to draw their own names in those characters. If you provide that option, explain that they can choose to draw a flower or any other design on their piece of bark.

4. When everyone has completed their project, be sure to give them time to share their design with the others at the table. Each project will be as different as the bark patterns on a Sycamore by the roadside, and the feeling of artistry with such a simple project is quite evident.

SPECIAL NOTES: To adapt this idea to a very low functioning group, simply eliminate the actual drawing on the bark. Instead, focus on the sensory stimuli of the bark, leaf, seed ball, photos and the ensuing discussion. Ask the participants if they ever looked at the clouds in the sky and found animal shapes there. Can they see any familiar shapes in the bark designs on the table in front of them? Different people will obviously see different things and this activity provides interesting social interaction…again a therapeutic tool.

RESPONSES TO THIS SESSION:

Upon looking at one of the sample pieces of bark, one participant pointed out what she thought looked like the shape of a duck's head, in profile. We all agreed that it did indeed. "Wait! I think now I see a hand in mine!"

"Well, my hand isn't that shape," said another participant. Laughter followed and laughter is always the best medicine.

SESSION TITLE: A Rose is a Rose is a Rose

PROGRAM DESCRIPTION: The three different projects that are included under this title all involve dried rose petals being glued onto a variety of objects - straw hats, pictures, and framing mats. All of these projects are a delight for the nose and since many people have had rose gardens in years past, a lot of conversation "stems" from this flower. Even the non-gardeners enjoy the fragrance of a rose!

At least one of the following projects will appeal to, and be suitable for, all but the lowest functioning group of participants. In one of the latter, a patient thought that the dried yellow rose petals were potato chips and you know the rest of that story!

BACKGROUND INFORMATION: The background information for this group of sessions is the same as described under Background Information in the "Hearts and Flowers" session found in the February section of this book.

MATERIALS REQUIRED:

- a vase of fresh roses , if possible to initiate the olfactory stimulation
- dried rose petals of various colors
- white glue for everyone
- handy wipes for cleaning sticky fingers
- plastic bags to cover the working surface
- pictures of different kinds of roses from flower catalogues
- a finished sample of whichever project you choose to present:
    - a) the 8 x 10 black and white picture of a rose *
    - b) the smaller "Love is Like a Rose" picture or a family photo with 4x6 mats
    - c) small straw hats
- a black marker for identifying each person's completed project (optional)
- scotch tape for securing pictures behind the mats

HANDS-ON INSTRUCTIONS:

1. After talking about the various types of roses, and passing around the fresh ones to smell, show the completed sample of the project that you are about to undertake.
2. Distribute the bags, glue and one of the above-mentioned objects to each participant.
3. Spread the dried petals on the table in front of everyone and encourage their touching them and smelling them. The dried petals still have a fragrance, all their own.
4. Encourage conversation while working on this project.
5. Be sure the project remains flat until the glue has dried sufficiently, before hanging or standing it upright.

* A copy of this black and white picture of a rose is transformed into a real-looking rose by gluing on dried rose petals. I have purchased silk green leaves and instructed the participants to glue those on in place also. Who would have thought that a picture of a rose could be fragrant and look so realistic?

SPECIAL INSTRUCTIONS: After completing the decorating of the 4x6 mats, ask each participant if they have a family picture or other special photo they'd like to put behind their mat once they return to their rooms. If the answer is "no", then give them one of the copied "Love is Like a Rose" picture to put behind their mat to complete their project. Scotch tape the four corners of the picture to the back of the matting. Enjoy the look of pride on the faces around the worktable!

RESPONSES TO THIS SESSION:

An Alzheimer resident with macular degeneration, and therefore extremely pessimistic, began the session very negatively with the comment, "It's so hard to do anything when you can't see. I just won't join you." There was nothing good about the beginning of that session for her. She stayed at our table, however, and by the middle of the hour, she had decided that she would like to make a frame, if I would help her. She said, “I’ve always just loved roses so.” By the end of that session she was not only completing her project, but was also laughing about not putting the petals where the glue was. “This is such an adorable, precious and lovely project. I just love it!” What a transformation in a personality in just one hour’s time. Horticultural therapy does work. Just stop and smell the roses!

SESSION TITLE: Flower Arranging

PROGRAM DESCRIPTION: This is a simple program. This is not a lesson on the different styles of arranging flowers, or the methodology and technique of arranging, it is simply a program whose purpose is to enjoy the color, fragrance and sheer beauty of the flowers themselves. Participants will create a bouquet to take back to their rooms. Some of my participants have displayed a real knack for the placement of the flowers in their vases and all have enjoyed the random colors of the blooms in their finished product.

BACKGROUND INFORMATION: Flower arranging is not something new to the homemaking scene. Martha Stewart did not introduce this pastime, she has just helped perfect it. As we look back at the remains of ancient cultures, we have proof through their manuscripts and archeological findings that flowers were used in many ways to decorate.

In a Neanderthal gravesite dig, there were found the remains of bunches of flowers around the body. Analysis of their remaining pollen was found to be over 50,000 years old.

The Egyptians used plants and flowers for decoration as far back as 5,000 B.C. This is evidenced in their paintings on walls and in their decorated pottery. They would lavishly decorate their banquet tables with bowls of flowers. We know that the Lotus blossom, the Rose, Lily and Poppy were definitely used in these table arrangements.

The ancient Romans had many beautiful monastery gardens containing many of the plants that the elite would use. Roses were the most sought after and then the Iris, Honeysuckle, Ivy and Lilies were in demand.

One important link to flower arranging is the Roman artwork entitled, "Basket of Flowers," which was found in Hadrian's (a second century Roman Emperor) villa and is now housed in the Vatican Museum.

With the fall of the Roman Empire came war and religious strife in Europe, and so in the middle ages, the art of flower arranging was forgotten for a few hundred years. There were obviously more important things to tend to then.

When we look at artwork from the Renaissance Period however, we see beautiful floral paintings done by the Masters. They were on tables, in corners of rooms and held by beautiful women in elegant gowns.

By the fifteenth century flowers were used everywhere, by everyone, for decoration. They were used by royalty and common people alike. They were used to decorate churches and homes everywhere.

Flowers were used extensively throughout history, not just for medicinal purposes, but for their sheer beauty, which is our purpose in this hands-on program.

MATERIALS REQUIRED:

- fresh flowers
- a vase, (it can be just a plastic, colorful 16 oz. glass) / participant
- a block of floral foam (oasis) in the glass to give stability to arranging

- scissors
- watering can
- a marker to identify each persons vase for transport back to their room

HANDS-ON INSTRUCTIONS:

1. The most important beginning for this session is enjoying the fragrance of many flowers together in a small space.
2. Encourage conversation about the names of the flowers, familiarity with them, and reminiscences of their own gardens and flowers that were among their favorites.
3. Distribute the vases with the block of oasis already inside.
4. Using the marker, identify each person's vase.
5. Demonstrate the "magic" of the thirsty foam substance.
6. Distribute the watering can so that everyone can add water to their vases.
7. Begin by distributing the flowers in any way you think is the best. It can be that everyone gets two white flowers and then two red flowers, etc. or if you think it will work, let each person choose their own initial six flower stems.
8. Use the scissors and trim the stems to the desired length. Some participants like very tall, flowing arrangements and other will want little, close, compact ones. Remember, there is no one way to make these arrangements. They will all turn out beautifully!
9. Allow time for each participant to hold up his/her completed vases so that everyone else can also enjoy it.

RESPONSES TO THIS SESSION:

"Flowers do brighten my day."

"I'm so glad you came with fresh flowers today."

SESSION TITLE: Cacti and Succulents

PROGRAM DESCRIPTION: This is a "play in the dirt" type of session and is both visually stimulating and tactile. It is not a good session for low functioning participants who may be prone to eating the soil. It is a session that is ongoing, because of the care needed for the transplanted succulents. The photos and the sample plants that are passed around the table prompt a lot of conversation.

BACKGROUND INFORMATION: The group of plants known as cactus and succulents is indeed a most interesting group of plants. There is a simple difference between the two, however. All cacti are succulents but not all succulents are cactus! Both are capable of storing water in their stems or leaves, but succulents do not have the spines (thorns) that the members of the cactus family have on their stems.

There are almost thirty different plant families that have succulent members. Some of the common groups are; Cactus, Euphorbias, Agaves, Aloes; Jades and Kalanchoe. The Euphorbias, Jades and Aloes are Eastern Hemisphere plants, native to Africa and The Mediterranean, whereas the Cactus and Agaves are Western Hemisphere plants. The Euphorbias have a milky sap, which is poisonous and often times irritating to the skin. Some stems have thorns and these plants do produce leaves if enough moisture is present. The cactus family, however, does not have leaves. These two families sometimes look very similar growing in the desert.

The Agaves are actually in the amaryllis family. They may grow for many years before a flower stalk is produced. The Century Plant is a well-known agave and it usually takes about 50 years before it blooms. Once it blooms, it dies (Monocarpic),

Native Americans used an agave leaf with fibers still attached as a needle and thread. One variety of the agave is the source of sisal used for roping.

Aloe, a member of the lily family, blooms annually and the plants do not die following their beautiful bloom. There are a variety of flower colors produced by the aloes. Their leaves are fleshy, and the sap is well known to soothe the skin. The popular "burn plant" is Aloe Vera and is also known as the "miracle plant." This plant is mentioned in the Bible and in ancient Greek and Egyptian manuscripts for its ability to heal, cleanse and beautify. Legend tells us that the Mayan maidens, famed for velvety skin and luxuriant gleaming hair claimed Aloe Vera as their gift from Venus, the goddess of Love. It is said that Cleopatra used it to enhance her already legendary beauty. Aloe Vera has been used for over three thousand years, however, just recently, science has rediscovered its important properties. Research has shown that the gel is capable of penetrating to the water-retaining layer of the skin, thus helping to promote new skin cell renewal and helping to slough off the dead cells that collect and are a deterrent to beautiful skin.

The very popular Jade plant (Crassula argentea) is a very undemanding succulent. It can store water in its thick, fleshy leaves, which allows it to survive for a long time in between watering. Even when the thick leaves have become thin and shriveled due to lack of water, it will survive if given a thorough soaking. That is my kind of houseplant! If the leaf loss is excessive then you are watering it too frequently, which never happens in my house! It may produce flowers in the summertime, but it's grown for its beautiful jade green leaves and beautiful sculpture-like formation. Perhaps it looks like an Oriental sculpture, but it actually originates in South Africa.

The Kalanchoe is a short, compact succulent that provides beautiful flowers that are set by the shortened daylight, so it is at is blooming best around Christmas. They are very popular gifts because they come in such a beautiful variety of colors, ranging from pastels, to red, orange and bright yellow varieties. The flowers stay fresh for nearly two months and are easy to care for, as are all of the succulents. The cacti have very unusual and interesting shapes and range in size from the Giant Saguaros to the tiny pincushion cacti varieties. The desert is a surprisingly beautiful world of color in the springtime. It seems as if the smaller the cactus, the larger the flower!

Some of the Saguaro live to be about two hundred years old and often times it takes them seventy years to develop their first "arm". They are the ones that are always pictured with "The Roadrunner" cartoon figure!

It is true that cactus can provide a life saving drink to a lost traveler in the desert. It may not be the best tasting, but it will provide sustenance.

Mother-in-law tongue (Sansevieria) and Hen and Chickens (Sempervivum) are also popular varieties of succulents that are easy to work with in this session. None of these plants need to be "babied" and in fact do much better with a little neglect.

MATERIALS REQUIRED:

- container for dish garden
- gravel (or Styrofoam packing material) for drainage, if the container has no hole in the bottom
- potting mix + scoop
- "spoon shovels"
- small watering can
- plastic bags to work on
- wet ones for dirty hand clean-up
- photos of cacti and succulents for discussion
- live plants for show and tell
- larger decorative rocks for "landscaping"
- sample of completed dish garden
- plants for potting (hens and chickens, short variety of sansevieria, aloe or jade)

HANDS-ON INSTRUCTIONS:

1. After talking about the plants, touching the sample plants and looking at the desert pictures, it is time to get started with our gardening project.
2. Distribute the plastic bag, container, and spoon shovel to each participant.
3. If using the gravel or packing pieces, let each person scoop out the appropriate amount so as to cover the bottom of the container to at least a 1-2 inch depth.
4. Let each participant now scoop enough soil to fill the container half way.
5. Give each one their choice of 1-3 plants (depending on the container size) and show how to dig a hole with the "shovel-spoon."
6. Place the plant into the hole and using the spoon shovel, place dirt around the plants until the level is 1/2 inch from the top of the container.
7. Water when planting is completed and pat the roots into the soil with the back of the spoon or your fingers.
8. Let them choose their rock or group of rocks, for the finishing landscaping design.
9. Instruct on the perils of over-watering, and the fact that the plant needs some sunlight to thrive.
10. Clean dirty hands and notice which participants are the seasoned gardeners. They will be the ones who didn't care if they used the shovel or not. They just went right into the dirt with their hands and they will need additional wet ones!

SPECIAL NOTES: If your container is large enough, you may want to add a small marigold for color, as an option.

This same background material can be used for a complete program on just Aloe, Sansevieria planting, or Jade propagation instead of making the dish garden.

RESPONSES TO THIS SESSION:

"I used to live near the desert in Arizona and I remember digging them up for our front yard. Of course I guess that's against the law now!"

"My mother always had an Aloe plant on our kitchen windowsill."

During my background presentation and show and tell segment of the session, I was quizzed by one of the participants on what I referred to as "the skeleton" of the Cholla cactus that I had taken for discussion. "Do you know what it really is?", I was asked. "It's an extensive vascular system for that dry climate plant," she explained. She just sparkled as she talked about it! I told her I was impressed with her knowledge of the cactus and she told me that she had been a Botany Professor at a local University and had written the textbook used!

Thank heavens I had done my homework before that presentation.

WASTE NOT, WANT NOT

Horticultural therapy is not only gardening know-how and people skills, it also encompasses being creative, inventive and frugal! In the nine years that I have been developing programs that stimulate, satisfy and encourage developmental skills, I have realized the limitations of my budget as well as that of the Activity Directors' budgets.

I have been successful at keeping the cost per person per session to $1.00. In order to do this, I am always on the lookout for things to be utilized in ways that they weren't necessarily intended to be. I look outside the box, or bowl as it sometimes becomes! For example, the black plastic salad bowls from Wendy's make perfect fairy garden containers, and Little Jimmy's baby food jars are now filled with Queen Anne's lace and decorated with a ribbon. Not even the colorful spray paint can lids go unnoticed. What cheerful little containers for a dried flower arrangement they can become! Material scraps or old neckties become sachet bags or sleep pillows when filled with the appropriate fragrant herbs and flower petals.

I love to eat a fresh orange in the morning, and when I know that the potpourri sessions are upcoming, I eat more and more of that healthy fruit because their skins, when scrapped and dried, add a wonderful fresh fragrance to a mixture of flower petals.

Occasionally my house runs short on hangers because they make the perfect topiary frame for a pot of ivy, which of course comes from my yard. All told, my yard and gardens are the backbone for many of my successful sessions. Have you ever noticed how beautiful the pictures of the flowers on the seed packets are? I just knew I could find a use for them. Check out the SEED ART SESSION in February's chapter! The flowers that I grow are picked, pressed, propagated, hammered or dried to fit the needs of the week. The plastic flats and empty cell packs from the nursery can have a second life as your seed starter kit. "Waste not, want not," my grandmother used to say.

I also grow many different kinds of herbs, and their delightful fragrances find themselves in sachets, sleep pillows, bath powders and potpourris.

Even the fallen branches in my yard are useful during the time we are making fairy gardens. Clipped, they are the perfect fence posts in the magical world of the fairies. Walnut shell swings, milkweed pod bathtubs, bark bridges and wood shaving pathways are necessities for our fairy friends. Imagination is a wonderful thing and my participants have responded with their own child-like enthusiasm to this fairy whimsy.

I walk four to five miles every day and my route takes me past fields of Queen Anne's Lace, and roadside "weeds." We all know that weeds are just misplaced flowers and they provide many sessions with their flowers or unusual seedpods. The Pinecones, Buckeyes, Locust pods and Osage orange balls are certainly worth picking up for some future project. Laminated sun catchers and colorful autumn leaves go together like peanut butter and jelly. Wait; do not throw away those laminating paper scraps! They will be the perfect size for your pressed flower and/or grass bookmarks project.

Did you know that the parchment-like bark from the beautiful Sycamore tree takes the color from a magic marker quite well? This is another fall project in the making. Some people find walking for exercise boring. Not me. I find it stimulating for both body and mind - so many treasures, so few pockets. When my imagination is sluggish, I put on my walking shoes and Mother Nature provides the inspiration that I need. How fortunate I am to have a job where my work supplies are often obtained through a morning's walk instead of an office supply outlet.

It is very important to try to find a supermarket, funeral home or florist shop that will give you their left over flowers. Not only will you have the necessary flowers for the one-on-one patient visits, but also here is your source of materials for potpourri, hammering, and pressing. Don't overlook the little plant food packets that are included in many bouquets or the pretty wrap that the bouquets are packaged in. Many an enclosed plastic trinket from a bouquet has found its way into another session months later. Yes, I have drawers and bins and cabinets and closets filled with treasures waiting to be used… and they will be, with no sales receipt attached. Baby's Breath and Eucalyptus dry beautifully and the fragrance of the latter can be part of many sessions. A participant told me that, "breaking up the pieces of dried eucalyptus sounds like a walk in the woods." Who is to say what smell or texture triggers a pleasant memory!

One of my favorite, if not messiest, attempts at being frugal comes after Christmas. My dried Christmas tree doesn't get put out for the garbage man or laid over my perennial garden. I cut off the branches and store them until they are sufficiently dried and then the needles get stripped from the branches and put into a blender and chopped into fine pieces. Pine scented projects are favorites with most everyone because of the memories that fragrance provides. The holidays are also a time of gift giving, and boxes provide a great source of cardboard that can be used for backings on wreaths and frames.

Certainly, you keep those Styrofoam packing pieces don't you? If they are NOT the water-soluble kind, they make great drainage systems for a flower container without a hole in the bottom. They also keep the containers lightweight and provide a few laughs as the participants try to shake them off their hands and arms.

The plastic bags from shopping days make the perfect work area mat. No one worries if dirt or glue is spilled on him or her instead of on the table.

An obvious frugal exercise is to buy the huge white glue refill bottles and just keep refilling those little bottles instead of purchasing new ones. I'm conducting my own study on the life of one of those little bottles. I wonder if I will have a tenth birthday party for any of them.

"But What Can We Do In Between Times?"

Some Activity Directors ask this question of me. They have seen, and understand the value of horticultural therapy for their residents but their budgets will stretch only so far. They want to have some simple things that they or a staff assistant can do that will keep horticulture flourishing for their residents in between my visits with them. They know their limitations in both the gardening know-how, as well as their time restraints. "What can we do?" I've been asked. Below are the suggestions that I have given them to fill in the gaps:

1. Something as simple as keeping existing plants, on patient's windowsills, watered and alive can raise the spirits tremendously. There is nothing more frustrating for a bedridden gardener than watching a plant wilt and droop because he or she can't water it. Having someone come in and do that for them and perhaps let them smell it, is a real morale booster and such a simple thing to do. Sometimes horticultural therapy is just the enjoyment of seeing, and smelling the flowers, not necessarily working on them.
2. Along the same lines as above, it is a real plus if someone makes sure that fresh cut bouquets have enough water in the vases and that the spent flowers are discarded. This

is a great morale booster. Fresh, crisp looking bouquets are uplifting. Droopy, dead looking ones are depressing.

3. If fresh flowers are obtainable, let some of the more capable residents arrange them in small vases for the dining room tables. Not only will the area look bright and cheerful, but the participants will have quite a sense of accomplishment and pride in their work. The other residents will also benefit from the cheerfulness that a vase of flowers provides.
4. As a patient's vase of flowers starts to wilt, assist them in pressing the flowers between napkins in between the pages of heavy books. When they are thoroughly dried and flattened, provide some small pieces of self-stick laminating paper so that they can create a bookmark or small picture. The finished product could be a pleasant reminder of the friend that sent them the fresh bouquet.
5. If the budget allows, a lighted grow cart is a wonderful addition to any unit. The capable residents could be in charge of tending the plants within it and even propagate some of the simpler varieties, such as African Violets or Aloe. Seed starting kits could also be part of the grow cart's function. There is nothing more intriguing than watching the progress of a germinating seed. These seedlings can be transferred to larger pots when they are mature enough. That is horticultural therapy at its basic level.

EPILOGUE

* *

Give fools their gold and knaves their pouch.

Let fortune's bubbles rise and fall,

Who sows a field or trains a flower

Or plants a tree, is more than all.

- John Greenleaf Whittier

* *

Horticultural Therapy is not a profession that will place you on the Fortune 500 list! I like to think that what "I make" isn't measured in dollars and cents. I would like to think that what "I make," is a difference; a difference in people's attitudes and lives, even if only for a few hours a month. I'd like to think that "I make" their former pleasant times seem real again, through the fragrances and textures and fresh flowers or photos that I bring to them. I would like to think, "I make" their confining life a little more enjoyable, meaningful and upbeat, by my programs and by my presence. I know that "I make" their recuperation and therapy less threatening by the garden environment. Ultimately these are the things that count and I know "they make" my day!

The mental health benefits of gardening have been recognized in America for over two centuries, but it's only been in the last decade or two in which this therapy has flourished as a distinct discipline, similar to Occupational Therapy, Music Therapy, and Physical Therapy. We are the "new kid on the block" but our time has definitely come. Activity Directors and Administrators are seeing the difference we can make in the lives of their residents. They are taking notice when the families of these patients make very positive comments concerning the progress their loved one is making, or can see the pride in the face of a participant when they talk about what they did, or made, on their own. A sense of accomplishment at the completion of a task is an important concept not to ignore.

After planting a flower, I've been told by a patient, "I never dreamed I'd ever have anything to care for again." And, "You bring joy to our day here." What does a horticultural therapist make? She makes patients feel good about themselves!

As I sit at my computer finishing this book, I can hear the beautiful crescendo of the seventeen year cicadas Brood XIV, which have emerged in our area a few weeks ago. Some people may call their beautiful sound an annoying drone, but I find it very soothing, almost hypnotic.

During my walk this morning, I noticed the overpowering fragrance of honeysuckle along the country roadside and I stopped to pick one of those blossoms. I pulled out the little protruding stamen and tasted the honey at its tip. I was a child again. I could hear the cicadas as they began their morning mating song and I found my footsteps matching their rhythm. The tiny purple flowers of the Canada Thistle seemed to be covered with the small, white, flitting, Cabbage Butterflies, who have escaped the birds beaks due in part to the over abundance of cicada meals. My morning is wonderful! My senses are overflowing and I am filled with overwhelming gratitude for this start to my day. There are many sessions along this stretch of roadside just waiting to happen.

Plants possess life-enhancing qualities that encourage people to respond them. In a judgmental world, plants are non-threatening and non-discriminating. They are living entities that respond directly to the care that is given them, not to the intellectual or physical capacities of the gardener. In short, they provide a benevolent setting in which a person can take the first steps towards confidence.

- Charles A. Lewis

Somewhere I have read the following, "Getting old is a gift from God. Not everyone has been given that gift."

My hope is that I can help these geriatric patients enjoy and appreciate their gift from God by helping them to feel young again, through remembering or laughing or feeling pride in what they have accomplished when we are together.

People may not remember exactly what you did or said, but they will remember how you made them feel. That is a thought that I try to remember as I approach each session.

A wise person once said, "No amount of professional skill can make up for a lack of human sympathy and love." That should be our mantra.

Activity Directors Comment On Horticultural Therapy

"What better way to open one's senses and their mind to memories gone by than with the sights and smells only flowers can bring! Our residents look forward to our monthly horticulture therapy sessions, as they love learning new ways to display nature's beauty. Days after a session you can hear them talking about how they made framed prints from flower petals or how beautiful their potted flower is. Horticulture therapy is truly a blessing in the disguise of plants!"

- Tracie Reynolds, CTRS, Activity Director
Scarlet Oaks Retirement Community

"I just missed you (Jan Doherty) this morning, but I wanted to say Thank You for being so great with the residents, and for bringing your love of gardening. I just wanted to let you know how wonderful I think your program is! The residents are lucky to have someone like you!"

- Joanne Perry, Activity Department
Eastgate of Cincinnati Health Care and Rehabilitation Center.

"Our Horticultural Therapy Program reaches all levels, from our most independent residents to residents in our skilled care and Alzheimer's units. The program allows all participants to see, touch, smell, feel and, sometimes, even taste nature year round. Our horticulture program has brought us slides of the flower shows, wonderful craft projects and homemade tea and treats that are good for the soul. The program draws people with a variety of interests together. Some come because they always loved nature and gardening, some because they enjoy the crafts, yet others to continue learning in retirement by learning or doing something new!"

- Debbie McClain, Program Coordinator

- Marjorie P. Lee.

"Jan (Doherty) has been providing our residents with Horticulture Therapy for the last several years. Her program has given our residents the opportunity to continue their love of gardening as well as the chance to learn new things. Jan incorporates many variations in her program ranging from basic gardening, gardening crafts and educational teachings. Jan not only delivers her gardening talent within a group setting, but through one on one-room visits. Our residents look forward to the monthly visit from the "gardening lady" and the many joys she brings with her. Gardening has been a life -long hobby for many of our residents. It is a hobby that also has many therapeutic benefits for the elderly. It is a sensory stimulator that brings back precious memories of the past. Growing Healthy has aided in our residents' physical abilities by exercising hand-eye coordination and fine motor control. The program also helps decrease depression and increase self-worth by allowing the residents to continue a leisure interest instead of feeling like yet another part of their life was taken away or out of reach. The Horticulture Therapy program has been a great asset to our activity department. I would highly recommend her program to any elderly setting."

- Amy White, CTRS

Eastgate of Cincinnati Health Care and Rehabilitation Center

"Horticulture therapy is a relaxing activity that stimulates our residents' minds and bodies regardless of their disability. They participate to the best of their ability and gain self-confidence and self-worth while completing a project that they take home and continue to nurture. It provides an opportunity for reminiscing and developing meaningful social relationships with peers. It provides a sense of purpose and enjoyment for them. I strongly encourage the use of horticulture therapy in activity programming. The residents at my community look forward to Jan's visit each month."

- Sherry Otten, Activity Director

Norwood (Ohio) Retirement Community

JANICE HOETKER DOHERTY

Jan Doherty was president of Growing Healthy Inc., a horticultural therapy service that used horticultural products to stimulate response from persons in retirement communities, health-care and assisted-living facilities as well as in Alzheimer's units.

A retired microbiologist from Cincinnati's Christ Hospital, Jan wove her love of gardening into her tradition of health care service and started Growing Healthy Inc. in 1995.

A lifetime in the garden has also embraced more than a quarter of a century of volunteer service in horticultural activities. A long association with the Cincinnati Nature Center culminated in her direction of the Herb Wall restoration program there. Soon after Cincinnati's internationally acclaimed Flower Show debuted, Jan volunteered to participate. Her flower show activity led to her being chosen as one of the 1999 Volunteers of the Year for the Cincinnati Flower Show. During that year's show, she served as crew chief for the Low Allergen Garden, which won a gold medal. In 2000, she co-chaired the Alzheimer's garden at the show and won a gold medal and the Cincinnati Horticultural Society's Professional Award. A third gold medal was awarded in 2001 for a floral interpretation of a work of art.

Her writing on horticultural therapy has appeared in The Herb Quarterly and DreamWeaver magazines.

Jan holds a Bachelor of Science degree in biology from Our Lady of Cincinnati College and is an Ohio Master Gardener.

She and her husband live in Cincinnati, Ohio and have four grown children and six grandchildren.

* *

Look deep into nature, and then you will understand everything better.

- Albert Einstein

I have a tee shirt with the following message on it. I think it speaks volumes in itself!

All I need to know about life I learned from gardening.

- *It's OK to be a late bloomer.*
- *Always try to be outstanding in your field.*
- *Remember it's important to branch out.*
- *We've all got our own rows to hoe.*
- *You always reap what you sow.*
- *Some problems are perennial.*
- *Weed out all the annoyances in your life*
- *People with lawns have mow fun.*

Janice Hoetker Doherty

A retired microbiologist from Cincinnati's Christ Hospital, Jan wove her love of gardening into her tradition of health care service and started Growing Healthy Inc. in 1995.

Her writing on horticultural therapy has appeared in The Herb Quarterly and DreamWeaver magazines. Jan holds a Bachelor of Science degree in biology from Our Lady of Cincinnati College and is an Ohio Master Gardener.

She and her husband live in Cincinnati, Ohio and have four grown children and six grandchildren.

48259269R00207

Made in the USA
Charleston, SC
29 October 2015